FULL EMPLOYMENT: A PLEDGE BETRAYED

By the same author

BUSINESS STRATEGY

Edited by the same author

STRATEGIC PLANNING IN NATIONALISED INDUSTRIES

and with Jonathan Michie

UNEMPLOYMENT IN EUROPE
MANAGING THE GLOBAL ECONOMY
CREATING INDUSTRIAL CAPACITY: Towards Full Employment
EMPLOYMENT AND ECONOMIC PERFORMANCE: Jobs, Inflation and Growth

Full Employment: A Pledge Betrayed

John Grieve Smith

First published 1997 by
MACMILLAN PRESS LTD
Houndmills, Basingstoke, Hampshire RG21 6XS
and London
Companies and representatives
throughout the world

ISBN 0-333-68736-1 hardcover
ISBN 0-333-68737-X paperback

A catalogue record for this book is available from the British Library.

This book is printed on paper suitable for recycling and made from fully managed and sustained forest sources.

10 9 8 7 6 5 4 3 2 1
06 05 04 03 02 01 00 99 98 97

Printed and bound in Great Britain by
Antony Rowe Ltd, Chippenham, Wiltshire

For Jean

Contents

Tables

Preface

This book is addressed to all those interested in the problems of economic policy and unemployment, whether they be politicians, journalists, civil servants, readers of the economic columns of the press or members of the economic profession. In trying to make it as widely accessible as possible, I am particularly grateful to Kit Jones, Brian Reddaway, Michael Stewart, Geoff Harcourt, Andrew Glyn, Robert Neild and Mića Panić for commenting on all or part of the manuscript. I should also like to thank John Wells for help with data on unemployment and poverty. Once again I am totally indebted to Lesley Haird for typing and retyping successive drafts with such patience and good humour.

As the reader may detect, Chapters 4 and 5 on the postwar period rely heavily on the various works of Alec Cairncross, Christopher Dow and Frank Blackaby and the National Institute.

I should like to take this opportunity to thank some of the many people to whom I have been indebted over the years for help and encouragement in getting to grips with the problems of economic and industrial policy, of which I believe that the problem of restoring full employment is now the most pressing. My longest standing debt is to Brian Reddaway, my Supervisor throughout the time I was a student at Cambridge, who taught me with tolerance and good humour, and confirmed my belief that economics should be a practical and useful subject. Next came my first boss, Robert Hall, head of the Economic Section of the Cabinet Office (and then the Treasury), who was unsurpassed as a government economic adviser in the postwar period: if Keynes was the architect of postwar full employment policies, Robert was the journeyman builder, who played the major role in turning them into reality. Returning to Whitehall in the 1960s I had the good fortune to work for Donald MacDougall in the Department of Economic Affairs on tackling what would now be called 'supply-side' problems. I am also deeply grateful for the good comradeship and support of John Jukes and Peter Evans with whom I worked so closely on and off for 20 years.

I have been much encouraged by a number of Cambridge

economists as well as those mentioned above, including in particular Wynne Godley, Bob Rowthorn and Frank Wilkinson who commented on previous papers on this subject. It has been especially rewarding to organise a series of conferences on different aspects of full employment, and edit the ensuing books, with my colleague at Robinson, Jonathan Michie.

I am also indebted to Patricia Hewitt, who was instrumental in the publication of my reports on Pay Strategy and Full Employment in the 1990s for the IPPR.

None of the above is, of course, responsible for the views expressed.

JOHN GRIEVE SMITH

Cambridge
May 1996

Acknowledgements

This book draws heavily on a variety of papers and articles which the author has published on aspects of economic policy in recent years and he is grateful to the respective publishers for permission to make use of material from the following: *Pay Strategy for the 1990's* (1990) and *Full Employment in the 1990's* (1992), Institute of Public Policy Research; 'Policies to Reduce European Unemployment' in *Unemployment in Europe*, ed. J. Michie and J. Grieve Smith (1994), Academic Press; 'A Programme for Reform' in *Managing the Global Economy*, ed. J. Michie and J. Grieve Smith (1995), Oxford University Press; 'Rebuilding Industrial Capacity' in *Creating Industrial Capacity*, ed. J. Michie and J. Grieve Smith (1996), Oxford University Press; 'Economic Policy and Constitutional Change after Maastricht' in *EMU after Maastricht*, ed. D. Currie and J.D. Whitley (1995), Lothian Foundation Press; 'The Delors White Paper on Unemployment', *International Review of Applied Economics*, volume 8, no. 3, Carfax Publishing Co.

1 A Pledge Betrayed

In its 1944 White Paper on *Employment Policy* the wartime Coalition Government committed its postwar successors to eliminate the disease of mass unemployment which had plagued the economies of the industrial countries in the interwar years. Speaking for the Government in the House of Commons in June 1944 while London was under attack by flying bombs, the Minister of Labour, Ernest Bevin, said that 'we can start out on this road this week and begin to say that we have left the old vexed disease of unemployment behind us'. For a long time this hope was fulfilled. Unemployment in the UK remained below 3 per cent for the next 25 years. This bipartisan achievement, spanning the periods of office of both Labour and Conservative governments, reflected the success of the postwar consensus to achieve full employment.

Since the 1970s, however, that promise had been betrayed. The commitment to full employment has been abandoned and mass unemployment has become tacitly accepted as a permanent feature of industrial society. Over the ten years from 1986 to 1995 unemployment averaged almost 9 per cent.[1] Despite the fall in unemployment from its 1993 peak, there were still over 2 million people claiming unemployment benefit in the first half of 1996 and another million or so who would like to work if jobs were available. Some key groups of the population have been particularly hard hit. In Greater London, nearly one-third of 16 to 17 year olds not in full-time education are unemployed and nearly two-thirds of young black (Afro-Caribean) men between the ages of 16 and 24. It is surprising that with so many young people unable to find work, there has not been more social unrest.

The rise in unemployment has been a major cause of the growth of poverty, homelessness and other social problems. It is not only the source of great personal misery and suffering; it also poses an eventual threat to the stability of Europe's economic and political institutions. Just as the 1929–31 slump stimulated the growth of fascism in Europe, so today there are already signs of the growth of racialist and extreme right-wing political movements in many parts of Western Europe.

There is nothing out-dated about the concept of full employment as a fundamental political and economic objective, merely because it was first established as such more than half a century ago – any more than the basic concepts of political liberty or universal suffrage, which date back even further, have had their day. Indeed the more advanced our industrial society becomes, the greater its failure in excluding some of its citizens from active participation. As William (later Lord) Beveridge recognised in his 1944 Report on *Full Employment in a Free Society*: 'A person who cannot sell his labour is in effect told he is of no use.' Industrial society based on the existence of substantial unemployment is irrational and indefensible. It is one thing to rely on a market economy to encourage managers to increase efficiency and productivity when the labour force is fully employed – another to use every endeavour to economise on labour when a substantial portion of the labour force is already unemployed.

The pursuit of full employment runs deeper than the technicalities of economic policy. It is bound up with the nature of the society in which we wish to live. Mass unemployment not only brings financial hardship to those directly involved; but when demand for labour is weak, the less educated or skilled have their wages depressed as they compete for a footing at the bottom of the employment ladder. Inequality increases and ghettos of deprivation and unemployment develop: nearly half of all council tenant householders of working age now have no wage earner.[2] Management becomes prone to rely on authority and fear rather than cooperation and participation. Full employment, on the other hand, reflects a strong demand for labour where employers have to take heed of the views and needs of their employees, and all workers have the chance of a decent wage, where 'flexibility' means flexibility of working conditions to meet the needs of the family as well as the firm, and where management has to operate by leadership and consent. In which kind of society would we prefer to live?

Many of the problems which are the subject of contemporary debate are caused or aggravated by heavy unemployment. The heavy cost of the welfare system is to an important extent a result of high unemployment. Discussion of the so-called 'demographic time bomb' – that is, the cost of supporting the growing number of retired people – is seriously distorted by the weak demand for labour. If the demand for labour were stronger, many people would want, and be able, to work (either full or part-time) well after the conventional retiring age.

Unemployment, and our attitudes towards it, raise fundamental questions about the political and moral values and objectives of the society in which we live, as well as technical questions about economic management and analysis. It is a mistake to think that the two can be kept in water-tight compartments. It is no coincidence that those forms of economic analysis, such as monetarism, which assume or conclude that unemployment cannot be tackled by economic management are associated with a set of political values which regard unemployment with equanimity. The re-emergence of mass unemployment reflects a change in attitudes as much as a change in circumstances.

We are concerned here to examine the origins of the wartime commitment to full employment, its successful achievement until the mid-1970s and subsequent abandonment, and how it can be restored. It is a story of the interplay between events on the one hand, and ideas and policy on the other. Although our account centres on the UK, it is common in varying degrees to all the main industrial countries, and the problems and the solutions lie as much on an international as a national plane.

UNEMPLOYMENT BEFORE 1939

Before the First World War, unemployment was not seen as a matter of general economic policy, as it was to be in later years, but solely as a consequence of imperfections in organisation of the labour market. In his first major study of unemployment in 1909, Beveridge described it as a 'Problem of Industry'. As he saw it then, the problem did not lie in securing a general balance between the supply and demand for labour but in 'perfecting the adjustment in detail'. To improve the working of the labour market he proposed a national system of Labour Exchanges, backed up by a national unemployment insurance scheme. The aim should be to reduce the 'reserve of labour' associated with fluctuations in demand and changes in industrial structure. Beveridge saw casual employment, with the insecurity and low level of earnings entailed, as a wasteful imperfection of the labour market that should be abolished; not, as some suggest today, as something to be encouraged in the name of 'flexibility'.

It was only after the First World War, with the emergence of mass unemployment on an unprecedented scale, that it came to be recognised as a major problem of economic policy. Rereading the history of the interwar years, it is striking how much of what is going on today closely resembles the events and arguments that took place then. The 'globalisation of finance' in the 1990s may appear to have made national economies uniquely subject to the whims of international finance, but in the 1920s and 1930s countries were even more vulnerable to international capital movements and the spread of recession through international trade. Then as now, discussion about the ways to tackle unemployment polarised between those who saw the remedy in the labour market and those who saw it as a problem of macro-economic policy. Then as now, deflationary policies in the name of 'sound finance' were the stock-in-trade of finance ministers and central bankers. Recent discussion and remedies break surprisingly little new ground, but represent for the most part a revival of old ideas (not even dressed in very new garb) that the wartime generation of political leaders and their economic advisers had seen to be ineffective and rejected.

The interwar experience of unemployment (discussed in Chapter 2) reflected both an intensification of the prewar trade cycle and the deflationary impact of a series of international financial crises, which led to a tightening of credit or other restrictive measures. In the UK, a short-lived postwar boom was followed by the 1921 slump with unemployment in that year averaging 17 per cent. Thereafter international factors became increasingly important in the British unemployment situation. The problems of our staple export industries, particularly coal and cotton textiles, had been intensified by the relative increase in British wages and prices during the war. This handicap was aggravated by the return of sterling to the Gold Standard in 1925 at the prewar exchange rate parity with the dollar. The resulting over-valuation of the pound was a classic case of the consequences of sacrificing industry and employment to the apparent interests of financial orthodoxy – in this case the desire to return to prewar 'normality' in the form of the Gold Standard and the pound's traditional parity. Ironically, although it was Winston Churchill who as Chancellor of the Exchequer took the fatal step, he had earlier summed up his misgivings by saying that 'I would rather see Finance less proud and Industry more content.'[3] The decision has many present day parallels. The tendency to sacrifice industrial competitiveness to inappropriate or inflexible exchange rate policies has now become a major theme in the development of European economic integration.

Interwar unemployment reached dramatic heights in the Great Slump, averaging over 20 per cent in the UK in 1931–3. Although the start of the Slump coincided with the Wall Street crash in 1929, it basically represented a severe but conventional trade cycle in many countries, including the US and UK, aggravated by national and international financial factors. In Britain a long-running debate over budgetary policy – whether to step up public works to reduce unemployment, or cut public expenditure to balance the budget – culminated in the collapse of the Labour Government in 1931. The Treasury and the Bank of England, in response to pressure from overseas financial institutions, were urging the Government to cut expenditure and in particular unemployment benefit. Unable to secure support for such measures from his colleagues in the Labour Cabinet, the Prime Minister, Ramsay MacDonald, resigned and formed a National Government. But within a few months the attempt to maintain the exchange rate had proved abortive and the UK went off the Gold Standard. One of the clearest, but least well learnt, lessons of the period was the danger of letting economic policy become dominated by the desire to cling to an unsustainable exchange rate.

The controversy about the role of budgetary policy in combating unemployment (which still continues today) started in the second half of the 1920s with an intense debate about the efficacy of 'public works' or increased public investment as a means of reducing unemployment. The case that such investment, worthwhile in its own right, could be legitimately financed by increased public borrowing was most closely argued in a series of Liberal Party publications inspired by Maynard (later Lord) Keynes and backed by Lloyd George; such proposals had also been put forward for many years by the Labour Party. But such measures were virulently opposed by the Treasury, who argued (in what became known as the 'Treasury View') that any increase in public investment would be ineffective and would automatically lead to a corresponding reduction in private investment.

KEYNES AND BEVERIDGE

The intellectual response to this opposition was eventually crystallised in Keynes' *General Theory* published in 1936. He set out there to convince his fellow economists that the common-sense observation that unemployment reflected lack of demand for goods and services was the correct one; and that the belief of the classical economists that the demand and supply for labour would automatically be brought into balance by adjustments in wages was not realistic (see Chapter 3). The power of Keynes' arguments, his position in the establishment and the evident facts of the time all combined to ensure that within five years his approach dominated the formulation of postwar economic policy. What was later to be known as the 'Keynesian Revolution' had begun.

Keynes ranks alongside John Stuart Mill and Karl Marx in his influence over political thinking, partly because he directed his powerful intellect to the key problems of his times, but also because he was always prepared both to engage closely with other policy makers in numerous intergovernmental conferences and official committees and to take the argument to the general public, whether it be in the pages of the *Evening Standard* or on the BBC. My endeavour has been to make this book Keynesian in that spirit, in the belief that in a democracy it is essential that the key issues of economic policy should be as widely understood and debated as possible. Incidentally in the present political climate it is worth recalling that both Keynes and Beveridge (whose names inevitably recur continually in any discussion of full employment) were Liberals, and from the centre rather than the left of the political spectrum.

Keynes defined 'full employment' in the *General Theory* as a situation where unemployment was either 'frictional', as people moved between jobs, or 'voluntary'. Beveridge publicised the concept most effectively when he published his report on

Full Employment in a Free Society in 1944 as a sequel to the Beveridge Report on Social Security. He wrote there that 'The adventure of full employment must be undertaken if free society is to survive.' Like the Government White Paper on *Employment Policy* published in the same year, Beveridge's proposals for ensuring full employment were based on Keynes' concept of the need to ensure adequate levels of demand, particularly investment in new plant and buildings which had historically been unstable and a major cause of the traditional trade cycle. The Beveridge Report and the 1944 White Paper inaugurated a new approach to the annual budget, whereby changes in taxation (or expenditure) were primarily directed to stabilising demand and keeping the economy on an even keel.

As widely expected, pent-up demand for goods ensured that demand would remain high in the immediate aftermath of war. The Keynesian approach underlined the need to curb, rather than stimulate, demand and in so doing avoid a boom followed by a slump as after the First World War. Both in the UK and elsewhere unemployment was successfully kept low from the end of the war to the early 1970s. Contrary to subsequent mythology, this did not involve any systematic deficit financing. Despite the interest burden of wartime debt, the ratio of national debt to national income went down from 2.7 in 1946 to 0.6 in 1973. A high level of employment and activity kept up tax revenue and kept down the cost of unemployment pay so benefiting the Budget – just as, conversely, the high level of unemployment in recent years has been a major factor in the general emergence of budget deficits.

BRETTON WOODS

In parallel with the preparation of the 1944 White Paper on *Employment Policy*, discussions had been taking place between British and American officials about proposals to stabilise commodity prices and establish a postwar international financial regime which would avoid the chaotic conditions which so frequently occurred in the interwar years and assist the achievement of full employment. The origins and nature of the eventual agreement reached at Bretton Woods in 1944 are discussed in Chapter 3. It attempted to achieve stability in exchange rates by a form of modified Gold Standard which would reduce the deflationary pressures that had become a feature both of attempts to restore the prewar Gold Standard and the successive international financial crises as it broke up during and after the 1931 Slump. Exchange rates were to be 'fixed' but could be adjusted where there was a 'fundamental disequilibrium'. Countries in temporary balance of payments difficulties could be assisted by being able to draw on the International Monetary Fund (IMF). Recognition of the need for creditor countries as well as debtors to assist in the adjustment process was most strikingly embodied in the 'Scarce Currency Clause'. Although in the event this was never applied, it would have enabled other countries to use discriminatory import restrictions against the currency of a persistent creditor – in practice the dollar.

The Bretton Woods regime did not eliminate foreign exchange crises. These were still inherent in one-way speculation against currencies expected to devalue; and the Fund's prescriptions for countries in difficulties were frequently deflationary. But it successfully presided over an orderly dismantling of wartime foreign exchange controls and liberalisation of trade, and provided the machinery for governments to cooperate in tackling the evolving problems of international payments. The fixed exchange rate regime re-established at Bretton Woods eventually broke up, however, in the early 1970s with a general move towards floating rates. Since then, apart from sporadic attempts to coordinate exchange rate policy, governments have increasingly withdrawn from any attempt to make a coordinated approach to international economic problems as free market ideology has taken hold.

INFLATION AND UNEMPLOYMENT

The period of full employment from the end of the Second World War to the 1970s was also one of low inflation: from 1946 to 1970 inflation in the UK averaged 3.6 per cent a year. This ran counter to the fears of Beveridge and the other architects of postwar full employment policy that the strengthened bargaining power of labour might drive up wages and lead to inflation. This was indeed a potential problem, but one that was avoided, albeit in a hand-to-mouth way, by a succession of incomes policies (discussed in Chapter 7). Successive governments of both major parties relied on a series of what proved to be short-term expedients, but never succeeded in establishing permanent machinery or institutional changes for dealing with the problem. Although there was effectively an inter-party consensus on the need for income restraint there was hardly ever any agreement on the actual measures involved: it was too easy for those in Opposition to find fault with whatever policy the Government of the day was pursuing at the time. In Denis Healey's words, 'Adopting a pay policy is rather like jumping out of a second floor window: no one in his senses would do it unless the stairs were on fire. But in postwar Britain the stairs have always been on fire.'

The commodity price boom of the early 1970s and the two successive oil crises stimulated price increases and put pressure on wages, and it became increasingly difficult to operate an effective incomes policy. Political disillusion with this approach reached its peak after the public sector strikes in 1979 during the so-called 'Winter of Discontent' in the final months of the Callaghan Government.

The perception of inflation, rather than unemployment, as the major threat to economic stability was, perhaps, a natural reaction to the outbursts of inflation following the oil crises in the 1970s. The memory of double digit inflation became part of the folk memory of the 1970s, as mass unemployment was of the 1930s. The damage done by the inflationary spasm itself was nothing compared with the havoc it subsequently wrought by giving policy makers an excessive fear of inflation when this was no longer a present danger.

The emergence of more acute inflationary problems in the 1970s led governments to adopt tighter fiscal and monetary policies which resulted in substantial increases in unemployment. From then on the creation and maintenance of a high level of unemployment policy became the crucial weapon in the fight against inflation. Unemployment, which had risen to 6 per cent in the late 1970s, reached a peak of 13 per cent in 1982 and remained in double figures to 1987. After a temporary drop to around 6 per cent in 1989 and 1990 during the so-called 'Lawson boom', it rose to a further peak of 10 per cent in 1993.

The fact that more effort was not made to reduce the high level of unemployment when inflation eased seems to have reflected two main factors. First, after a time such increases in unemployment are not easily reversible. Second, political attitudes had become more tolerant of unemployment. Kalecki's warning to liberal Keynesians in 1943 had eventually come to pass: 'The assumption that a government will maintain full employment in a capitalist economy if it only knows how to do it is fallacious.'[4] High unemployment did not, as formerly assumed, necessarily lead to governments losing elections. One reason for this must be that while initially increases in unemployment may be spread fairly widely across the community (and are associated with a highly visible increase in business failures), eventually they become concentrated on the most disadvantaged and least vocal sections of society. This would explain the fact that temporary increases, such as those experienced in the early 1990s, attract far more attention than the emergence of a permanently high level of unemployment over the course of the last decade. Higher unemployment remained acceptable to what J.K. Galbraith has called 'the Contented Majority', at least until they became a prey to general and pervasive insecurity.[5]

THE MONETARIST LEGACY

As the emphasis of economic policy changed at the end of the 1970s the postwar Keynesian revolution gave way to a monetarist counter-revolution, the legacy of which still dominates economic policy-making. The essence of monetarism was the theory that inflation is a purely monetary phenomenon and hence that if the money supply is properly controlled there will be no inflation. The monetarists predicted that restricting the money supply would not affect unemployment, save in the short run. Unemployment reflected 'imperfections' in the labour market to be tackled by such measures as legislation to curb the trade unions, and by abolishing or weakening machinery to regulate wages (such as Wages Councils). Short of such structural changes there was a 'natural rate of unemployment' (a telling phrase!) to which the economy would eventually revert. The history of full employment, however, suggests that on the contrary the strength or weakness of labour has been a *consequence* rather than a *cause* of the level of unemployment – with those features of the labour market said to be inimical to high employment, such as strong unions and protective legislation, most evident in the postwar period of full employment.

The monetarist approach was put to the test in the early days of Mrs Thatcher's government in Sir Geoffrey Howe's Medium Term Financial Strategy (MTFS). It was a costly experiment whose failure was later apparent in the persistence of inflation despite the fact that unemployment rose to over 3 million.

The pure monetarists maintained, wrongly, that budgetary policy was only of relevance in so far as government deficits or surpluses affected the supply of money. But as had been clearly understood in the previous Keynesian consensus, both monetary policy and budgetary policy directly affect the demand for goods and services and hence put pressure upwards or downwards on output, prices and employment. Monetary policy acts through changes in interest rates and the ease or difficulty of obtaining credit; budgetary policy affects demand through changes in public expenditure or tax rates. In practice, throughout most of the 1980s vigorous use was made of both monetary and fiscal policy to clamp down on demand in the UK and elsewhere with the aim of eliminating inflation. These attempts met with varying degrees of success, but the price paid was an almost universal rise in unemployment.

THE NEW ORTHODOXY

While few of those concerned with economic policy would still describe themselves as 'monetarists', the flirtation with monetarism in the 1980s has given rise to a new orthodoxy to which most finance ministers, central bankers and their officials now subscribe – as indeed do most financial and economic commentators. It is a doctrine which is essentially monetarist in origin. The New Orthodoxy in its purest form may be summarised as follows:

(a) inflation should be controlled by the use of interest rates, preferably by an independent central bank;

(b) budgets should be balanced and not used as an active means of influencing demand; and
(c) unemployment should be tackled by removing imperfections in the operation of the labour market.

The doctrine initially found ready political acceptability among those whose prime objective was to cut back the role of the state. It became a natural part of the Thatcher and Reagan ethos. At its core lies the fallacy that modern economies are self-stabilising mechanisms that will operate effectively without any government intervention or international cooperation. 75 years of history belie the case. But as well as appealing to the political right, the New Orthodoxy has now gained a hold across the whole political spectrum and is rapidly establishing a new consensus to which the centre and left throughout Europe also subscribe. It is difficult to discern exactly how this has come about. One factor has been that those in power, or hoping to gain power, have been increasingly concerned to assuage the doubts of financial markets about their policies. This has certainly been the case with the Labour Party in Britain. By some mysterious process of osmosis, as the Labour Party has seen power within its grasp, its policy statements have increasingly tended to embrace the assumptions and attitudes that now prevail in official and financial circles.

At present the underlying assumption governing economic policy is that unemployment cannot be allowed to fall below something in the range of 1.5 to 2 million because inflation would accelerate. As a result, over a million of our fellow citizens are increasingly condemned to unemployment because it has become the only politically acceptable way of regulating inflation. If full employment is to be restored, we must find an alternative to the maintenance of mass unemployment as the means of controlling inflation once again. This makes a reform of the pay bargaining system a key part of any full employment policy.

One consequence of the prolonged period of high unemployment in recent years is the erosion of our industrial capacity, which is no longer sufficient to employ the whole of our potential labour force. The rate at which this capacity can be rebuilt will be a key factor in determining the pace at which unemployment can be reduced.

The most crucial respect in which our present position varies from that of the past era of full employment is our position in the European Union (EU). Not only is the British economy now more closely linked to those of other members of the EU, but UK government economic policy is liable to be influenced by the Treaty of Maastricht and its general attitudes towards future political and economic integration in Europe. At present European economic policy is dominated by the New Orthodoxy; but the history of the rapid spread of Keynesian ideas in the 1940s, and then of monetarist ideas in the 1980s, gives grounds for hope that once the battle of ideas is won and full employment is again accepted as a primary objective of economic policies in the UK, it will soon become fashionable elsewhere. But for this to happen, there must be protagonists, as strongly convinced as Mrs Thatcher was in her free market beliefs, to fight the ideological and political battle for restoration of full employment.

THE KEY ISSUES

Amid the sometimes confusing welter of recent economic theory and statistical analysis, five practical issues stand out as those which need to be addressed in developing policies to restore full employment:

1 re-establishing the use of both budgetary and monetary policy as a means of influencing output and employment, rather than solely as a means of controlling inflation;
2 reforming the pay bargaining system to obviate the reliance on unemployment to avoid a wage/price spiral;
3 remedying the lack of adequate capacity to employ the labour force fully, along with other 'supply-side' measures to enable the economy to operate at a higher level of demand;
4 establishing full employment as a major objective of the EU and extricating it from the deflationary straitjacket of the EMU convergence conditions in the Treaty of Maastricht;
5 establishing a new international financial regime to ensure greater exchange rate stability and combat speculative pressures, and so reduce the deflationary bias of the present system.

These five key policy areas are discussed in Chapters 6 to 11, following a review of the emergence of the postwar full employment consensus and its subsequent abandonment in Chapters 2 to 5.

The long-term rise in unemployment has not been the result of uncontrollable events, but of changing economic policies and political values. It can be reversed. We can to a large extent control our economic destiny. But to do so, we must revolutionise our approach to economic policy and the values which underlie it.

2 Unemployment and Economic Policy before 1939

History, if faced with courage, need not be lived again.
(Maya Angelou)

UNEMPLOYMENT BEFORE 1914

Unemployment first became a major economic problem in the years between the Wars. Although unemployment before the First World War had become recognised as a serious social problem, it had been much less widespread. Recorded unemployment in that period was very much a cyclical problem, mainly apparent in times of trade recession. Before the institution of general unemployment insurance in 1920, the only figures available refer to trade union members. From 1881 to 1914 the percentage of trade union members unemployed each year ranged from 2 to 10 per cent, averaging 4.7 per cent (see Table 2.1). Although the trade union returns probably understate the level of unemployment compared with the later insurance figures, unemployment before 1914 was still not much over one-third of the levels reached in the 1920s and 1930s.[1]

William (later Lord) Beveridge, best known for his 1942 'Beveridge Report' on Social Insurance and his subsequent book, *Full Employment in a Free Society*, published his first major study of unemployment in 1909, entitled *Unemployment: A Problem of Industry*. Even then, he considered that the problem of unemployment lay, in a very special sense, at the root of most other social problems. In his personal Odyssey through the unfolding history of unemployment, however, Beveridge saw the problem before 1914 as one of industrial organisation, – how to make the labour market work more effectively and humanely. At that time the unemployment problem did not appear to be bound up with general economic policy – a concept that in any case had hardly been recognised. It was not until after the

Table 2.1 UK unemployment, 1881–1918 (annual averages)

Year	*per cent*	*Year*	*per cent*
1881	3.5	1900	2.5
1882	2.8	1901	3.3
1883	2.5	1902	4.0
1884	5.8	1903	4.7
1885	8.8	1904	6.0
1886	9.8	1905	5.0
1887	8.7	1906	3.6
1888	4.9	1907	3.7
1889	2.1	1908	7.8
1890	2.1	1909	7.7
1891	3.5	1910	4.7
1892	6.3	1911	3.0
1893	7.5	1912	4.0
1894	6.9	1913	3.6
1895	5.8	1914	4.2
1896	3.3	1915	1.2
1897	3.3	1916	0.6
1898	2.8	1917	0.7
1899	2.0	1918	0.8

Notes: (a) Before 1912 the figures cover members of trade unions paying unemployment benefit (which covered some 1.4 million members in 1912).

(b) From 1912 to 1916 the figures refer to people covered by the 1911 National Insurance Act (about 2.25 million manual workers in a limited number of industries).

(c) From 1916 to 1918 the coverage was extended by a further 1.25 million workers by the 1916 Unemployment Insurance Act.

Source: *Labour Market Trends*, January 1996.

1914–18 War that unemployment both reached a new order of magnitude and took on a new dimension as an aspect of what were clearly major economic problems posing inescapable problems of policy.

In his 1909 study, Beveridge saw no general imbalance between the growth of the supply and demand for labour, only specific problems of adjustment which led to unemployment. He attributed the unemployment problem to three main factors: changes in industrial structure; fluctuations in industrial activity; and industry's reliance on a reserve of unemployed labour. It was the wasteful and unnecessary nature of the last of these factors to which he addressed particular attention. Study of labour conditions in the docks and in building highlighted the problems of casual labour, and the way in which it drove down earnings.

Beveridge distinguished two features of casualisation. One was the inevitable variations of labour requirements of individual employers and trades. The other was the fact that employers were relying on picking an ever-changing labour force from the available pools of labour; so that the dock employers, for example, had more men dependent on them than could be fully employed even at peak times. (The recent spread of casual work has revived this phenomenon, with unattached unemployed people drawn to London by the chance of getting at any rate some casual employment.) Beveridge argued that employers should be encouraged to maintain a constant labour force even if they could not fully employ them all the time, rather than keep two men perpetually half employed though one regular man would serve. Decasualisation in the docks was only eventually achieved when Ernest Bevin set up the National Dock Labour Corporation during the Second World War. In Beveridge's eyes if the principle of the 'living wage' meant anything, it meant not simply a certain rate of pay, but also a minimum continuity of employment – a comment with renewed application today.

Beveridge's principal remedy was to improve the working of the labour market by setting up a national system of Labour Exchanges. This should lessen the impact of fluctuations in demand for labour by different employers and industries by making it easier for workers to find other employment. The financial problems of those who still remained out of work would best be met from a general insurance scheme, rather than under the inhumane provisions of the Poor Law. But in commenting on the age-old problem of avoiding making such assistance more attractive than seeking work, he commented that 'A nation cannot treat its dependents less badly than it treats its citizens. Only when it has humanised industrial relations can it safely humanise the Poor Law'. (During the 1980s, however, there has been a desire to dehumanise both: industrial relations have been degraded by 'deregulating' the labour

Table 2.2 UK unemployment, 1919–39 (annual averages)

Year	*per cent**	*Thousands†*	*Year*	*per cent**	*Thousands†*
1919	6.0	–	1930	16.0	2,014
1920	3.9	–	1931	21.3	2,718
1921	16.9	–	1932	22.1	2,813
1922	14.3	1,541	1933	19.9	2,588
1923	11.7	1,292	1934	16.7	2,221
1924	10.3	1,153	1935	15.5	2,106
1925	11.3	1,289	1936	13.1	1,822
1926	12.5	1,441	1937	10.8	1,557
1927	9.7	1,142	1938	12.9	1,881
1928	10.8	1,287	1939	9.3	1,590
1929	10.4	1,276			

* The percentage of people covered by the National Insurance Acts of 1920 and 1930.
† Those who had registered at Labour Exchanges whether insured or not, including those who had not lost their jobs but had reregistered because of short-time working or temporary stoppages.
Source: *Labour Market Trends*, January 1996.

market; and unemployment benefit has been reduced in relation to wages and made subject to more severe conditions.)

UNEMPLOYMENT BETWEEN THE WARS

The 1914–18 War was followed by a short-lived boom as wartime shortages were made good. But this soon collapsed, with the help of sharp increases in the Bank Rate (which reached what was then the high level of 7 per cent in April 1920) and unemployment rose to 17 per cent in the 1921 slump. From then on unemployment remained at levels well above anything experienced before 1914 (see Table 2.2): Although the figures were still heavily influenced by the trade cycle, unlike earlier years the problem remained severe even at the top of the cycle, and in the two best interwar years (1927 and 1937) one person in ten was still out of work. At the worst of the depression in the early 1930s over one in five of the insured population was unemployed. From 1921 to 1939 unemployment averaged 14 per cent of the insured workforce.

Along with the high general levels of unemployment, the incidence of unemployment in the worst hit industries and areas was devastating throughout most of the 1920s and 1930s. Textiles and coal, the main exporting industries, were particularly badly affected. Exports of coal fell from 73 million tons in 1913 to 25 million tons in 1921. There was some recovery during the 1920s, interrupted by trade disputes, but coal production in 1929 was down to 258 million tons from 287 million tons in 1913 and output per manshift rose. Cotton suffered equally severely. Recovery was slow. In 1932 over one-third of coal miners were unemployed, but in 1937 this had only fallen to 15 per cent. Iron and steel had recovered rather better: whereas nearly half the labour force was unemployed in 1932, this was down to around 10 per cent by 1937. But in Wales, the North and Northern Ireland up to one-quarter of the insured population were still unemployed. Mining towns were particularly badly hit, with 37 per cent still unemployed in Pontypridd and 42 per cent in Merthyr Tydfil at the peak of the 1937 boom.[2] Events such as the Jarrow march, to publicise the plight of the unemployed in the shipyards there, symbolised the frustration and suffering of the depressed areas. Both the severity and the nature of the unemployment problem had changed beyond recognition since 1914. The new problem of mass unemployment became a major political issue.

THE PRE-1914 GOLD STANDARD

Two critical events which crystallised the debate about unemployment and economic policy between the Wars were the return to the Gold Standard in 1925 and the budgetary crisis which led to the break-up of the Labour Government in 1931. The return to the prewar Gold Standard is now remembered as much for what Keynes wrote about it in his famous pamphlet *The Economic Consequences of Mr. Churchill* as for the event itself. But the lessons for exchange rate policy not only permeated the postwar Bretton Woods agreement, but have striking parallels today, most obviously in sterling joining the European

Exchange Rate Mechanism (ERM) in 1990 at an unrealistically high rate. The story of the return to the Gold Standard is the all too familiar one of what is mistakenly conceived as financial rectitude having disastrous effects on industry and employment.

The whole of the interwar period was dominated by the desire of most governments and central banks to re-establish the Gold Standard which had come to be regarded as the embodiment of the financial stability of prewar years. In this there was a strong element of nostalgia not wholly related to the facts. The problems of returning to the Gold Standard are a crucial part of our story, because the need to recreate some form of international payments system without repeating the mistakes of the 1920s and 1930s dominated the discussions of postwar policy.

Prior to the 1914–18 War, the United Kingdom had been on the Gold Standard, which meant that the pound was freely convertible into gold at a fixed rate, as were the currencies of the main industrial countries in Europe and North America. We were thus effectively part of a fixed exchange rate system. For those industrial countries who were members of the Club, the pre-1914 Gold Standard had come to serve two purposes. The first was that the use of gold as backing for domestic currencies served as a guarantee of their continued value, given that gold itself could be assumed to remain a scarce and valuable commodity and the weight of gold represented by a pound or a franc remained unchanged. This was the rationale of the continued reliance on gold backing after the introduction of paper money, and was essentially a matter of national policy and legislation. The informal consequence of this was the establishment of gold as a medium for the final settlement of international payments and a system of fixed exchange rates between members of the Club – as long as they did not change the value of their currencies in terms of gold.

The system was 'informal' in the sense that there were no formally agreed rules of the game. Neither was it consciously designed as a self-regulating mechanism. This was an attribute given it by successive economists, starting with David Hume in the eighteenth century. Central bankers operated the way they did because of the dictates of their own national monetary systems, not in response to any formal rules of the Gold Standard, although in later years the principles on which they worked came to reflect a tacit understanding of the way the system should work.

The self-regulating feature of the system was the expectation that interest rates would rise (either because of contraction of the money supply or from central bank action) when gold was flowing out of the country, and fall when it was flowing in. In the former case, as a consequence of the decrease of the money supply, prices and activity in the country concerned would fall: this would reduce imports and increase exports; the balance of payments would improve and the gold outflow be stemmed. This was the process that circumstances enforced on debtors. The converse process for creditors experiencing an inflow of gold was an expansion of the monetary supply and lower interest rates, leading to higher prices and activity, lower exports and higher imports and a deterioration in the balance of payments. This self-adjusting process also applied where gold outflows and inflows were the result of capital movements. Higher interest rates would help to stem the outflow by making inward investment more attractive and *vice versa.* To the theoreticians of the system like Hume, the adjustment process was symmetrical, with what we would now call 'creditor' nations expanding credit and stimulating their economies while 'debtors' were restricting credit and deflating. But in practice, then as now, the pressures on debtors to stem the outflow of gold (i.e. a movement out of the currency) was much greater and more immediate than the expansionary pressures on creditors.

Up to 1914 the system appeared to work relatively smoothly, particularly when viewed from the crisis-ridden years after 1918. The members were not subject to the enormous strains resulting from reparation payments and war debts which were to dominate the scene in the interwar years. Long-term investment flowed from the industrial countries, particularly the UK, to those newly developing. The flow of immigrant labour went in the same direction as capital, to the United States, Canada and Australia, thus easing the need for new industrial investment in the old European countries. In addition, whereas the UK had no tariff barriers, most of the newly developing countries had substantial tariff protection. These three factors helped to establish broadly compatible trends among members of the Club, but there were still temporary imbalances in the total payment flows.[3] These were, however, largely isolated from the politically charged question of unemployment: partly because unemployment was both lower and less visible than post 1918; and partly because unemployment was regarded as a problem of poverty largely unrelated to financial policy. Prices and wages were also much more variable than they came to be in the interwar years.

THE DISRUPTION OF WAR

The First World War disrupted the operation of the system. The extent to which the Gold Standard was formally suspended during the War varied from country to country but most central banks took steps to ban or limit gold shipments. The War also radically changed the economic conditions under which the Gold Standard had previously worked. Differing rates of wartime inflation set up cost disparities which were bound to make the restoration of prewar exchange rates inappropriate. By the end of the War sterling was overvalued against the dollar by around 10 per cent, and the franc by 35 per cent.[4]

There had also been striking changes in the net creditor or debtor position of the major industrial countries. Most of the foreign securities which the UK sold from 1914 to 1920 to help pay for the War went to the US, but it still incurred large war debts primarily to the US. Although the UK remained a major lender, its weak balance of payments was only sustained by substantial short-term borrowing. The US moved from being a net debtor before the War to being a major creditor at the end of the War, and effectively supplanted the UK as the dominant force in international economic relations. Whereas before 1914 Europe had been a source of capital for the rest of the world, after 1918 it became a net borrower, and the US became the major source of new foreign investment. These changes would in themselves have been more than enough to create serious payments difficulties, but the situation was further aggravated by the attempt to extract reparations from Germany on a vast scale to compensate the Allies for wartime damage and costs: these reparations would have required an enormous increase in German exports to finance the payments required. Despite all these traumatic changes, the financial community and governments saw a re-establishment of the Gold Standard as the only means of returning to 'normality'.

THE 1925 RETURN TO THE GOLD STANDARD

During the war the convertibility of sterling into gold was suspended but sterling remained effectively pegged to the dollar. But in March 1919 sterling began to float and fell to levels well below the prewar rate of $4.86 to the pound. At the end of the war the Committee on Currency and Foreign Exchange with Lord Cunliffe in the Chair had recommended a return to the Gold Standard at the prewar parity. Action was delayed until 1925, when after the fall of the short-lived minority Labour government in 1924, Winston Churchill, the new Conservative Chancellor of the Exchequer, announced the decision to return to gold at the prewar parity – an appreciation of about 10 per cent. The consequent over-valuation of the pound accentuated the difficulties of Britain's major export industries. (Taking 1913 as 100, the average of export prices for 1927–9 was France 101, Italy 123, Switzerland 149 and UK 162. The corresponding figures for the volume of exports were France 147, Italy 136, Switzerland 101 and UK 85.)[5]

Although Churchill eventually succumbed to the pressure from the Treasury and the Bank of England, initially at least he had serious doubts about their approach. After reading an article by Keynes, he wrote:

> The Treasury have never, it seems to me faced the profound significance of what Mr. Keynes calls 'the paradox of unemployment amidst dearth'. The Governor shows himself perfectly happy in the spectacle of Britain possessing the finest credit in the world simultaneously with a million and a quarter unemployed. The community lacks goods and a million and a quarter people lack work. It is certainly one of the highest functions of national finance and credit to bridge the gap between the two . . . I would rather see Finance less proud and Industry more content.[6]

Keynes' criticisms in *The Economic Consequences of Mr. Churchill* were devastating. British prices and wages were now at least

10 per cent higher than those of its competitors. Unless the general level of prices in Britain were to be reduced by 10 per cent, cutting the wages of miners, textile workers and other employees in export industries to make them more competitive would mean reducing their real wages by a corresponding amount. The high exchange rate would be bad for the balance of trade and interest rates would have had to be raised to attract funds to London.

> This, in the circumstances, is the orthodox policy of the gold party; the adverse trade balance indicates that our prices are too high, and the way to bring them down is by dear money and restriction of credit . . . By what *modus operandi* does credit restriction attain this result? *In no other way than by the deliberate intensification of unemployment* . . . This is the so called 'sound' policy . . . Deflation does not reduce wages 'automatically'. It reduces them by causing unemployment.[7]

Keynes saw that the attempt to reduce prices and costs by deflation was certain to involve unemployment and industrial disputes.

> Our export industries are suffering because they are the *first* to be asked to accept the 10 per cent reduction. If *everyone* was accepting a similar reduction at the same time, the cost of living would fall, so that the lower money wage would represent nearly the same real wage as before. Deliberately to raise the value of sterling money in England means, therefore, engaging in a struggle, with each separate group in turn, with no prospect that the final result will be fair.

There was no guarantee that the money incomes of other classes would be reduced in line with those of wage earners.

The inevitable clash with the miners was postponed by a temporary government subsidy and another Royal Commission under Lord Samuel was set up to inquire into the industry. When the government accepted the Commission's recommendation in 1926 that the subsidy should be stopped, the employers renewed their demand for wage cuts and the General Strike ensued. Although the General Strike only lasted nine days, the miners' dispute continued for over six months, until they were eventually forced to return to work and accept wage reductions. But the trauma of the dispute contributed to the failure of employers to reduce wages in other export industries, which remained relatively uncompetitive.

The return to the Gold Standard looms large over the history of unemployment in the 1920s because of its direct impact on unemployment in our staple export industries. As Churchill himself saw, the return to gold symbolised the ascendancy of financial interests over those of industry – a central theme throughout the history of economic policy to this day. A return to the Gold Standard was widely believed to be essential to restore the financial standing of the City of London, and little heed was paid to the possibility of going back at a lower exchange rate than that prevailing before the War. The attraction of the Gold Standard as a source of stability was a reflection of the breakdown in the prewar international financial system. The lesson which Keynes and others sought to embody in the 1944 Bretton Woods agreement was that any 'fixed' exchange rate system should where necessary permit adjustments in rates rather than enforce deflation and unemployment.

THE GREAT SLUMP

The international financial system had made some return to prewar 'normality' by the end of the 1920s but was still in a fragile state. One source of instability was the increase in the value of assets quoted and saleable in a number of different markets in addition to those in which they were issued: for example, reconstruction loans and shares in the new international corporations.[8] The international financial crisis in 1931 thus had two related aspects. One was that falling commodity and share prices threatened the solvency of the banking system. The other was that the associated atmosphere of panic stimulated major movements of short-term capital. Any idea that the countries' economies were relatively independent was dashed after 1931, when all the industrial countries caught the virus of depression and the primary producing countries were hard hit by over-production and declining demand.

Following Britain's return to the Gold Standard, the level of unemployment remained substantially above prewar levels for the rest of the 1920s. The Slump which started in 1929 then raised it to new heights. The start of the world-wide Slump is popularly attributed to the Wall Street Crash in October 1929, but industrial production in the United States had started to fall and unemployment to rise some months before. The rise and fall in share prices was initially an exaggerated accompaniment of the movement in real business activity rather than a causal factor; but after the Crash the ensuing financial crisis in the United States and its international repercussions became a contributory factor to the Depression. Whereas in the 1920s the American economy seemed set on an expansionary course, between 1929 and 1933 output (GDP) fell by 30 per cent and unemployment rose from 3 per cent to 25 per cent. In the United Kingdom output fell by 6 per cent and unemployment doubled, from 10 per cent to 21 per cent, between 1929 and 1931. Other countries suffered in a similar fashion, and unemployment in the industrialised world as a whole is estimated to have reached 25 per cent in 1932.[9]

Falling commodity prices and deflationary conditions put a strain on the banks throughout Europe and North America, which was then reinforced by the movement of short-term funds looking for the safest refuge. In Europe the critical moment came in 1931 when the Credit-Anstalt, Austria's largest bank, got into difficulties and was only saved by international assistance and negotiating a partial suspension of payments with its foreign creditors. The consequence was a lack of confidence in Germany and elsewhere in Europe. This led in turn to a withdrawal of funds from London and a serious loss of gold. A rise in Bank Rate failed to staunch the flow and a credit of £50 million was then arranged with the Bank of France and the Federal Reserve Bank of New York.

THE 1931 BUDGET CRISIS

In 1931 the Labour Government faced a major budgetary crisis. As usual, financial institutions' attention focused on the public sector deficit, in particular that of the Unemployment Insurance Fund. A Royal Commission on Unemployment had criticised the funding of the Unemployment Insurance Fund. The Report of the May Committee, which was set up to recommend ways of cutting government expenditure, then provoked the final crisis by recommending increased taxation and expenditure cuts, particularly in unemployment benefits, in order to cope with the forecast budget deficit of £120 million for the year.

The Labour Cabinet was unable to agree on the reductions in expenditure proposed by the Treasury. By the last week of August the foreign line of credit was almost exhausted and the Government resigned. It was succeeded by the National Government in which Ramsay MacDonald remained Prime Minister and Philip Snowden, Chancellor of the Exchequer. New credits were obtained in Paris and New York and Snowden introduced new Budget proposals to remove the deficit. But pay cuts in the Navy led to the Invergordon 'Mutiny' and further financial panic. Again the international line of credit was almost exhausted and on September 21st the United Kingdom went off gold for the last time. The pound fell from $4.86 to $3.80 and the six years' return to prewar financial orthodoxy came to an end.

THE BREAK-UP OF THE GOLD STANDARD

The Gold Standard had in common with the subsequent postwar fixed exchange rate systems, Bretton Woods and the European Exchange Rate Mechanism, the advantage of ensuring a degree of international order but the disadvantage of setting in motion deflationary pressures which led to higher unemployment whenever a particular country came under pressure. In his study of the interwar years A.J. Youngson wrote:

> Britain's abandonment of the Gold Standard was a turning point in modern economic history. Britain had tried to restore nineteenth century financial stability so as to facilitate the international movement of foods and transfer of capital; and she had failed . . . As far as Britain was concerned, the direct consequences were almost wholly favourable; the indirect and remote consequences, on the other hand, most conspicuously the set-back to international cooperation in general and the resultant rise of nationalism, anarchy, suspicion and hatred in Europe, were in most ways, without doubt, disastrous.[10]

After the UK went off gold, the main survivors were those in the European Gold Block: France, Belgium, Italy, the Netherlands, Luxembourg, Switzerland and Poland. But after a succession of speculative crises the bloc eventually broke up in 1936, when France devalued as part of a Tripartite Agreement with the USA and UK in an attempt to stabilise foreign exchange markets. Any remnants of the prewar Gold Standard had finally come to an end.

The movement of 'hot money' (in effect any form of easily realisable asset) from one financial centre to another played a major part in the various interwar financial crises. The word 'financial' is important because the foreign exchange aspect of the crisis was generally a corollary of banking or budgetary difficulties; whereas, after the Second World War, foreign exchange crises have more often been directly related to pressure on the exchange rate itself, as for example in the UK leaving the ERM in 1992. This reflected in part the fact that at the beginning of the 1931 Slump and in the following few years some key movements of deposits were caused by fear of actual banking collapses, rather than, as in recent times, the opportunity to make a quick profit through gambling on the devaluation of a weak currency. This type of crisis created difficulties for central banks who were torn between the need to create credit to preserve the solvency of their banking system and the pressure to restrict credit and raise interest rates to attract money from abroad. Fortunately when the United States banking system was faced with a solvency crisis in 1933 internal conditions took precedence. Individual States declared a series of bank holidays in the run-up to the inauguration of Franklin Roosevelt. Within days Congress had given the new President sweeping powers to control the banking system and by the end of the year changes in the official price of gold had effectively devalued the dollar.

RECOVERY IN THE 1930S

The history of the 1930s was of various attempts by individual countries to achieve greater control of their economic situation and reduce unemployment through the use of tariff protection, exchange control or, in the case of Nazi Germany by rearmament and a high degree of economic autarky. The retreat from the Gold Standard was followed by an era of protectionism in the United Kingdom and elsewhere. Import duties were introduced in 1932 with a general duty of 10 per cent on most imports, excluding food and raw materials, but with Imperial Preference giving free entry to goods from other countries in the British Empire. The effects of protection on imports were, however, heavily diluted by free entry for Empire products, although in the special case of steel the tariff and its use as a bargaining counter with the European Steel Control gave the industry some measure of protection.

The other main instrument of recovery, cheap money, had a much more discernible effect on output and employment, particularly in the field of housing. Bank Rate was reduced to 2 per cent in June 1932 and remained at that level until 1939. As an indicator of the general level of longer term rates, the rate on 2.5 per cent consols averaged 3.15 per cent from 1933 to 1938 as compared with 4.26 per cent from 1920 to 1929. Cheap money played a key part in stimulating an unprecedented boom in house building. Over 3 million new houses were built in the 1930s. Of these little over one-fifth were built with state assistance; and the remainder were built by private enterprise unaided. Lower interest rates both encouraged investment in houses to rent and house-buying financed by building society mortgages. The use of low interest rates to stimulate the economy had the advantage of avoiding any doctrinal argument. It had long-standing antecedents going back to the days of the Gold Standard. Moreover it helped, rather than hindered, budget probity by keeping down the cost of the national debt.

BALANCING THE BUDGET

In terms of the development of thinking about economic policy and unemployment, the travail of the Labour Government over balancing the budget in 1931 crystallised the debate between the orthodox economists, the Treasury and the financial community on the one hand, and Keynes, the Liberal Party and the major part of the Labour movement on the other. Although orthodoxy triumphed on that occasion, little more than a decade later the Keynesians seemed to have won a permanent victory in the formulation of postwar economic policy; but today the same arguments that prevailed in 1931 have become fashionable once again.

The key economic dispute underlying the policy debates about public finance in the late 1920s and early 1930s was whether increased expenditure on 'public works' (i.e. public investment) financed by borrowing would reduce unemployment. The idea of public works as a remedy for unemployment started in the nineteenth century with the concept of local authorities providing work for the unemployed who would otherwise be eligible for Poor Law relief. But during the 1920s the Liberal Party began to advocate more ambitious schemes of public investment financed by government borrowing. The Liberal 'Yellow Book', *Britain's Industrial Future* (published in 1928), proposed a major programme of public investment, and was followed by a further report, *We Can Conquer Unemployment,* in the following year which constituted a central plank of the Party's 1929 election programme. This included a massive road-building programme, and investment in new low-rent housing, telephone installation and London transport, estimated to employ in total about 600,000 men for two years at a cost of £250 million, to be financed by a loan.

As Keynes and Hubert Henderson pointed out in a supporting pamphlet, *Can Lloyd George Do It?,* there would be a further stimulus to trade as those brought into employment had their effective purchasing power increased by receiving wages instead of unemployment pay. The cumulative effect of increases in employment would lead to increased consumer spending and hence further increases in employment – a process later to be formally expressed as the 'multiplier effect'. This would be reinforced by the creation of a more optimistic mood in the business community and greater willingness to invest in new capacity. The same process in reverse could be seen as a major factor behind the severe fall in employment in the Slump. As expenditure on investment in new plant and buildings eased off, those thrown out of work in the building and engineering industries spent less on consumer goods leading to a further loss of jobs in other industries. This again meant a further decline in consumer spending and further job losses in a cumulative downward spiral, reinforced by a loss of confidence.

The Treasury consistently expressed strong opposition to any proposals for increasing public investment. They set out their views (along with those of certain other departments) in 1929 in a special White Paper, *Memoranda on Certain Proposals Relating to Unemployment* (Cmd 3331), when the Government took the unusual step of publishing official comments on the Liberal proposals (even mentioning 'Mr Keynes' personally). The Treasury argued that public investment which generated sufficient revenue to meet the interest and sinking fund payments on the loans (e.g. telephones) could legitimately be financed by borrowing, but that to pay for other public investment by borrowing was unfairly placing the burden on later generations. There was, however, the intermediate case of capital expenditure by local authorities, where the interest and amortisation was met by central government out of current revenue. In this case the argument about what should or should not be financed by borrowing had some element of flexibility. The Treasury's arguments about the placing of burdens on subsequent generations would have been reasonable if it had had no relevance to the employment position. It was their insistence that increased public investment would not increase employment which was particularly damaging.

The 'Treasury View', as it became known, was based on the assumption that at any given level of interest rates there was a fixed supply of savings to be invested, and if the state invested more, private individuals and businesses could invest less. This reflected the assumptions of classical economic theory which did not take into account the possibility of unused resources and significant unemployment (which will be discussed in the next chapter), and the associated view that increased borrowing by the state was likely to raise interest rates and hence reduce private investment – a viewpoint still frequently put forward today in, for example, discussions about how to tackle unemployment in the EU.

Keynes' criticism of this view rested on the argument that when resources were unemployed the country could devote more resources to public investment without limiting other investment – indeed, the consequent increase in business activity would stimulate business activity. Greater government borrowing would bring into play what he then referred to as 'surplus savings', because 'the savings of individuals do not necessarily materialise in investments'. Without having yet formalised his approach, as he was later to do in the *General Theory*, Keynes and his allies saw clearly that at a time of massive under-employment of resources, the will to invest was the key factor, not the willingness to save. On the contrary, merely abstaining from consumption served to depress demand and employment; it was the positive decision to invest in new plant and machinery that would increase employment.

Theory apart, governments had long taken to borrowing when the need was urgent enough, the main example being in wartime, and the severity of the unemployment crisis might have been expected to lead to similar action. In the United States, it did with Franklin Roosevelt's programme for the New Deal. Part II of the National Industrial Recovery Act authorised the President to spend $3.3 million on public works to increase employment. Roosevelt's undogmatic approach and strong leadership rescued the US from a major economic crisis; but in Britain the instinct for financial orthodoxy and the baleful grip of classical economics continued to prevent any such action.

BEVIN AND THE LABOUR MOVEMENT

The strength of Lloyd George's personality and Keynes' skill as a publicist have ensured that the proposals of the Liberal Party to deal with the emerging unemployment crisis have received a good deal of historical credit, which indeed they deserve. But a decade earlier, the Labour Party had anticipated the inter-war debate on public works while the First World War was still in progress. A policy resolution proposed by J.R. Clynes and passed at the 1917 Labour Party Conference stated that:

> the Government can, if it chooses, arrange the public works, and the orders of the National Departments and Local Authorities in such a way as to maintain the aggregate demand for labour in the whole Kingdom (including that of capitalist employers) approximately at a uniform level from year to year; and it is therefore the first duty of the Government to prevent any considerable or widespread fluctuations in the total numbers employed in times of good or bad trade.[11]

By the eve of the 1929 General Election, however, the Labour Party was having one of its fits of financial orthodoxy and excoriated Lloyd George's schemes for public works financed by borrowing as 'Madcap Finance'. A pamphlet on *How to Conquer Unemployment: Labour's Reply to Lloyd George*, with a foreword by Ramsay MacDonald, described the Liberal proposals as 'a mere amateurish improvisation doomed to failure from the first because it ignores the need for taking the permanent reorganisation of our leading industries fairly and courageously in hand'. The Party's election platform, *Labour and the Nation*, envisaged that any new measures to reduce unemployment could be financed by savings on existing expenditure, particularly on armaments, and increased revenue from direct taxation on the rich and higher duties on large estates. These 'would provide resources for the abolition of taxes on necessaries, for the development of indispensable social services and further reduction of the National Debt'.

But one outstanding figure in the labour movement whose association with Keynes on the Macmillan Committee and the Economic Advisory Council led him to share Keynes' views was Ernest Bevin, who was then General Secretary of the Transport and General Workers' Union. Bevin's industrial experience and shrewd common sense had led him to see clearly the disastrous consequences of sacrificing the interests of industry and industrial workers to the obsessive preoccupation of the financial establishment with a return to the Gold Standard. 'We cannot do anything while we remain on the Gold Standard', he told the Macmillan Committee in November 1930.[12] He advocated devaluation in order to spread the burden of cost reduction fairly around the community, rather than concentrating it on particular sections, and also as a means of reducing the real interest burden of the national debt. He was convinced throughout the 1931 crisis that Britain would inevitably have to abandon the Gold Standard. As the crisis came to a head, Bevin played a leading part in defining the attitude of the TUC and the Labour movement as a whole to MacDonald and Snowden's proposals. When he later became Minister of Labour in the wartime coalition government, Bevin was one of the staunchest protagonists of postwar full employment policies.

After the formation of the National Government and MacDonald and Snowden had left the Party, Labour became more radical. In its 1933 policy statement, *Socialism and the Condition of the People,* its analysis of the causes of the slump closely anticipated Keynes' *General Theory,* to be published three years later. 'The national income is the national expenditure on consumption, plus national savings . . . when savings are not absorbed by the expenditure on capital goods, including additions to stocks, there is less income to spend on the consumption of goods . . . there is a fall in prices and a decline in employment.' This was a cumulative course of events leading to the current slump. Conversely, in a boom, 'money is spent on capital goods faster than actual savings are accruing for investment', with the opposite result. But by then Labour had also became a strong proponent of planning combined with public ownership. Investment would be kept in line with savings by means of a public investment programme, including the re-equipment of key state-owned industries, railway electrification, constructing oil extraction plants in coal mining areas, investment in housing, schools, hospitals, roads, and other public works – proposals which foreshadowed much of Labour's successful General Election manifesto in 1945.

3 The Birth of Full Employment

The adventure of full employment must be undertaken if free society is to survive. (Beveridge)

KEYNES' *GENERAL THEORY*

The publication of Keynes' *General Theory* (*The General Theory of Employment, Interest and Money*) in 1936 marked a turning point in the debates about the causes of unemployment and the conduct of economic policy: within little more than five years Keynes's ideas had become the basis of postwar economic policy. The book itself was intended for his fellow economists schooled in classical theory. Its aim was to put the ideas which he had been developing in policy debates into more rigorous theoretical form and show why existing theory failed to explain the existence of mass unemployment. In Keynes' words, 'the ideas which we have expressed so laboriously are extremely simple and should be obvious. The difficulty lies, not in the new ideas, but in escaping from the old ones.'[1]

Effective Demand

The key to his new approach raised no difficulties for those not burdened with a grounding in classical economics: namely that the volume of goods produced and sold, and hence the level of employment, depended on the willingness of consumers or business to purchase them – what Keynes called 'effective demand'. (The description 'effective' distinguishes demand backed up with the necessary purchasing power and resulting in actual expenditure, from demand in the sense of what we should like to have if we could.) He was therefore primarily concerned with the factors that determined effective demand, in particular the willingness of businessmen to invest in new plant and equipment and consumers to spend their incomes on goods and services. Investment depended on the expected returns in relation to the cost of capital goods and the cost of borrowing, as determined by interest rates. Consumer expenditure depended on the level of incomes and on people's 'propensity to consume' rather than save. This led on to an explanation of why effective demand could fall short of the level needed to ensure 'full employment', defined as a situation where existing unemployment was either 'frictional', as the labour force adjusted to the jobs available, or 'voluntary'.

Both Keynes and the classicists started with the assumption that investment and saving have to be equal. This follows from the fact that national output can either be regarded as reflecting expenditure or generating incomes. Hence (appropriately defined) national income equals national expenditure; they are the different sides of the same coin. On one side of the equation incomes can then either be spent on consumption or saved. On the other, expenditure can be divided into two categories: consumption and investment. So by definition saving must equal investment. In other words, what people and businesses do not spend on consumption, they save; and the output which does not go into consumption goes into investment. Keynes' simple model disregarded government expenditure and taxation, and the balance of payments, but they can be fitted neatly into the same pattern.

Where Keynes took issue with the classicists was in his analysis of the causal relationship between saving and investment. The classicists tended to imply that saving was the key to investment, whereas in Keynes' view investment determined the level of saving. As James Meade later put it, they had to shift from thinking 'in terms of a model of reality in which a dog called Savings wagged its tail labelled Investment, to thinking in terms of a model in which a dog labelled Investment wagged his tail labelled Savings'. The mere act of saving, or abstaining from consumption, did not itself lead to investment. Entrepreneurs took decisions to invest in plant and machinery on the basis of expected profits and the cost of capital. It was the task of the banking and financial system to mobilise the necessary finance out of available savings, past or present. The equation of investment with saving did not reflect a direct financial link between new saving and new investment, but the simple fact that output not consumed was invested. If people wanted to save more out of their incomes than business was prepared to invest, lack of effective demand would lead to a fall in output, and hence employment and incomes, until the level of savings had fallen to the same level as investment. There was no reason why investment and saving should equate at a level high enough to ensure full employment. If the desire to invest was too weak, or the desire to save rather than consume was too strong, unemployment would result.

Keynes' approach was heavily influenced by his debates over the previous decade with those who held the 'Treasury View' (discussed in Chapter 2): namely that increased investment in public works would correspondingly reduce other forms of investment. This reflected the classical assumption that saving and investment were brought into balance by changes in interest rates: higher interest rates encouraged saving and reduced investment, and lower interest rates discouraged saving and encouraged investment. Hence on this view, once this equilibrium was reached at any given interest rate, the supply of saving was fixed and no further investment was possible. Additional saving would only be forthcoming if interest rates were raised, and indeed the additional demand for capital arising from the extra government borrowing to finance the public works would increase interest rates. But higher interest rates would choke off some private investment.

Keynes pointed out that the flaw in this approach was the tacit assumption that the nation's available manpower and capital were already fully employed. If they were not, higher investment would automatically generate the additional saving required out of the higher incomes generated directly or indirectly. This was the situation in the 1920s and 1930s.

The Multiplier

The mechanism by which changes in investment affected national income and output had been established some years earlier by Keynes' close collaborator, R.F. (later Lord) Kahn,[2] and is known as the 'multiplier'. Once stated it is a simple enough concept and, as Keynes said, should be obvious. The multiplier effect reflects the fact that an increase in investment not only has a direct effect in increasing output and employment in industries such as building and engineering, but also gives an indirect boost to industries producing goods and services for consumption. This reflects the fact that as more workers are taken on in building and engineering, and they receive wages rather than the dole, their spending on consumption will rise by a substantial proportion of their increase in income – the remainder will be saved or go in taxes. This raises employment in the consumer goods industries and leads to a further round of spending by the additional workers employed there. Each successive way of spending will be lower than the last until the multiplier effect peters out. The magnitude of the multiplier will depend on how high a proportion of the additional wages (or profits) are saved or taxed – the higher the proportion saved, the lower the multiplier. The result will also depend on the leakage of the additional spending into imports (either imports of materials or finished goods). At that time a typical value of the multiplier for the UK or US economies was considered to be 2 to 3: that is, the eventual increase in expenditure and output would be 2 to 3 times that of the initial increase.

The *General Theory* sought to explain fluctuations in the level of activity and the existence of massive unemployment primarily in terms of the behaviour of investment. This approach reflected the key historical role of investment in booms and slumps (e.g. in the late 1920s and early 1930s). As investment moved up (or down), the level of incomes and employment moved with it, until the higher (or lower) level of saving required was equal to the new level of investment. The increase (or reduction) in saving came about through a change in incomes, the key assumption being that in given conditions people would save more, the greater their incomes. Thus in Keynes' model, saving and investment were brought into balance by changes in the level of incomes and employment. Whereas the classicists tacitly only examined the case of full employment, Keynes' theory was 'general' in that it covered the possibility of employment fluctuating well below this level. He was thus bringing economic theory into line with the economic reality as it was after the First World War, whereas the classical approach was more in tune with the position prevailing in earlier times when unemployment appeared to be considerably lower, except in recessions (see Chapter 2).

In view of Keynes' previous immersion in controversy about public investment and borrowing, it is interesting that budgetary policy goes almost unmentioned in the *General Theory*. The simple model in the *General Theory* did not explicitly take government expenditure and revenue into account. (But Keynes, unlike many of his successors, did not make the mistake of assuming that a model constructed for a particular purpose told the whole story.) Following the same approach, government expenditure can be seen as a component of effective demand, and taxation as something which reduces it. In respect of taxation, his main concern, then and later, was with the effects of making the new system more redistributive, so increasing the propensity to consume, as taxes on the rich are less likely to reduce consumption than those on the poor. The *General Theory* does not explicitly discuss the use of variations in taxation or public expenditure as a means of influencing effective demand. It was the parallel development of national income and expenditure accounts which soon focused attention on the now familiar categories of national expenditure, including public sector current and capital expenditure, exports and imports.

Unemployment and Wages

The central contention that Keynes set out to demolish was the proposition that the supply and demand for labour would automatically be brought into balance by appropriate changes in real wages (i.e. money wages adjusted for changes in prices). The classical view was that if the price of labour was right, there would be no unemployment problem. If there was a problem, it was because wages were being held too high by collective bargaining or some form of artificial restriction. Keynes dealt with this in two ways. The first was to demonstrate in his own terms that there was no reason to assume that the effective demand for labour would necessarily be adequate to ensure full employment – an easily observable fact at the time. The second was to argue that the level of real wages appropriate for any particular level of employment would come about without cutting money wages. As demand and output expanded, rising prices would make the additional output profitable and, because money wages would lag behind the rise in prices, real wages would be brought down to the appropriate level.

In adopting the latter approach, Keynes was meeting the

classicists on their own ground by assuming 'decreasing returns' i.e. that labour productivity would fall as output grew. In the *General Theory*, Keynes accepted this assumption without debate, although three years later he modified his views,[3] in response to work by Dunlop and others showing that in fact real wages could go up in a period of recovery. The classical assumption of decreasing returns has strong overtones of Ricardo's classic theory of rent, based on the principle that the most productive and profitable land is brought into production first and then successively less fertile land until the marginal land is only just profitable to cultivate. But in modern industry increasing, rather than decreasing, returns from scale are more generally the rule. Productivity tends to go up, rather than down, as output is increased. When factories are underused, additional output does not normally require a commensurate increase in the total labour force. Typically it will require more shop-floor workers with much the same productivity as those already at work, but no immediate increase in supervisory and managerial staff. If new plant has to be built, it will generally be more advanced technically and more efficient than existing plant. Hence it is misleading to think that increased output and employment mean lower productivity and require reductions in real wages: additional output is generally profitable at existing wage and price levels, if the demand is there to absorb it.

This is a point of major significance in any consideration of policies to reduce unemployment, and I shall return to it in Chapter 8. The *General Theory* in effect suggested that while reducing real wages was not a sufficient condition to restore full employment, it was a necessary consequence. But if it is accepted that we live in a world of increasing returns, then the idea that cutting real wages is essential for restoring employment falls to the ground. The only terms in which it is valid is that by cutting wages one country may improve its competitive position and increase its employment at the expense of others.

Although at that time Keynes still thought that lower real wages were a necessary concomitant of higher employment, he argued strongly against cuts in money wages as a means of reducing unemployment. He opposed attempts to reduce unemployment by wage cutting on two grounds: it would not work, and it was not fair. It would not work because of the effect of lower wages on workers' purchasing power. The classical advocates of reducing wages implicitly assumed that effective demand would remain unchanged if wages were cut, and lower prices and wages would therefore increase sales. But what might be valid for one firm (or even one industry) in isolation was not valid for the economy as a whole. Lower wages would affect demand. Suppose employers were to increase their labour force in expectation of higher sales; demand would only rise sufficiently to absorb the increased value of output if *all* the extra incomes (wages and profits) were being spent on additional consumption – which was almost certain not to happen, particularly in the case of profits – or any additional income not spent was matched by a corresponding increase in investment. In so far as lower wages reduced the incentive to invest in new plant and machinery, higher investment would not come to the rescue.

Wage cuts were unfair because reductions would fall disproportionately on certain industries (coal being a classic example) and certain classes of worker, while leaving those on fixed incomes better off. 'If important classes are to have their remuneration fixed in terms of money in any case, social justice and social expediency are best served if the remuneration of all factors are somewhat inflexible in terms of money.'[4] Keynes came to the ironical conclusion that 'To suppose that a flexible wage policy is a right and proper adjunct of a system which on the whole is one of *laissez-faire*, is the opposite of the truth. It is only in a highly authoritarian society, where sudden, substantial, all-round changes could be decreed that a flexible wage policy could function with success.' He was, of course, assuming that in either case social justice was a key consideration, something with which recent advocates of flexible wages seem blithely unconcerned.

Inequality

In his conclusion to the *General Theory* Keynes wrote that 'The outstanding faults of the economic society in which we live are its failure to provide for full employment and its arbitrary and inequitable distribution of wealth and incomes.' Achieving full employment depended on raising investment and increasing the propensity to consume. Since investment determined saving rather than the reverse (as formerly assumed), low interest rates should be a fundamental part of a full employment regime. He defended the liberal society and saw no case for state socialism or public ownership. What was required was the 'socialisation of investment', a concept he did not spell out in detail, save to refer to 'all manner of compromises and devices' by which public authority will combine with private initiative to stabilise investment at a high level.

Another consequence of his approach was that when there was a chronic shortage of demand, the arguments against death duties and taxation on the rich – that they would discourage savings – were no longer valid. There was no bar to a more egalitarian pattern of taxation on these grounds. Indeed such a shift in the tax burden could help to achieve full employment by increasing the propensity to consume, because the rich were able to and likely to pay their taxes by reducing savings, whereas taxes on the poor forced them to reduce consumption. He did not at that stage consider general reductions in taxation, and a consequent increase in borrowing, as a means of stimulating demand. The idea of varying the general level of taxation as a means of regulating demand was a logical corollary of this approach but was not something that Keynes advocated at the time, or was very enthusiastic about later.

PLANNING FOR POSTWAR FULL EMPLOYMENT

Although the *General Theory* was aimed primarily at Keynes' professional colleagues, the influence of its ideas quickly spread and fell on fertile ground in the early 1940s when politicians and the public began to consider postwar economic policy. By 1944 unemployment had fallen to a little over 100,000; public opinion was strongly behind the idea that the full employment attained by mobilisation for war must be maintained in peacetime and that a repetition of the experience of the 1920s and 1930s must be avoided. All parties to the Coalition Government were agreed on this theme and their formal commitment to this aim was expressed in the 1944 White Paper on *Employment Policy*. At virtually the same time as the White Paper was published, Beveridge completed his more detailed report, *Full Employment in a Free Society*, intended as a sequel to his previous 1942 Report on *Social Insurance and Allied Services.* Although the first 'Beveridge Report' was published nominally on his own responsibility to avoid political difficulties, it was in fact the report of an interdepartmental committee of officials. Beveridge wanted to undertake a similar exercise on full employment but the Government was not prepared for him to do so, and he wrote the Report on Full Employment in a personal capacity, but with much assistance from other experts, in particular Nicholas Kaldor (later to become a Treasury adviser himself).

This cautious approach on the Government's part was reflected in the White Paper's commitment to 'a high and stable level of employment' rather than 'full employment' *per se.* What was remarkable, however, was the willingness of Treasury officials and the Conservative members of the Coalition Government to subscribe (even if with some reluctance) to a document that represented such a reversal of prewar attitudes. Indeed the White Paper itself says:

> Not long ago, the ideas embodied in the present proposals were unfamiliar to the general public and the subject of controversy among economists. Today, the conception of an expansionist economy and the broad principles governing its growth are widely accepted by men of affairs as well as by technical experts in all the great industrial countries.

Full Employment in a Free Society

Although the term 'full employment' is defined and used in the *General Theory,* it is generally associated in the public mind with Beveridge's report and it is interesting therefore to look back on his definition of it at the time. Beveridge made it clear that 'full employment' did not literally mean there would be no unemployment. There was bound to be some frictional unemployment, however high the demand for labour. Full employment:

> means having always more vacant jobs than unemployed men, not slightly fewer jobs. It means that the jobs are at fair wages, of such a kind, and so located that the unemployed men can reasonably take them; it means, by consequence

> that the normal lag between losing one job and finding another will be very short.

In Beveridge's view:

> the labour market should always be a sellers' market rather than a buyers' market. For this, in the view of society underlying this Report – that society exists for the individual – there is a decisive reason of principle . . . A person who cannot sell his labour is in effect told that he is of no use.[5]

The aim should be to reduce unemployment to not more than 3 per cent as compared with the 10 to 22 per cent experienced between the Wars. He regarded this as conservative rather than unduly hopeful, and in fact unemployment did not exceed 3 per cent for the first 25 years after the War.

Beveridge spelled out how the effect of the continuous heavy unemployment in the interwar years had changed his and others' approach to the problem. In his 1909 Report he had assumed that apart from the trade cycle, demand would look after itself, and was mainly concerned with the way in which industry responded to demand. Thirty-five years later, after the experience of the 1930s and the Keynesian revolution in economic thought, it was evident that the demand for labour could no longer be taken for granted. Unemployment must now be attacked 'on three lines – of maintaining at all times adequate total outlay; of controlling the location of industry; of securing the organised mobility of labour'. The State must assume a new responsibility for ensuring adequate total outlay – what came to be known as 'demand management.' The annual Budget had to be seen as 'an instrument not only for determining public outlay, but also for influencing private outlay'. Beveridge thus set out the new approach to the Budget which underlay fiscal policy in the postwar years. (As we shall see later, however, for much of this period the emphasis was not on raising demand but on keeping it down to avoid excessive pressure on resources when the economy was already fully employed.)

Budgetary policy in any particular year should be based on forecasts of national income and expenditure and take whatever corrective action was needed to keep effective demand at a level consistent with full employment. This process became formalised in the annual Economic Surveys starting in 1947.

Beveridge considered in some detail a number of different Budgetary policies varying expenditure, taxation or both with the aid of Kaldor's Appendix on the Quantitative Aspects of the Full Employment Problem in Britain.

The 1944 White Paper

The official White Paper on *Employment Policy* had its origins in studies of the problems of postwar full employment in the Economic Section of the Cabinet Secretariat, starting with a paper by James Meade (later to win the Nobel Prize) as early as 1941.[6] Meade's original proposals closely followed Keynes in advocating counter-cyclical variations in public investment and measures to influence private investment. But in addition Meade argued for measures to stabilise consumers' expenditure: e.g. hire purchase controls (varying minimum deposits and the maximum period of repayment) and variations in income tax and indirect taxes. Keynes, however, remained doubtful about the usefulness of measures to influence consumption. His reluctance to envisage changes in taxation as a means of influencing the demand for consumer goods and services was a constant theme in the internal discussions leading up to the White Paper. It was generally couched in terms of caution about reducing taxes when demand was weak, partly because of the political difficulty of raising them. As it turned out, however, the practical arguments in the immediate postwar years, when the need was to hold down pent-up demand, were mainly about raising taxes.

The White Paper was naturally somewhat restrained about Budgetary policy in deference to the views of senior Treasury officials, but it still showed a remarkable shift from the interwar doctrine, largely under the influence of Keynes and Meade. Following Keynes it focused on the instability of private investment and the possibility of using variations in interest rates to help steady it. But monetary policy alone would not be sufficient to defeat the inherent instability of capital expenditure. High interest rates were more effective in depressing excessive investment in periods of prosperity than low interest rates in encouraging investment in periods of depression. Public investment should be used more directly as an instrument of employment policy and in a remarkable *volte face*, as far as the Treasury was concerned, the White Paper said that 'The

Government believe that in the past the power of public expenditure, skilfully applied, to check the onset of a depression has been understated.'

The approach to public borrowing and Budget surpluses or deficits was cautious. As in the Treasury's prewar statements, borrowing by local authorities for their capital expenditure was taken for granted, as was borrowing for remunerative capital assets bringing in revenue, like the telephone system. Financial inducements to public authorities to expand capital expenditure would mainly take the form of an annual grant towards meeting current charges on the loan raised. Policy towards public borrowing should be determined in the light of the magnitude of the debt charge in relation to the rate of growth of the national income – an approach much in use today. In a rather schizophrenic section reflecting the tussles between the traditional Treasury and the Keynesian economists, it was stated that:

> None of the main proposals maintained in this Paper involves deliberate planning for a deficit in the National Budget in years of sub-normal trade activity . . . [But this] does not mean a rigid policy of balancing the Budget each year regardless of the state of trade . . . they certainly do not contemplate any departure from the principle that the Budget must be balanced over a longer period.

In considering this approach in relation to the recent doctrine that the Public Sector Borrowing Requirement should be zero, at least in the long run, it is important to note that the Treasury at that stage was talking about the central government budget deficit or surplus, excluding capital expenditure and excluding borrowing by local and public authorities. What was being fudged was whether the budget surplus should merely be allowed to oscillate with the state of trade bringing into play what were later termed the 'built-in stabilisers' or whether tax revenue or expenditure should be deliberately altered as an act of counter-cyclical policy. The main built-in stabilisers were the fact that tax revenue automatically goes down in a recession and social security payments go up, thus mitigating the fall in demand. The White Paper did, however, include in an Appendix proposals for a possible scheme of James Meade's to vary social security contributions for employers and employees as unemployment varied – reducing them as unemployment rose, and raising them as unemployment fell in an endeavour to help stabilise effective demand. Such changes would be easier and quicker to implement than changes in income tax. Keynes had initially been sceptical of this proposal, which Meade originally intended for the Beveridge Report on Social Insurance, but had later became a supporter. Powers to make such changes were embodied in the 1946 National Insurance Act.

The Strength of Labour

The authors of the White Paper were conscious of the danger of a stronger demand for labour driving up wages and prices. In the light of interwar experience they, like Beveridge, took stable prices as their objective. The White Paper said that to maintain stable prices 'increases in the general level of wage rates must be related to increased productivity'. The Government also undertook to seek power to take action on restrictive practices which might drive up prices.

Beveridge saw the achievement of full employment in a wider context as shifting the balance of power from employers to workers and thus achieving a fairer society. He took strong issue with a contemporary comment in *The Times* that unemployment 'is part of the essential mechanism of the system . . . it maintains the authority of master over man',[7] a concept revived in the 1980s (in non-sexist language) as 'managers' right to manage'. But to Beveridge:

> The challenge to management that will be presented by full employment is a challenge that enlightened employers will welcome. The essence of civilisation is that men should come to be led more by hope and ambition and example and less by fear . . . A civilised community must find alternatives to starvation for preservation of industrial discipline and efficiency.

Beveridge saw, however, that the strengthened bargaining power of labour could cause inflationary problems: 'There is a real danger that sectional wage bargaining, pursued without regard to its effects upon prices, may lead to a vicious spiral of inflation, with money wages chasing prices and without any gain in real wages for the working class as a whole.' He had two suggestions for dealing with this problem. The first was that the TUC General Council should evolve the machinery for a 'co-ordinated wage policy'. The second suggestion was that 'collective bargaining in each industry should in general include a clause for arbitration, in default of agreement between the parties'. Employers for their part should be prepared 'to put all facts as to profits, costs and margins unreservedly at the disposal of the arbitrator'. Beveridge's comments were far-sighted and we shall return again to this theme.

Public Reaction

In a brief postscript Beveridge commented critically on the Government's White Paper (which came out just as he was finishing his report), mainly on the lines that it did not go far enough. He was critical in particular of the lack of adequate measures to stabilise investment: 'The substantive policy of the White Paper is one of public works, to be expanded or contracted to compensate for contraction or expansion of private investment.' He proposed a more radical approach to the stabilisation of private investment with a National Investment Board encouraging and controlling investment: control which, to be effective, would depend on there being some excess demand to invest so that if some projects were turned down the total of what were passed would be adequate. Beveridge also argued for the extension of the public sector of industry so as to bring monopolies under control and increase the scope for stabilising investment. This thesis reappeared in the Labour Party's 1945 election manifesto *Let Us Face The Future*, that one reason for creating a substantial public sector of industry was to help stabilise employment. Beveridge also commented that the White Paper appeared to be more concerned with ironing out the trade cycle than establishing a permanently lower level of unemployment.

The White Paper was debated in the House of Commons in June 1944. Introducing it on behalf of the Coalition Government, the Minister of Labour, Ernest Bevin said that 'In laying down that it is the primary responsibility of the Government to maintain a high and stable level of employment, we are turning our back, finally, on past doctrines and past conceptions and looking forward with hope to a new era.' He emphasised the need for public authorities to have investment plans ready to bring forward if needed to forestall a recession. Commenting on the vexed question of counter-cyclical budgetary policy, Bevin said that: 'The practice hitherto in local authorities, as in Government, has been to reduce taxation when we are doing well, and to increase it when we are hard up. I would rather pay it when I am doing well, than when I am hard up', thus dismissing the alleged political difficulty of using taxation to influence consumer demand! The Chancellor of the Exchequer, Sir John Anderson, was more cautious, saying that 'we ought in my opinion to be very wary how we play about with our taxation, for the purpose of producing a desired economic policy.'

The White Paper commanded general cross-party support, with many speakers taking the line that there was bound to be a mixture of both public and private ownership after the war and the difference between parties was as to where the boundary should lie. But James Griffiths put the Labour view that 'The larger the proportion of the capital investment of the country that is publicly owned, the easier it will be to find full employment.' Two Communist and Independent Labour Party members, together with Aneurin Bevan, dismissed the White Paper on the grounds that full employment was incompatible with capitalism. If unemployment could be avoided by this means, there was no justification for public ownership. Nye Bevan scornfully dismissed the Treasury's conversion to Keynesianism, saying, 'The great British Treasury has caught up with the soap-box orator of Hyde Park . . . Every worker knows that the reason he is idle is because he has not enough money to buy things.' But Ernie Bevin summed up the overwhelming feeling of the House in his concluding statement that 'we can start out on the road this week and begin to say that we have left the old vexed disease of unemployment behind us'.

A NEW INTERNATIONAL REGIME

The Keynes Plan

Postwar planning was not confined to the problems of the UK economy. Keynes and others were equally anxious to devise a new postwar regime for international payments which would obviate the crises and deflationary pressures leading to unemployment of the interwar years. The experience of these years vividly illustrated the problem of trying to operate a fixed rate system, such as the Gold Standard, without any provision for dealing with foreign exchange crises or the orderly adjustment of exchange rates. It was also evident that every crisis tended to invoke a deflationary response, either in the form of higher interest rates or efforts to reduce a budget deficit. There was an increasing realisation, particularly on the left, of the need to devise some orderly system of international payments which would minimise the deflationary tendencies of any residual payments difficulties. In a 1933 policy statement, the Labour Party said that 'the world has become a single economic unit' and governments must 'pursue an active policy of International Economic Cooperation'.[8]

In wartime Whitehall, Keynes first put down his thoughts about the postwar currency problem in 1941.

> The problem of maintaining equilibrium in the balance of payments between countries has never been solved, since methods of barter gave way to the use of money and bills of exchange . . . the failure to solve this problem has been a major cause of impoverishment and social discontent and even wars and revolutions . . . To suppose there exists some smoothly functioning automatic mechanism of adjustment which preserves equilibrium if only we trust to methods of *laissez-faire* is a doctrinaire delusion which disregards the lessons of historical experience without having behind it the support of sound theory.[9]

He emphasised the asymmetrical nature of the pressures for adjustment under the Gold Standard.

> It is characteristic of a freely convertible international standard that it throws the main burden of adjustment on the country which is in the *debtor* position on the international balance of payments – that is on the country which is (in this context) by hypothesis the *weaker* and above all the *smaller* in comparison with the other side of the scales which (for this purpose) is the rest of the world.

This remained the key problem throughout the discussions leading up to Bretton Woods, and indeed in the whole postwar period.

Keynes produced proposals for an 'International Currency Union', later to become an 'International Clearing Union', which after lengthy discussion in Whitehall and numerous revisions eventually formed the basis for the official British proposals in the 1943 White Paper.[10] The two key elements in Keynes's initial proposals were to establish: (a) a multilateral clearing system for international payments; and (b) arrangements for dealing with creditors and debtors in such a way as to minimise the impact on employment.

Writing at a time when trade and payments were tightly controlled, Keynes was concerned to establish that, after the necessary period of postwar adjustment, there would be a dismantling of wartime controls and other obstacles to current trade and payments. But from the very start, Keynes consistently maintained the need to maintain control over capital movements in order to deal with refugee or speculative movements of funds. To make this possible all foreign exchange transactions would need to continue to be controlled in order to be able to rule out unlicensed capital transactions. The emphasis on the need to control capital transactions had been a constant theme of Keynes before the War, but the practicality of doing so was enhanced by the existence of wartime currency restrictions and the probable need to maintain them for some years.

Keynes' original proposals were revolutionary in a number of respects. They would have set up an International Central Bank (ICB) managing a world currency, with each national currency having a fixed value in terms of the world currency, 'bancor'. There were provisions for changing exchange rates where countries were out of balance, but these took much of the power to vary rates out of the hands of individual countries and into the hands of the new central bank. Statutory provisions were made to force creditors as well as debtors to get back into balance. Indeed the system was in principle asymmetrical in the opposite direction to the Gold Standard, in that the powers over creditors were more stringent than those against debtors; but, of course, ordinary market pressures would continue to fall more heavily on debtors than creditors.

The official UK *Proposals for an International Clearing Union*, eventually published in 1943 as a White Paper,[11] were somewhat less radical. They reflected discussions not only in Whitehall but with the American government. The published proposals did, however, emphasise the concept of an international central bank with an international currency whose volume was 'capable of deliberate expansion and contraction to offset deflationary or inflationary tendencies in effective world demand'. The proposed new bank would re-lend credit balances to other countries as a domestic bank could re-lend to another customer. But these loans would only be introduced to give time for adjustment rather than to perpetuate existing imbalances.

The White Plan

At the same time as the British proposals were published in April 1943, the Americans also published their own plan, originating from Harry White in the US Treasury. Since both the original Keynes Plan and the original White Plan had been discussed between British and American officials, the two sets of proposals had come closer together. White envisaged both a Stabilisation Fund (to become the International Monetary Fund) and a Bank (later to become the International Bank for Reconstruction and Development). Like the Clearing Union, the Stabilisation Fund would have quotas for each country and an international currency, in this case called the 'unitas'. Exchange rates would be fixed and could only be varied with the agreement of three quarters of the members' votes, but with more elastic provisions for an initial three years' postwar transition period.

The most radical feature of the US Plan was the treatment of creditors whose currency became scarce. The Fund would report on the reasons for the scarcity and make recommendations. In addition, the Fund would 'apportion its sales of such currency', which meant that other countries could be free to restrict their imports from the scarce currency country. As the most likely target of any such action was the United States, and in view of their anxiety to reduce discriminatory restrictions as soon as possible, this was a remarkably altruistic proposal; but one which was eventually embodied in the Scarce Currency clause in the Bretton Woods agreement.

Looking back in the light of subsequent history, White's proposals for making the fixing of exchange rates a collective responsibility of members of the Fund pinpointed the stumbling block in all subsequent attempts to run a fixed exchange rate system, whether on a global or a European scale. This is the dilemma that, save in the case of relatively small countries, exchange rates are a two-way concern with a conflicting interest in terms of trade competition, in that each party has an interest in seeing the other's rate raised rather than lowered. For this and other reasons, it has proved virtually impossible to arrive at any rational pattern of exchange rate adjustments by intergovernmental agreement, as we shall see in Chapter 11. The question of how an international body could make an effective contribution to facilitate agreed changes is one of the key questions which now needs urgent re-examination.

Bretton Woods

After extensive talks between US and UK officials on the Keynes and White plans a *Joint Statement by Experts on the Establishment of an International Monetary Fund*[12] was published in April 1944 without any formal commitment by either Government. The United Nations Monetary and Financial Conference was eventually held at the disused Mount Washington hotel at Bretton Woods, New Hampshire, for three weeks in July 1944. (As befitting a conference of Treasury officials, the first of the pre-conference documents[13] set out with some precision how delegates were to be charged. The daily charge was $11 a day computed 'on the basis of four six-hour quarters, calculating from the beginning of that quarter of the day during which the individual enters upon residence'. Swimming, tennis and the movies were free, but golf, horse-riding, etc. would be available at 'the customary rates'!)

The final Bretton Woods agreement was a striking testimony to the spirit of cooperation and determination that pervaded the discussions. Although it was not as revolutionary as the original British proposals for an international currency and central bank, it created both a new set of international financial institutions and for the first time a formal framework of rules governing exchange rates and international payments. The agreement reflected a wide-ranging vision of how the postwar economic system might work, including a liberal regime for trade and tariffs, and measures to stabilise commodity prices. It was designed to overcome both the problems experienced in the interwar period and those emerging from the Second World War, in particular restrictions on trade and payments and the dollar shortage. The rules were intended first to encourage a speedy, but orderly, dismantling of wartime restrictions on imports and movement to currency convertibility, and then to establish (as a permanent regime), a liberal system of trade and payments and fixed exchange rates which would be compatible with the pursuit of full employment. The operation of the international payment system was to be supervised by the International Monetary Fund controlled by the leading Allied Powers with a system of weighted voting ensuring a dominant voice for the USA.

As set out in Article I, the purposes of the International Monetary Fund were to: promote international monetary co-operation; facilitate the expansion of international trade and 'contribute thereby to the promotion and maintenance of high levels of employment'; promote exchange rate stability; assist in establishing a system of multilateral trade and eliminating foreign exchange restrictions; facilitate correction of balance of payments maladjustments without destroying national or international prosperity; and minimise international balance of payments disequilibrium.

It was a fixed exchange system in which members could not change the par value of their currencies except to correct a 'fundamental disequilibrium' – a key phrase in the IMF epistemology. There was no provision for the Fund (formally) proposing changes in exchange rates, but members could only change rates after consultation with the Fund (which would make no objections to changes of less than 10 per cent). Countries' quotas were fixed in the agreement, and they could borrow 25 per cent of their quota from the Fund automatically, provided they were below 75 per cent of their quota. Further drawings must in total not exceed 200 per cent of their quota. There was explicit provision for control of capital movements, but current transactions were to be unrestricted. Harry White's scarce currency proposal was embodied in Article VII and, if a currency was declared 'scarce', members could take restrictive measures against it.

The Conference also set up the International Bank for Reconstruction and Development (which came to be known as the 'World Bank'). Although its principal function came to be that of making long-term development loans out of its own resources (including money which it borrowed on world capital markets), its original terms of reference were rather wider. They included the promotion of private foreign investment by means of guarantees or participation to be supplemented by loans from the Bank's own resources when private capital was not available on reasonable terms. With interwar problems in mind, the Bank was also 'to promote the long-range balanced growth of international trade and the maintenance of equilibrium in balances of payments by encouraging international investment . . . [and] To conduct its operation with due regard to the effect of international investment on business conditions.'[14]

Bretton Woods itself did not deal with the issues of tariffs and trade; these took longer to resolve. But eventually the foundations of a liberal international economic regime were completed in 1948 with the General Agreement on Tariffs and Trade (GATT) providing for the gradual reduction of tariffs by international negotiation.

In his final address to the assembled delegates at the Closing Session at Bretton Woods, Keynes said:

> I am greatly encouraged, I confess, by the critical, sceptical and even carping spirit in which our proceedings have been watched and welcomed by the outside world. How much better that our projects should begin in disillusion than that they should end in it! . . . If we can continue in a larger task as we have begun in this limited task there is hope for the world . . . We have been learning to work together. If we can so continue, this nightmare, in which most of us present have spent too much of our lives, will be over. The brotherhood of man will become more than a phrase.

4 The Years of Full Employment: 1946–70

LABOUR GOVERNMENTS, 1945–51

Demobilisation and Reconversion

The Second World War left a legacy of pent-up demand and a battery of controls over the home economy and foreign trade and payments which had been used to give priority to the war effort. The immediate postwar task was to ensure a smooth demobilisation of the armed forces and rebuild peacetime production. It was particularly vital to rebuild exports, not merely to prewar levels, but to the new higher levels needed to make good the decline in income from invisibles due to shipping losses together with the liquidation of assets and borrowing incurred to pay for the war. In the immediate aftermath of war, continued controls on imports, materials and investment played an important part in the process of reconversion. Prices were held down by price controls, rationing and food subsidies, despite a substantial 'inflationary gap' between potential demand and the available supplies. This would be reduced as output expanded, but there remained a need to restrain demand. The process of 'disinflation' (i.e. reducing demand by fiscal means) was started in the autumn 1947 Budget of the Labour Chancellor, Hugh Dalton, and continued by his successor Stafford Cripps in the three years up to the end of 1950. As demand and supply got into better balance, controls were gradually abolished and the economy returned to more normal peacetime conditions.

In the event demobilisation and redeployment went smoothly, and exports replaced war production as the top priority. Between 1945 and 1950 approximately half the increase in national output went towards improving the balance of payments: exports rose 77 per cent in volume between 1945 and 1950 while the increase in imports was held down to only 14 per cent by import controls. The 'austerity' regime associated with Stafford Cripps, first as President of the Board of Trade and

Table 4.1 UK unemployment, 1945–70 (annual averages)

Year	*per cent*	*Thousands*	*Year*	*per cent*	*Thousands*
1945	1.3	202	1958	2.2	501
1946	2.5	390	1959	2.3	512
1947	3.1	496	1960	1.7	393
1948	1.8	331	1961	1.6	377
1949	1.6	338	1962	2.1	500
1950	1.6	341	1963	2.6	612
1951	1.3	281	1964	1.7	413
1952	2.2	463	1965	1.5	360
1953	1.8	380	1966	1.6	391
1954	1.5	318	1967	2.5	599
1955	1.2	265	1968	2.5	601
1956	1.3	287	1969	2.5	597
1957	1.6	347	1970	2.7	640

Note: see Appendix 1, Measuring Unemployment.

then as Dalton's successor at the Treasury, limited the rise in personal consumption over the five years to only 6 per cent.[1] The cost of living increased by an average of 4.5 per cent a year in the first five years after the war, and wage rates at a similar rate. Unemployment stayed low. Apart from the period of the fuel crises in the winter of 1947, unemployment remained between 1.5 and 2.5 per cent (see Table 4.1). But the feared acceleration in wage demands did not occur.

The gradual return from a tightly controlled wartime economy to a situation where there were only limited controls, and demand and supply were broadly in balance, was mainly accomplished in the first five years of peace. In November 1948, Harold Wilson, the young President of the Board of Trade, had his well publicised 'bonfire' of controls and the process of decontrol continued until building licensing was eventually abolished under the Conservative Government in 1954. (Our postwar experience of gradual and successful conversion from a controlled economy to a market economy with demand and supply in balance could have provided important lessons for the former Soviet Union in the post-Communist period; it would have helped them to avoid the disastrous effects of the precipitant attempt to liberalise their economy overnight without the advantage of any previous experience of a market economy or the associated institutional framework.)

As after the First World War, the external legacy proved more difficult to overcome than the internal one. The decline in invisible earnings from overseas investments and shipping was aggravated by continued high military expenditure abroad. (In 1946, although the visible trade balance was better than the 1936–8 average thanks to tight import controls, the current deficit of £230 million was £186 million greater.) The practical problem was, however, not so much the general deficit as the dollar position, aggravated by the UK's continued position as banker for the Sterling Area (mainly the countries of the Commonwealth). Not only did we have a substantial trade deficit with the dollar area, but so did other members of the Sterling Area on whose behalf we held the Area's gold and dollar reserves.

The sudden cessation of Lend Lease at the end of the war in the Far East left the UK facing a serious crisis which was only averted by the American Loan Agreement finalised in 1946. The Loan of $3,750 million, with no interest payable for the first five years, eased the immediate payments position, but one of its key conditions soon proved unsustainable. This was the obligation to re-establish the free convertibility of sterling into dollars (which had been suspended by wartime controls) in mid-1947. The consequent run on the reserves was disastrous and convertibility had to be suspended five weeks later. The convertibility crisis dramatically demonstrated that the 'dollar shortage' was a key fact in the postwar world and that the objective of removing all restrictions discriminating against the dollar would not be possible for some time. Sterling was not made formally convertible again until 1958, and the Bretton Woods regime described in Chapter 3 did not come into full operation until then.

The dollar shortage, however, led to one of the greatest acts of international statesmanship of the post-war era, the Marshall Plan. A speech by the American Secretary of State, George Marshall, speedily followed up by the British Foreign Secretary, Ernest Bevin, led to the 1948 agreement on an aid programme which helped Europe through the key years of postwar reconstruction and avoided the succession of payments crises which occurred after the First World War. Apart from the economic assistance which the aid provided, the need for participating countries to cooperate in its distribution through the formation of the Organisation for European Economic Cooperation started a process of intergovernmental cooperation which paved the way for the formation of the European Payments Union (EPU) and the European Community.

Despite the renewed suspension of convertibility, sterling remained under pressure and the issue of devaluing sterling became a live issue. The Government was initially opposed to devaluation in the belief that the problem was more appropriately dealt with by controls rather than the price mechanism – a factor which later influenced Harold Wilson's decision not to devalue in 1964. Stafford Cripps (later referred to by Winston Churchill as the 'soul of honour') was forced to state repeatedly that there was no intention of devaluation and (like many finance ministers after him) came under some personal attack when the exchange crisis in the summer of 1949 finally forced the Government to devalue from the wartime parity level of $4 to the pound to $2.80. But as most other countries devalued against the dollar at the same time, the trade-weighted devaluation of sterling was only about 9 per cent. This was the first postwar example of the difficulty of making necessary adjustments in a fixed exchange system, whether it be a global one like Bretton Woods, or a regional one like the European Exchange Rate Mechanism (ERM). At that time, however, there was at least no penalty to be paid for the delay in the form of damage to industry or unemployment.

The Korean Boom

The 1949 devaluation crisis had not been over very long before the Korean war broke out in June 1950, and the new Labour Government – elected in February with a majority of only five – embarked on a major rearmament programme. The outbreak of war coincided with, and further stimulated, the first postwar boom. Between 1949 and 1950 world industrial production rose by 13 per cent as the USA recovered from the recession it experienced in 1949 and the West German economy got under way again. The boom had started before the steep rise in US military expenditure took place at the end of 1950 and the more gradual rise in defence expenditure in Europe had started. US government stockpiling of raw materials and speculative purchases elsewhere helped to drive up commodity prices, which rose dramatically. British import prices rose by 25 per cent in the course of 1950 and another 25 per cent before they reached a peak in the middle of 1951. This was the first of what later came to be called 'shocks' to the global economic system which had such dramatic effects in the 1970s.

The events of 1950 placed a dual strain on the British economy. The rise in material prices threatened the relatively high degree of price stability which had prevailed since the end of the war, and the burden of the new rearmament programme put a renewed strain on productive potential, particularly in the engineering industries. Competition for resources from increased defence production thus fell on exports and home investment rather than personal consumption. The Government accepted that there would have to be some deterioration in the balance of payments. To curb investment the new Chancellor, Hugh Gaitskell, in his 1951 Budget, suspended initial depreciation allowances on new plant and machinery and industrial building. He also raised direct and indirect taxes in order to curb consumption, and introduced the Health Service charges which precipitated the resignation of Aneurin Bevan and Harold Wilson from the Cabinet. The tax on distributed profits was raised and dividend control was to be introduced. (Dalton is said to have commented that 'Gaitskell's speech, whatever else it has done, has thrown the Stock Exchange into complete disorder, and that is good fun anyway.'[2] We could do with a little of the good Dr Dalton's iconoclasm today!)

The rise in import prices of over 50 per cent between 1949 and 1951 was the main factor behind a 13 per cent increase in retail prices. It also led to a severe deterioration in the balance of payments, which swung from a surplus of £300 million in 1950 to a deficit of £370 million in 1951. Another sterling crisis helped to bring down the Labour Government and greeted the new Conservative Government after the October 1951 election.

Managing Demand

Before moving on to examine the 1950s, we should consider how far economic policy in the immediate postwar period was influenced by Keynesian ideas on demand management. The main product of Keynesian thinking was the idea of an inflationary gap between potential demand and supply. As long as such a gap existed, price controls and rationing remained essential to avoid price inflation and ensure a fair distribution of scarce goods. The possibilities of closing the gap by increasing the supply of consumer goods by raising production was limited by the need to export, so that measures were also needed to curb demand by taxation or other measures such as hire purchase restrictions. As a result the three Labour Chancellors all followed what were effectively stringent budgetary policies despite the substantial decline in government spending on defence.

At that time, the conventional budget classification distinguished between a surplus or deficit on 'ordinary' revenue and expenditure 'above the line' and an 'overall' surplus or deficit. The distinction between above and below the line was in broad terms between current and capital transactions, but not in a very satisfactory manner. The conventional wisdom had been that the budget should be balanced above the line, so that running substantial surpluses represented a positive effort to reduce demand by the use of fiscal policy, one which required some political courage when the public were looking for relief from wartime stringency and fellow ministers wanted to increase their departmental spending programmes. A deficit of nearly £600 million in 1946–7 gave way to a surplus of over £600 million in 1947–8; and in the following three years the realised surpluses averaged £700 million. This fell to £380 million in 1951–2 with rearmament. From Dalton's autumn 1947 Budget onwards, the Budget was seen as a major instrument for reducing the pressure of demand. It did so successfully. Excess demand was gradually reduced, controls and rationing eased and the economy moved nearer to peacetime conditions without a re-emergence of prewar unemployment.

With the help of Marshall Aid, the 1945–51 Labour Governments had effectively accomplished the enormous task of postwar conversion, the greater part of which had been achieved before the set-back of the 1950 boom and the war in Korea. In contrast to the experience after the First World War there had been no run-away boom followed by a severe slump. Unemployment and inflation had both been kept low. The balance of payments remained the danger point, although thanks to strict import controls a substantial surplus was achieved in 1950.

But Gaitskell and his Conservative successors then had to meet the first of the postwar shocks in the form of a world-wide commodity price boom complicated by what later proved to be an over-ambitious rearmament programme.

CONSERVATIVE GOVERNMENTS, 1951–64

Churchill's new Conservative Government that took office in November 1951 was naturally highly critical of their Labour predecessors. But in retrospect the practical differences in policy were mainly ones of emphasis. As one close observer put it,[3] 'Conservative governments, no less clearly than Labour governments before them, in fact put full employment first as the main object of policy.' The broad similarity between Gaitskell and Butler's policies led to the term 'Butskellism' to describe them both.

Faced with a balance of payments crisis, the first act of the new Chancellor, Rab Butler, was to impose a series of drastic import cuts. One innovation, however, was the use of Bank Rate which had been frozen at 2 per cent since 1939. This was raised to 2.5 per cent in November 1951 and to 4 per cent in the following March, the first use of this instrument since before the war. This was more a signal to the outside world than an indication that the Government had embarked on a deflationary policy. The March 1952 Budget was broadly neutral. Demand was already falling and unemployment rose to over half a million in April and May 1952.

Stimulating Demand

The year 1953 saw the first deliberately expansionary budget of the post-war period. Butler introduced a number of tax changes which in total were estimated to cost just over £400 million in a full year (2.7 per cent of GDP). The initial investment allowances were restored to stimulate investment. Income Tax was reduced by sixpence and Purchase Tax was cut to boost consumer demand. A further expansionary factor was Harold Macmillan's housing programme with a target of 300,000 houses a year, which was achieved in 1953. (An interesting feature of this achievement was the fact that the Conservative Party's public commitment to the programme made it sacrosanct in Whitehall, despite misgivings about its feasibility and the absorption of so much of the building industry's resources. It suggests that a Government which is dedicated to reducing unemployment would be well advised to make a public commitment to a numerical target for reducing unemployment, thus ensuring that the administration's efforts are unequivocally devoted to this end.)

Unemployment fell in the two succeeding years from an average of 463,000 in 1952 to 265,000 in 1955. The Treasury's response to the emerging boom and deteriorating balance of payments was to rely increasingly on monetary, rather than fiscal, policy to restrain demand. Bank Rate, which had been reduced slightly in the preceding year, was raised to 3.5 per cent in January 1955 and 4.5 per cent in May. The new found emphasis on monetary policy to restrict demand was not solely a matter of raising interest rates. More direct measures were also taken to restrict bank advances. But with a General Election pending, Butler's April 1955 Budget cut Income Tax with a loss of revenue equivalent to 0.9 per cent of GDP, despite the already high pressure of demand. The intention to offset the effects of the tax cuts by tightening up on bank lending proved ineffective. After the election in the summer, there was a run on sterling and Butler was forced to introduce a further Budget in October withdrawing in effect two-thirds of the concessions made earlier in the year; this was the first of the 'election budgets' to give fiscal policy a bad name.

Thorneycroft's Chancellorship

The pressure on sterling then abated until the Suez crisis in the autumn of 1956 which led to a further sterling crisis. This was surmounted with the help of a large standby credit obtained from the IMF with American support once we had agreed to withdraw our forces from the Canal. But yet another sterling crisis developed in 1957 despite the fact that the balance of payments was in surplus. In the third quarter of the year the reserves fell by £500 million. The new Chancellor, Peter Thorneycroft (who took over from Harold Macmillan when the latter became Prime Minister), reacted to the crisis by announcing a series of measures designed to deflate demand. He was concerned about the apparent threat of inflation: retail prices had risen by 5 per cent in 1956, although the rate of increase had abated by the middle of 1957. Ministers had also become concerned about the accelerating rate of wage increases (which reached 8 per cent in 1956) and, for the first time since the war, the question of deliberately raising the level of unemployment in order to restrain wage increases became a live issue. Thorneycroft envisaged that a rise in unemployment would check wage increases without the political embarrassment of having to face a series of major strikes: he was thinking of unemployment rising to something in the range of 2 to 3 per cent. At the same time, however, he set up the Council on Prices, Productivity and Incomes in a parallel attempt to moderate wage claims by persuasion. This was the body of 'Three Wise Men' which issued a series of reports on the need for wage restraint but which did not make a great deal of public impact. It was boycotted by the Unions and wound up in 1961.

The now forgotten feature of Thorneycroft's brief Chancellorship was his concern with the quantity of money. He was in a sense a monetarist before his time. In August 1957 Robert Hall, the Government's Economic Adviser, recorded in his diary that 'the Chancellor's holiday seems to have increased his conviction that it is too much money which is at the root of all our troubles'.[4] Bank Rate was raised to 7 per cent in September 1957, its highest level since 1921. The banks were required to hold the level of advances down to the average of the preceding 12 months. Public investment and government current expenditure were to be stabilised at the then current levels. The Chancellor stated that 'so long as it is generally believed that the Government are prepared to see the necessary finance produced to match the upward spiral of costs, inflation will continue and prices go up'. He made it clear for the first time that the Government was willing to sacrifice employment to counter inflation. His tight objectives for government expenditure proved too much, however, for the Prime Minister and the rest of the Cabinet, and Thorneycroft and the two junior Treasury ministers, Nigel Birch and Enoch Powell, resigned in January 1958 – an incident that Macmillan described as 'a little local difficulty'. Thorneycroft was succeeded by Heathcoat Amory.

Thorneycroft's deflationary measures virtually coincided with the top of the boom. Output peaked in the middle of 1957, and remained flat throughout 1958. By the autumn of 1958 Ministers were concerned at the rise in unemployment which exceeded 550,000 (2.5 per cent) in the last two months of the year. Robert Hall referred in his diary to ministers' 'panic' about increasing unemployment.[5] The Prime Minister, Harold Macmillan, whose prewar experience on Teesside had made him a firm protagonist of full employment policies, ordered prompt measures to expand demand. Hire purchase restrictions were completely withdrawn and increases in public investment were approved.

Unemployment reached a peak of 666,000 (3.0 per cent) in January 1959 and then began to decline. Further expansionary measures were taken in Heathcoat Amory's April Budget, with tax reductions worth £359 million (1.7 per cent of GDP) in a full year: next to Butler's 1953 Budget, this was the second most expansionary budget since the war. Despite differences in emphasis, the Conservative Government remained firmly committed to the need to maintain full employment at a level below the 3 per cent post-war target. Output expanded rapidly: GDP rose by 4.5 per cent in 1959 and 5 per cent in 1960. Unemployment fell to 2 per cent by the end of 1959 and averaged 1.7 per cent in 1960.

Themes for the 1960s

The start of the 1960s saw an increasing concern to find long-term solutions to what were beginning to be seen as endemic problems of the British economy: 'Stop-Go', alternating packages of deflationary and expansionary measures; the perpetual danger of wage inflation; and the slow rate of growth (i.e. output per head) in the UK economy as compared with other major industrial countries.

Avoiding Stop-Go

Concern at the Stop-Go cycle was brought to the fore by a further speculative foreign exchange crisis in 1961 following the revaluation of the Deutschmark in March. This led to another deflationary package in July. In his first Budget a few months earlier, Selwyn Lloyd, who had succeeded Heathcoat Amory as Chancellor, had introduced two 'regulators' to enable measures to be taken to influence demand between Budgets. The first, following the Meade scheme in the 1944 White Paper, would have given the government the power to increase national insurance contributions but was quickly abandoned. The second was the power to raise or lower indirect taxes by up to 10 per cent across the board. This provision was used to raise indirect taxes in the July package. At the same time, Bank Rate was raised from 5 to 7 per cent; government expenditure was to be curbed; exchange controls were tightened; and a 'pay pause' was imposed on wage increases in the public sector, in the hope that the private sector would follow suit.

The consequently intensified criticism of Stop-Go policies was partly a natural political reaction to unpopular measures, but also reflected dissatisfaction with the way the economy was being run. There were a number of elements behind this dissatisfaction, some of which are reflected today in recent calls for greater 'stability' in macro-economic policy. Perhaps the most important distinction which needs to be made is between the external and internal factors. The crisis nature of the packages introduced in 1955, 1957 and 1961 was in each case due to a run on sterling, partly, but not necessarily entirely, due to a deterioration in the balance of payments in conjunction with a low level of gold and foreign exchange reserves. If the balance of payments had been stronger to start with, and the reserves greater, the fluctuations in internal demand would not have been so serious.

Another source of criticism was that action to expand or restrict demand tended to be taken too late, partly because of the delay in the relevant statistics becoming available, and partly because of the time needed to get political decisions and the fact that the annual budgetary cycle did not necessarily coincide with the need for policy changes. The statistical problem led Macmillan, when he was Chancellor, to complain that 'we are always, as it were, looking up a train in last year's Bradshaw'.[6]

The point then (as now) was that governments cannot keep the economy on a steady growth path without varying interest rates or taxation to try to offset the inevitable fluctuations in demand, particularly for industrial investment. The objective must be to make such policy adjustments in a non-disruptive way, such as by gradual adjustments in interest rates and modest changes in tax arrangements. But to be able to do this, the key requirement is to be in a position where neither the weakness of the balance of payments nor the position of sterling make the economy vulnerable to external financial pressures, which (whatever the merits of the case) lead to the adoption of crisis deflationary measures as a sop to international financial opinion. (The problem of minimising such pressures will be discussed in Chapter 11.)

Pay Policy

Another element in the situation was that if the average level of unemployment was to be kept reasonably low (as Macmillan was determined that it should) there was a need to prevent periodic booms from setting off excessive wage increases and hence leading to an outbreak of inflation. Moreover if the problem of pay bargaining was to be solved without major industrial disputes, some new machinery was needed to influence the settlements reached. Macmillan came to believe that an incomes policy was 'necessary as a permanent feature of our economic life'.[7] A year after the announcement of the pay pause the Government set up a National Incomes Commission (NIC). It had very limited terms of reference. It could review certain pay matters where the cost was met wholly or partly from the Exchequer, and examine retrospectively any pay settlement referred to it. But rising unemployment damped down wage increases and it only received one reference under the first head, and four under the second, before it was succeeded by the National Board for Prices and Incomes (NBPI) in 1964.

The idea of a 'norm' for wage increases was by then becoming common parlance. The Three Wise Men in their reports had discussed what the norm should be, and in January 1962 the Chancellor sent a letter to the TUC asking for their cooperation on keeping increases in earnings to 2 to 2.5 per cent: this was the Treasury's estimate of the probable rise in productivity and hence implied, if successful, no overall increase in prices. The norm was later increased to 3 to 3.5 per cent on the grounds that the target rate of growth accepted by the National Economic Development Council implied a 3.2 per cent rise in productivity.

Long-Term Growth

The other new theme to emerge in the early 1960s was increasing concern with the long-term growth of the economy and an interest in the apparent success of French 'indicative planning'. This led to the setting-up of the National Economic Development Council (NEDC), which was to remain a forum for tripartite discussion for government, employers and unions for two decades. In announcing the setting-up of the NEDC, the Chancellor said that he envisaged 'a joint examination of the economic prospects of the country stretching five or more years into the future . . . Above all it would try to establish what are the essential conditions for realising potential growth.' In May 1962 the NEDC agreed to examine the implications of an annual rate of growth of 4 per cent a year from 1961 to 1966. This growth target was deliberately set well above the past trend rate of growth (put at about 2.7 per cent) and nearer that of other countries, with the object of investigating the problem of faster growth, and eventually influencing individual firms' planning.

A study was conducted of the implications of a 4 per cent growth rate for 17 major industries covering over half of national output. The results of the inquiry were presented to the Council in February 1963 with a general economic assessment. The responses from firms and trade associations were regarded as generally encouraging. Then in April a study on *Conditions Favourable to Faster Growth* was published. This outlined possible ways of overcoming eight major obstacles to growth. It covered regional development, research and development, the tax system, wage inflation, management education and industrial training. The Government took the report and its implications seriously, and, for example, asked the Central Electricity Generating Board to make its investment plans on the basis of the NEDC growth target, which meant in effect assuming a 10 per cent rather than 8.5 per cent annual increase in electricity demand.[8]

THE LABOUR GOVERNMENT, 1964–70

The achievement of faster growth was the major theme of the new Labour Government under Harold Wilson when it took office in October 1964. The distinctive feature of its approach to economic policy was its concern with what would now be called 'supply-side' (i.e. industrial) issues and the attempt to relegate macro-economic policy to second place. This approach was embodied in the creation of the Department of Economic Affairs (DEA) under the Deputy Prime Minister, George Brown, to work in parallel with the Treasury. The role of the DEA was to take into the government machine the work on planning for faster growth that had hitherto been concentrated in the National Economic Development Office set up to service the NEDC, and to coordinate action in Whitehall to achieve it. But in the event an equally demanding task was to devise an effective incomes policy.

Although planning for faster growth and incomes policy were the two major concerns of the new Government, their immediate preoccupation lay with yet another balance of payments crisis. When Reginald Maudling succeeded Selwyn Lloyd as Chancellor in July 1962, the Conservative Government was (as Macmillan later wrote) 'definitely set upon an expansionist course'.[9] Credit restrictions were relaxed. In the following year the Budget, if anything, leant the other way, but with a General Election in the offing no major increases were made in taxation. The pressure of demand increased, unemployment fell to 1.5 per cent and the balance of payments deteriorated sharply. The 'Maudling experiment' of trying to accelerate out of the Stop-Go cycle and reach a path of permanently faster growth appeared to have failed.

By 1964 the chronic weakness of the balance of payments raised the question of whether sterling should be devalued in an attempt to allow the economy to expand without the continual threat of balance of payments crises. But a decision not to devalue was taken in the first hours of the new Government at a meeting between the Prime Minister and his two economic colleagues, the new Chancellor, James Callaghan, and the Secretary of State for Economic Affairs, George Brown. Thereafter devaluation became the 'Great Unmentionable' in Government circles and was not discussed by the Cabinet until 1966.[10] Wilson's desire to avoid the opprobrium of devaluation meant, however, that the fear of balance of payments crises remained a major inhibiting factor on faster growth.

The crisis compelled the new Labour Government to take

policy decisions at breakneck speed. Ten days after taking office they announced the imposition of a 15 per cent import surcharge and a system of indirect tax rebates on exports to improve the balance of payments. The surcharge was introduced as a temporary measure, and following the strong reaction of Britain's trading partners it was first reduced, and then abolished completely after two years. A few days after the statement on the balance of payments, the Chancellor introduced an Autumn Budget. This raised pensions and national assistance benefits from March 1965 and abolished prescription charges. This additional expenditure was rather more than covered by increases in national insurance contributions, petrol taxes and income tax. The Chancellor also announced that he would be introducing a capital gains tax and altering the system of company taxation.

Despite the broadly neutral impact on demand, the Budget was followed by a run on sterling: City reaction was probably due as much to political, as economic, factors. After some hesitation Bank Rate was raised by 2 per cent. In an unfortunate throwback to 1931 the Governor of the Bank, Lord Cromer, pressed the Government to cut public expenditure in order to reassure the financial markets; but the Prime Minister's response was to threaten to float the exchange rate and go to the country again. Wilson asked Cromer to mobilise support for sterling from fellow central banks and he raised $3 billion in a round of telephone calls the following day.[11] The initial crisis was followed by two further sterling crises in July 1965 and July 1966 before the pound was eventually devalued in November 1967.

Planning

The concept of planning in the early 1960s had mixed origins. Before the War there had been some discussion of economic planning on both sides of the Atlantic. This was reflected in the creation of such bodies as PEP (Political and Economic Planning) in the UK and the NPA (National Planning Association) in the US. It represented mainly a natural extension of the planning activities which were essential in large corporations rather than a response to planning in the Soviet Union, although at that time planning was associated mainly with the totalitarian countries. One of the influences of wartime experience, however, was to make the concept of a 'planned economy' consonant with a basically capitalist economy and liberal state.

The essential prerequisite of wartime and immediate postwar planning was the existence of surplus demand for particular products and hence the necessity to control their distribution and use. This control had then to be geared to some planning priorities – in wartime, for example, ensuring that factories producing fighter aircraft got labour and materials at the expense of those producing civilian goods. In the immediate aftermath of war, planning of a similar kind enabled priority to be given to building up exports and investment in industrial capacity. With consumption tightly constrained by rationing and controls, one connotation of 'planning' was 'fair shares for all' (Labour's 1945 election slogan) as opposed to leaving the distribution of scarce goods to the price mechanism. This form of planning was thus dependent on the economy being run with an excess of demand, otherwise there would be no need or scope for any controls to restrict consumption or investment. As demand and supply were brought into balance, however, planning of this kind became otiose.

Contrary to 1990s mythology, Labour had effectively become committed to running a market economy by the time it took office in 1964 and the 'planning' then introduced had virtually nothing to do with controls, as it had done in the early years after the War. The first postwar Labour Government's views were exemplified in a ministerial paper by Hugh Gaitskell, when he was Minister of Fuel and Power in 1950, which concluded that 'certain physical controls are essential to the effective planning of full employment and fair distribution of income'.[12] By the 1960s, however, when wartime controls had been abolished, support for planning was mainly based on the apparent success of 'indicative planning' in France. In the early postwar period the French Commissariat du Plan under Jean Monnet had produced a series of fairly *dirigiste* plans with particular emphasis on the public sector. But by the 1960s the emphasis was on indicative planning in the sense of setting targets for growth in different sectors with the idea that firms would take these as guidelines in making their investment decisions. The relatively rapid growth of the French economy led to considerable interest in this approach, which was instrumental in the original decision to set up the NEDC, and was one of the progenitors of the DEA's 1965 National Plan.

The National Plan set a growth target of 25 per cent between 1964 and 1970 equivalent to an annual rate of 3.8 per cent, rather less than the previous NEDC target of 4.0 per cent, but considerably faster than past trends. It contained detailed projections for key industrial sectors based on a further industrial inquiry, public expenditure plans, and a breakdown of the use of resources by major claimants, i.e. balance of payments, investment, defence, public and personal consumption. The Plan in George Brown's words was intended as 'a guide to action', and it contained a Check List of Action Required by the Government and other bodies concerned. What it did not cover, however, was macro-economic strategy, and on that it foundered.

There had been a further sterling crisis in July 1965 a few months before the Plan was published and a third crisis in July 1966 led to a severe set of deflationary measures and a voluntary freeze on wages and prices. These deflationary measures were opposed in the Cabinet by a group of ministers in favour of devaluation (including George Brown, Tony Crosland and Roy Jenkins). But eventually the measures were agreed. In the end, however, devaluation became inevitable and in November 1967 the parity of the pound was reduced from $2.80 to $2.40. By then the National Plan had become unrealistic. In the event the growth of national output from 1964 to 1970 averaged only 2.2 per cent against the 3.8 per cent envisaged in the Plan: total output rose by 14 per cent instead of 25 per cent. Although unemployment only rose 1 per cent between 1964 and 1970 (from 1.7 per cent to 2.7 per cent), total employment rose by 5 per cent less than predicted in the Plan.

The failure to achieve the growth target by so wide a margin reflected in the first instance the fact that the implicit macroeconomic strategy on which it was based was unrealistic – namely, that the balance of payments would be satisfactory at the existing sterling parity and this growth would not be interrupted by another 'Stop'. But with the balance of payments in deficit to start with, and faster growth of the economy involving higher imports and thus needing more exports to pay for them, a change in the exchange rate was essential to make British goods more competitive. It was too optimistic to assume, as the Plan implied, that any incomes policy could be so successful in slowing down inflation as to produce a significant improvement in our competitive position. As long as the balance of payments remained precarious, and foreign confidence fragile, there was always a danger of a crisis leading to the familiar series of deflationary measures.

It is, however, doubtful whether the required acceleration of the growth in output would have been achieved even if there had been a smooth growth in demand: output per head only grew at 2.6 per cent a year against the target of 3.4 per cent. The hoped-for acceleration in growth depended partly on a number of measures listed in the Plan to assist industry, but mainly on the hope that by setting up a scenario of possible faster growth, industry would in turn plan on that basis to achieve it. In so far as the achievement of the plan rested on stimulating more investment in new capacity, this was a possibility, certainly for large firms in highly concentrated industries. But in so far as faster growth depended on a more rapid increase in productivity by improvements in managing day-to-day operations, the Plan could not be expected to have much impact. Any progress in this field was more dependent on the 'Little Neddies', the Economic Development Committees set up for particular industries.

One of the weaknesses of the Plan was that the plethora of projections of investment, employment, and so on made no distinction between those referring to the public sector which were the Government's responsibility, and those in the private sector which were outside its control.[13] In addition it followed the pattern of industrial planning at that time in making no clear distinction between: (a) long-term strategy setting out long-term objectives and the means of achieving them; and (b) detailed quantitative plans which would require more frequent revision. Whereas it was obvious to those closely concerned that any such quantitative exercise should be revised, say, annually (as the Treasury's forecasts are today), it was then felt too embarrassing politically to make any (inevitably downward) revisions in the projections. The plan thus stood unamended until finally a new 'planning document', *An Economic Assessment to 1992*, was published in 1969, which merely stated a range of possible projections for the next few years.

The creation of the DEA and the National Plan represented a unique attempt in British postwar history (after the abolition of wartime controls) to relate economic policy more closely to the needs of industry, rather than regarding it as primarily a matter of macro-economic policy to be run exclusively by the Treasury. There was some justification by then for feeling that the problems of regulating demand to ensure full employment had been solved and demand management had become largely a routine operational matter; and hence that the more fundamental problems lay in the realm of industrial development and efficiency (what would today be termed 'supply-side' policies), including the long-term improvement in the balance of payments. The weakness was that devaluation was an essential precondition for such an improvement. Events demonstrated, however, that apart from weaknesses in the balance of payments *per se*, the continual eruption of foreign exchange crises led to short-term preoccupation with macro-economic measures. In so far as the short term inevitably took precedence over the long term, the Treasury remained effectively in control.

Incomes Policy

The other major preoccupation of the Wilson government was with incomes policy. The new government replaced the National Incomes Commission (NIC) by the National Board for Prices and Incomes (NBPI) under Aubrey Jones. The new Board, which was set up early in 1965, covered prices as well as incomes and initially had no statutory powers. The criteria for both wage and price increases were first set out in a White Paper in April which embodied the norm of 3 to 3.5 per cent for wage increases inherited from the NIC and agreed by the TUC. This initial phase of entirely voluntary wage restraint was, however, disappointing, and George Brown sought to reach agreement with the TUC on a more effective mechanism. This resulted in the TUC setting up a Vetting Committee which examined and commented on claims before they were put in to employers. This committee remained in existence from October 1965 to January 1970. It worked hand-in-hand with the Government's official Early Warning System and was a key factor in the practical operation of pay policy. There was a corresponding notification system for forthcoming price increases for 75 key items.

Before the policy had been in place very long, however, the July 1966 sterling crisis led to a six-month freeze on wages, salaries, dividends and prices, to be followed by a further six months of 'severe restraint'. The Government also took statutory powers to require advance notification of price or wage increases and to issue directions forbidding such increases. The period of 'severe restraint' ran from the end of January 1967 to August that year. During this period there was a nil norm for wage increases, with possible exceptions for productivity agreements and the low paid. These measures were effective in the short-term with wage rates rising only 2 per cent from July 1966 to June 1967.

Government policy for the succeeding twelve months from July 1967 was that there should be no publicly stated norm, on the grounds that the previous norm of 3 to 3.5 per cent had tended to be taken as a minimum. All increases would have to be justified on special criteria, basically as productivity deals. A similar line was taken in the next statement in 1968, despite the faster rise in retail prices following devaluation. The attempt to enforce such a strict policy proved abortive in these circumstances and hourly wage rates rose by 12 per cent in a year and a half (between the last quarter of 1968 and the second quarter of 1970); by then the policy was degenerating into a series of often spurious productivity deals, and the political scene was dominated by controversy about the proposals for trade union reform set out in the White Paper, *In Place of Strife*.

The survival of the Prices and Incomes Board for six years represented the most persistent attempt to maintain a supervisory institution in this field, and any lessons that can be derived from the Board's experience are obviously highly significant for any future policy. The Board placed great weight on the need for improvements in efficiency as the key to higher real wages. How far its investigations acted as a stimulus to such improvements it is difficult to tell. The investigators always tend to be much more sanguine about the benefits than those investigated. But one important side effect was that the productivity factor helped the Board to inject enough 'give' into the system to maintain the policy intact whilst extending some sort of special treatment to difficult cases.

The informal methods of the Board led to complaints from the unions. It made a point, for example, of not showing the parties its findings before publication and played down any attempts to conciliate rather than pronounce. Its decision not to hold public hearings also appeared to shut off a useful safety valve. But its initial success, and later weakness, depended primarily on the unions' relations with the government on the question of pay restraint rather than on the *modus operandi* of the Board.

Balance of Payments

While the Government had set out to tackle the fundamental problems determining growth and our competitive position in world markets, the weakness of the balance of payments effectively dominated macro-economic policy. The Labour Government inherited a current deficit of nearing £400 million in 1964 as a result of the Maudling 'dash for growth'. This was converted it into a small surplus in 1966 before it deteriorated again to a deficit of £300 million in 1967, and devaluation intervened. To free the resources needed to improve the balance of payments after devaluation, early in 1968 the new Chancellor, Roy Jenkins, announced major reductions in public expenditure which involved a withdrawal of British forces from East of Suez. The Budget two months later involved substantial increases in indirect taxes. The effect of devaluation reinforced by restricting home demand was to produce a massive improvement of over £800 million in the balance of payments, converting the 1967 deficit into a surplus of well over £500 million in 1970. But although the various deflationary packages introduced in response to balance of payments difficulties seemed severe at the time, unemployment remained relatively low: it averaged 2.5 per cent in 1967, 1968 and 1969 and rose slightly to 2.7 per cent in 1970.

Lessons for Labour

In line with the spirit of the time the Wilson Government had come into office with the prime objective of speeding up the long-term rate of growth. One means of doing so was to put an end to the Stop-Go cycle that seemed to be a chronic feature of the British economy and of which Labour had been so intensely critical when in Opposition. They were not, however, able to do noticeably better in this respect than their predecessors: there was a major 'Stop' in 1966 followed by further deflationary measures after devaluation. Not only did (and still does) the British economy have a natural instability, but in addition any period of excess demand tended to be dramatised by its effect on the balance of payments and sterling. There is perhaps a lesson for Labour in the 1990s: do not stake your reputation on being more successful than your predecessors in ironing out the cyclical ups and downs in demand and output!

The other principal means of tackling the growth problem was to concentrate on what would now be called 'supply-side' problems by setting up the Department of Economic Affairs, which was intended to be at least the equal of the Treasury: George Brown was deputy Prime Minister. In practice the Treasury still dominated economic policy, partly because it was the department effectively controlling the public sector, and partly because macro-economic policy was bound to be the predominant concern in the short-run. This was at a time when many people felt, reasonably enough, that full employment was now an accomplished fact which could be taken for granted, and macro-economic policy was a matter of routine maintenance. Today with unemployment a major problem, macro-economic policy is even more likely to take centre stage and any Labour Government should recognise this from the start.

5 Transition and Revolution: 1970–95

I. TRANSITION

The 1970s were a period of transition from the postwar years of full employment to the period of deflation and mass unemployment which started in the early 1980s. Between 1946 and 1970 annual unemployment did not exceed 2.5 per cent, but in the 1970s it remained between 2.5 and 6 per cent; and then from 1980 to 1995 it stayed up in the range 6 to 13 per cent, averaging 10 per cent, virtually the same as in the 1920s. The economic events which triggered this transition were a succession of world-wide booms in oil or commodity prices which set up sharp inflationary spirals throughout the industrial world. The difficulties in coping with these by existing means eventually led to a resort to deflationary measures which raised unemployment to a new order of magnitude.

THE HEATH GOVERNMENT, 1970–4

Although Edward Heath's Conservative Government came into office at the beginning of 1970, strongly wedded to reducing government intervention, in the event its broad economic policies had more in common with its Labour predecessors than with its Conservative successors in the 1980s under Margaret Thatcher. Devaluation had led to a substantial improvement in the balance of payments and the Heath Government inherited a surplus of £700 million in 1970. Unemployment was rising slowly, but wage rates were rising at a rate of 12 to 13 per cent and prices were also accelerating but not so sharply. Anthony (later Lord) Barber's first Budget in October 1970 was broadly neutral but planned longer-term reductions in government expenditure.

Having wound up the National Board for Price and Incomes and temporarily disengaged itself from private sector pay negotiations, the new Government quickly became involved in major disputes in the public sector. The winter of 1970–1 saw the 'dustmen's strike', a dispute affecting the pay levels of 770,000 local government manual workers, an overtime ban by electricity workers leading to power cuts, and industrial action by the firemen, all of which were eventually settled by substantial pay increases. These were the first clear signs that government involvement in unpopular industrial disputes was a consequence of their responsibility for public sector pay policy whether or not they had an all-embracing pay policy.

Early in 1971 unemployment passed the 3 per cent mark for the first time since the war (apart from the 1947 fuel crisis: see Table 5.1). The Heath Government, like its predecessors, remained firmly committed to full employment, and faced with forecasts of a continuing rise in unemployment it took a number of reflationary measures during 1971 to expand demand and output. Tax cuts in the March Budget were designed to increase the rate of growth of output from 2 to 3 per cent. They were followed by cuts in Purchase Tax in the Mini-Budget in July and the abolition of hire purchase controls (specifying minimum deposits and maximum periods of repayment). The summer package also contained £100 million for public investment in Development Areas. In December the Government announced the repayment of the £130 million outstanding postwar credits in the following year, thus giving effect to Keynes' original concept of forced saving during the War being used to stimulate demand when needed in the postwar period.[1] (Keynes envisaged the release of such deposits 'at the outset of the first post-war slump'.)

Monetary policy was also set in a reflationary direction. Bank Rate was cut by 1 per cent in April and September, and in September all ceiling limits were removed on bank lending, stimulating a sharp rise in bank advances. Bank lending increased by 37 per cent in 1972 and 43 per cent in 1973.[2] These unexpectedly sharp increases reflected the fact that measures to stimulate demand in the short term became entangled with structural reforms to alter the method of central bank control and encourage competition in the financial sector.

Despite these reflationary measures, by the start of 1972 unemployment had risen to over 4 per cent or nearly one million, whereas the Government's intention had been to get it down to 500,000. In response Barber introduced a further reflationary

Table 5.1 UK unemployment, 1970–95 (annual averages)

Year	*per cent*	*Thousands*	*Year*	*per cent*	*Thousands*
1970	2.7	640	1983	12.2	3,105
1971	3.5	797	1984	11.5	3,160
1972	3.8	876	1985	11.7	3,271
1973	2.7	619	1986	11.8	3,293
1974	2.6	619	1987	10.5	2,953
1975	4.2	978	1988	8.3	2,370
1976	5.7	1,359	1989	6.3	1,799
1977	6.2	1,484	1990	5.8	1,665
1978	6.1	1,475	1991	8.0	2,292
1979	5.7	1,390	1992	9.8	2,779
1980	7.4	1,795	1993	10.3	2,919
1981	11.4	2,734	1994	9.4	2,636
1982	13.0	3,119	1995	8.3	2,326

Note: see Appendix 1, Measuring Unemployment.

budget in March 1972 cutting Income and Purchase Tax. It was designed to secure a 5 per cent annual rate of growth of demand and output in the second half of 1972 and first half of 1973. In his Budget speech the Chancellor indicated that the exchange rate parity would be sacrificed if necessary, saying:

> I am sure that all honourable members in this House agree that the lesson of the international balance of payments upsets of the last few years is that it is neither necessary nor desirable to distort domestic economies to an unacceptable extent in order to maintain unrealistic exchange rates, whether they are too high or too low.

The dollar had been floated in 1971 and the pound was 'temporarily' floated in June 1972, soon after the Budget; but this soon became permanent as floating led to an immediate devaluation of the pound of 7 per cent against our trading partners, and it depreciated further in the autumn. But the balance of payments deteriorated dramatically with the deficit reaching over £1,000 million in 1973 as commodity prices shot up. By the third quarter of 1973 (before the rise in oil prices in mid-October 1973), the export prices of primary products (excluding oil) in dollar terms were over 80 per cent higher than in 1971, with food import prices rising by 70 per cent. Retail food prices in the UK rose 23 per cent in the same period, and the price of materials for manufacturing by 44 per cent. This added considerably to the pressure on wages and prices. With the balance of payments in heavy deficit and unemployment now down to little over 500,000, the Government introduced a restrictive mini-Budget in December 1973, reintroducing hire purchase controls, calling for Special Deposits to restrict bank lending and cutting public investment by 20 per cent.

Soon after the Arab–Israeli War broke out in October 1973 and OPEC raised oil prices by 66 per cent, the power engineers began industrial action and the miners started an overtime ban. Oil shipments to the West were cut by 25 per cent in November and oil prices doubled on the first of January. The Government were forced to introduce the 3 day working week.

Prices and Incomes Policy

When the Government and the TUC failed to reach any agreement to moderate wage increases, the Government introduced a 90 day freeze on wages and prices, starting in November 1972. This was Stage I of their new prices and incomes policy. Stage II, which was to run from March 1973 to the autumn, broke new ground in specifying limits on pay increases for the average pay bill per head in a firm as a whole: this was not to exceed 4 per cent or £1 per week per head and no individual was to receive an increase of more than £250 a year. No exceptions were allowed for increases in productivity. A Pay Board was set up with responsibility for ensuring that this policy was observed. A Price Commission was also established to control prices. Firms were only permitted to increase prices to recover 'allowable' costs. Profit margins were not to exceed the best two years of the last five.

A new pay code, Stage III, came into operation in November 1972. The limits for pay increases were raised to an average of £2.25 per week or 7 per cent, with an individual maximum of £350 a year. Provisions for greater flexibility included a 1 per cent margin for changes in pay structure and extra payments for genuine efficiency schemes for which evidence from three months' operation had to be given to the Pay Board. Most significant for the future was the introduction of threshold provisions as a permissible element in wage agreements. These could provide that when the retail price index had risen 7 per cent above the October 1973 level a pay increase of 40p per week could be given, and the same increase for every further 1 per cent rise in the index. (This would give full compensation on average earnings before tax.) This provision was intended to moderate immediate increases and by slowing down the rate of inflation render its application inoperative. But in the event the rise in oil prices a few weeks later meant that threshold agreements seriously aggravated the inflationary problem.

The greater flexibility of Stage III was intended to help deal with the looming miners' dispute and the Coal Board was able to make an offer worth about 13 per cent without breaching the Code. This was rejected and the miners' initial overtime ban was followed by a vote for an all-out strike to start on 10 February 1974. On 7 February the Prime Minister called a General Election for 28 February and was defeated by a narrow margin.

Although the Heath Government had not been able to defuse the explosive price and wage explosion that shook not only the British economy but other industrial nations, they had not abandoned the commitment to full employment. Unemployment when they left office was virtually back to the level of 2.5 per cent at which it had been when they came in.

Jekyll and Hyde

The history of incomes policy in the Wilson and Heath governments typified what Michael Stewart, in describing the development of economic policy between 1964 and 1977, called 'the Jekyll and Hyde Years'.[3] Despite the efforts of the Macmillan Government to achieve a workable incomes policy, the Conservatives in opposition bitterly criticised Labour's incomes policies in the late 1960s and then abolished them when they regained power. But when the Heath Government reintroduced a pay policy in the early 1970s, Labour was equally vociferous in its opposition. The problem was not, as was frequently suggested (e.g. by the Social Democratic Party) that the two main parties were too extremist or in fundamental ideological disagreement, but that the conduct of whoever was in Opposition made agreement on any long-term institutional changes in many fields, particularly anything which affected the trade unions, virtually impossible. As Stewart put it:

> The two main parties, of course, have different political and economic philosophies, and very largely represent different kinds of people. Nevertheless, such differences do not explain or justify the extent to which the essentially consensus policies which each party has eventually come to pursue when in office have been repudiated by it when in opposition.

The subsequent development of 'sound-bite' politics has, if anything, accentuated the problem in recent years. But, as we shall argue later, if there was one major lesson to be learnt from the events of the last 25 years it is the need for *permanent* institutional arrangements for non-inflationary pay bargaining if unemployment is to be kept down to tolerable levels.

LABOUR GOVERNMENT, 1974–9

Inflation

The second Wilson Government came to power at the beginning of March 1974 without an overall majority, but after a second General Election in October it had an overall majority of three. When it took over, wage and price inflation had reached unprecedented heights: in the first quarter of 1974 hourly wage rates were 14 per cent higher then a year before and retail prices 12 per cent higher. The miners' strike was settled on terms proposed by the Pay Board recommending 'exceptional' payments to the miners, which gave them pay increases ranging from 22 to 32 per cent and averaging 29 per cent. In true Jekyll and Hyde fashion, the Heath Government's pay policy was abandoned and the Pay Board abolished. In its place in June came agreement with the TUC on the Social Contract[4] under which wage increases were to match increases in the cost of living (with exceptions for the low paid). Payments under the threshold agreements were to continue. These were triggered in April 1974 by a sharp rise in the retail price index and by November, compensation for a rise of 11 percentage points above the threshold was due. These arrangements covered 7 to 7.5 million workers, mainly in the public sector.

Prices and wages rose sharply throughout 1974 and continued to do so in the first half of 1975. With price rises accelerating, threshold and cost of living agreements were stimulating a further acceleration in wage increases. In the year to July 1975 hourly wage rates rose by 33 per cent and retail prices by 26 per cent. The country was facing an unprecedented inflationary crisis and responsible trade union leaders were well aware that something had to be done to stem the flood of pay increases or the Government could be forced to take extreme deflationary action. Their response, led by Jack Jones, General Secretary of the Transport and General Workers' Union, was to agree a limit of £6 per week for all pay increases to August 1976 (with nothing for those earning more than £8,500 a year). This was equivalent to a 10.5 per cent increase on average for all workers, well below the current rate of inflation. For this reason, and because of the way it compressed pay differentials, Stage I was bound to be a temporary measure, but it did the trick. In the year to July 1976 the rate of increase of hourly wage rates fell by nearly a half to 18 per cent. The rate of inflation also slowed down to 13 per cent, partly as a result of a general deflation of the economy as the Government strove to contend with the effects of the quadrupling of oil prices in the balance of payments as well as unprecedented rates of inflation. By July 1976 unemployment had risen to over 6 per cent (nearly 1.5 million) as compared with 2.7 per cent when the Labour Government took office.

Fiscal Policy

The new Chancellor, Denis Healey's, first budget in March 1974 was primarily concerned with meeting political commitments and paving the way for agreement on the Social Contract. Pensions were raised, food and rent subsidies increased, and nationalised industries were directed not to raise prices. Income Tax was increased, particularly on unearned incomes; Corporation Tax was increased; and gift and wealth taxes were to be introduced. The PSBR was forecast to be reduced from the level of the previous year and the net effect on demand was officially estimated to be slightly deflationary.

Healey introduced a further mini-Budget in July designed to reduce prices by cutting Value Added Tax from 10 to 8 per cent. Then, after the October election, he introduced an additional budget aimed at improving profitability and liquidity in the company sector and shifting resources from consumption into investment and exports. It effectively reversed his previous approach to prices by easing price controls, but did not reduce food subsidies. More generous allowance was made for stock appreciation in calculating Corporation Tax liabilities. Banks were encouraged to give priority to lending to industry. VAT on petrol was increased. Pensions and family allowances were increased. The net effect on demand was difficult to assess.

The current balance of payments deficit in 1974 rose to £3.8 billion, partly financed by an inflow of capital from the greatly enriched oil producers. Shifting the additional resources into exports (or import substitution) in order to reduce the deficit to manageable proportions was bound to be a mammoth task. The critical break with the past appeared to have come in the next, April 1975, Budget. As one Keynesian commentator put it at the time:

> The latest budget was the clearest indication yet of the break which is occurring in the way in which economic policy has been conducted since the war. Against a background of falling output and rapidly rising unemployment (actual, as well as forecast) the Chancellor introduced a deflationary package. The last time unemployment reached 750,000 on an upward trend, in mid-1971, policy was already moving towards stimulation of demand, and this was the tendency on all previous occasions when the unemployment figures had been rising for any length of time. The different reaction this time is a measure of the seriousness with which the Chancellor views the balance of payments situation and more especially, wage and salary inflation.[5]

The Budget included increases in Income Tax and increases in VAT from 8 to 25 per cent on various consumer durable and electrical goods. The PSBR would be reduced by about £1 billion, but there would be some slowing down in the rate of increase of demand and output, and unemployment was expected to rise to perhaps one million by the end of the year. In the event it passed the one million mark for the first time since the Second World War in August 1975.

The 1976 Crisis

When James Callaghan succeeded Harold Wilson as Prime Minister in April 1976, the government were facing an economic situation at least as difficult as any since the end of the War. Wage and price inflation was slowing down, the balance of payments deficit had improved but was still running at over £1 billion a year, leaving sterling extremely vulnerable to external pressure. The balance of payments deficits of the UK and other non-oil producing countries were, however, the mirror image of the vast surpluses being run up by the OPEC countries following the quadrupling of the prices they were getting for their oil. Somebody else was bound to be in corresponding deficit unless the oil producers expanded their imports very substantially, and as far as the Middle East producers were concerned their capacity to absorb more imports was limited. (Some oil producers, like Nigeria, did increase their imports substantially, but then found themselves in difficulties later on.) Deficit countries like the UK were dependent on the reinvestment of the OPEC surpluses in London or elsewhere; and the non-oil developing countries were dependent on the surpluses being recycled by fresh loans through the banking system. Sterling was thus very susceptible to any changes in sentiment which led to those highly mobile funds being moved from London to New York or elsewhere. As a result sterling depreciated sharply against the dollar, though much less against our trading partners taken as a whole. It was not the time to be the home of an international currency. As long as the OPEC countries were running surpluses of this magnitude, the problem was essentially an international one and efforts by the main industrial countries to improve their balance of payments were bound to be either at each others' expense or to the detriment of the non-oil primary producers who were already in serious trouble.

The day after Callaghan took over as Prime Minister, Healey

presented a Budget primarily designed to win trade union acceptance of a continued social contract. He promised income tax concessions worth almost £1 billion a year provided the unions agreed to limit wage increases to only 3 per cent between August 1976 and August 1977. In other words workers would be compensated for the squeeze in real wages by cuts in tax rather than increases in pay. In the end the TUC agreed to a Stage II formula that was expected to result in average increases of about 4.5 per cent: there was a 5 per cent norm for the increase in a person's total earnings with a lower limit of £2.50 a week and an upper limit of £4. This resulted in a further drastic slowing down in the rate of wage increases. Hourly wage rates in the third quarter of 1977 were only 5 per cent higher than 12 months before.

The Callaghan Government's major misfortune was that although the balance of payments began to turn the corner and was in surplus by the second half of 1977, speculative pressures in the meantime led to a sterling crisis which put the Government into the hands of the IMF. Budgetary policy then became dominated by what the IMF would accept. It is astonishing in retrospect that in the midst of the most severe global payments crisis since the War, the IMF (with the active intervention of the US Treasury) should be trying to dictate a member Government's budgetary policy rather than putting together a comprehensive international package to deal collectively with the problems caused by the OPEC countries' surplus.

Sterling was declining throughout the summer of 1976 and the crisis came to a head at the end of September. The Chancellor applied to the IMF for a Stand-by loan, but agreement on the conditions was not reached until December. There was considerable discussion in the Cabinet about the deflationary effect of the proposed measures. Tony Benn, supported by Peter Shore, proposed an alternative strategy of reimposing import and exchange controls, and a system of import deposits. Tony Crosland also favoured import deposits, and argued for a cosmetic cut in the PSBR by selling £1 billion of BP shares. But the Chancellor supported by the Prime Minister prevailed.[6] The eventual package involved cuts of £1 billion in public expenditure in 1977/8 and £3 billion in 1978/9. Taxes on alcohol and tobacco were raised. The Letter of Intent to the IMF also included targets for domestic credit expansion and a proposal to sell part of the Government's holding in BP to raise £0.5 billion, both precursors of things to come in the form of the IMF's preoccupations with monetarism and privatisation. With further aid from a credit negotiated with the Bank of International Settlements, the Government weathered the storms in the markets, and the balance of payments improved, achieving a current surplus in the second half of 1977.

Although Stages I and II of the Pay Policy substantially reduced the rate of increase of wages, the rise in retail prices accelerated again over the winter of 1976–7. This was partly due to the fall in sterling in late 1976 which led to a sharp increase in the price of imported goods. In addition there were some relaxations in the Price Code. Food subsidies were cut and nationalised industry prices raised as part of the response to IMF pressure on public expenditure. But in the second half of 1977 the rate of increase of retail prices slowed appreciably. Another phase of Pay Policy, Stage III, began in August 1977 limiting increases to 10 per cent. The crunch came when the Government tried to tighten up still further in the following year when it set an unrealistically low guideline of 5 per cent for wage settlements under Stage IV. This led to the public sector strikes in the Winter of Discontent (1978–9) and the Government's defeat in the General Election in May 1979. In Denis Healey's words, 'Our hubris in fixing a pay norm of 5 per cent without any support from the TUC met its nemesis, as inevitably as in a Greek Tragedy.'[7]

The Verdict?

When the Labour Government took office in February 1974 unemployment was 2.7 per cent. Five years later it stood at 6 per cent, and apart from a brief period at the peak of the 1989–90 boom, it has been significantly higher ever since. Historically, therefore, their period of office saw the end of postwar full employment. It also saw a change in attitude towards the previous approach to economic policy. But this in retrospect appears more of a change in emphasis than an abandonment of full employment as a major objective of policy, even though it was an objective the Government failed to achieve.

Callaghan's much quoted speech to the Labour Party Conference in September 1976 during the sterling crisis is often taken as signalling the end of post-war Keynesian demand management. The key paragraph, in which Peter Jay (who had become a convert to monetarism) had an influential hand, said:

> We used to think that you could spend your way out of a recession and increase employment by cutting taxes and boosting Government spending. I tell you in all candour that the option no longer exists, and that insofar as it ever did exist, it only worked on each occasion since the War by injecting a bigger dose of inflation into the economy, followed by a higher level of unemployment.

As the brief review in Chapter 4 should have demonstrated, this statement bears little relation to the course of unemployment or inflation before 1970 or the few occasions on which the budget was actively reflationary. The 1970s saw both a rise in inflation and unemployment, but the prime causes were external to the British economy, accidently accentuated by the effects of threshold agreements on wage increases.

In his memoirs Callaghan himself stands by the speech[8] but qualifies it by saying that:

> The passage I have quoted does not say that Governments should never increase public expenditure or reduce taxation as methods of boosting employment. My argument was that in the circumstances of 1976 these measures were not appropriate, nor were they an alternative to facing up to the long-term changes that were required in our economy and our society.

These changes consisted of: 'long-term, intelligent cooperation between both sides of industry and the Government to build a modern manufacturing sector' and 'in the short-term, to harmonise the creation of wealth with the fair distribution of wealth'.

Denis Healey's later comment in response to a question by Milton Friedman was 'It just shows that you should not let your son-in-law write your speeches.'[9] Although in his memoirs

Denis Healey speaks of 'when I abandoned Keynesianism in 1975', he goes on to state that:

> Keynes was right in saying that adequate demand is a necessary condition for full employment; but given the inadequacy of the information available and the uncertainty about how people will use their money, fine tuning of demand is not possible. However, if demand is grossly above or below productive capacity, the economy will be in trouble[10]

– shades of Macmillan's 'last year's Bradshaw'.

Healey suffered particularly badly from misleading statistics and forecasts. The Treasury grossly overestimated the probable rise in the PSBR, thus accentuating our difficulties with the IMF. Reducing the PSBR became for a time an end in itself unrelated to the state of home demand. But by 1978 Healey felt able to introduce a reflationary budget in response to the higher level of unemployment. Moreover after the customary reversal of the previous Government's prices and incomes policies, the Callaghan Government (at the cost of great political anguish) stuck to the attempt to use such policies to bring down inflation rather than resort to deflation and higher unemployment.

One key lesson that emerges from this period is the extraordinary difficulties of bringing inflation down, when to do so means asking wage earners to accept pay increases which fail to compensate for the previous increase in prices. (Their Conservative successors found equal or greater difficulties when they adopted policies which tried to do the same thing without an incomes policy by reducing the bargaining power of labour.) In judging past economic policies or trying to formulate policies for the future, it is essential to distinguish between success or failure in (a) choosing appropriate strategies and (b) success or failure in implementing them. The interwar years were full of major disasters caused by following inappropriate policies, such as the return to the Gold Standard. The postwar years up to 1970 were strategically more successful, so that criticism focuses more on day-to-day economic management than on strategy. The conversion from war to peace was in retrospect outstandingly successful, and the main point of criticism was our long-term failure to improve our industrial efficiency as rapidly as many of our main competitors.

When it comes to the 1970s and the response to the boom in commodity prices and the oil shocks, it is difficult to judge governments' responses to the events even with the advantage of hindsight. Both the Conservative and Labour Governments strove to moderate inflation by acting on prices and wages with as much cooperation from both sides of industry as they could muster. Neither was immediately successful. The experience of their successors over the following ten years when circumstances were very much easier suggests that resort to deflation instead would not have been any more effective, and the cost in terms of lost jobs would have been enormous. But by trying and appearing to fail to cope with the new situation with existing policies, they left the door wide open for the Thatcherite revolution to come.

In retrospect those with most cause to regret their actions should have been the trade union leaders who failed to cooperate in achieving effective incomes policies. George Woodcock, former General Secretary of the TUC, had warned in 1975 that:

> The most likely alternative to cooperation is that governments will have to modify or abandon their commitment to maintain a high level of employment . . . If this country were to return to the industrial instability and the heavy unemployment of pre-war days, that would certainly not improve the ability of the trade unions collectively to secure greater social justice and fairness for their members.[11]

It was perhaps understandable that the unions should have taken the maintenance of full employment for granted, and with it the continued power of the unions and their members which had so much potential for improving the lot of the ordinary worker. But their failure to curb the use of this power when the country was faced with serious difficulties in the 1970s produced a disastrous reaction in the following decade. It helped to create a climate of opinion in which a combination of heavy unemployment and anti-union legislation in the 1980s were deliberately used to reduce the unions' power and influence at great cost to their members. (Indeed, given that Mrs Thatcher succeeded in virtually eliminating the miners and privatised much of the public sector, the unions were lucky to survive as well as they did.)

II. THE THATCHER REVOLUTION

The return of Mrs Thatcher's first Government in May 1979 heralded a revolution in economic policy. Its keynote was reliance on the market and control of the money supply rather than state intervention, and its prime objective was reducing inflation. Government expenditure and taxes were to be cut. There was to be no more resort to prices and incomes policies. Inflation was to be controlled by controlling the money supply. Free market ideology and reliance on monetary policy went hand in hand; both had a simplicity of appeal. All that was required to reduce inflation was to keep the rate of increase in the money supply in check.

Little was said about the implications for unemployment, which was regarded as essentially a labour market question and getting the right 'price' for labour. While at first the shift in emphasis from fiscal to monetary policy entailed in this approach was the most striking change, in the longer run it was not so much the technicalities of macro-economic management that were so important as the reliance on a continued high level of unemployment as a permanent feature of the new approach to inflation.

THE FIRST THATCHER GOVERNMENT, 1979–83

The first year of the Thatcher Government coincided with the second 'oil shock'. Oil prices doubled from $13 a barrel at the end of 1978 to $26 to $27 a barrel at the end of 1979. But as usual when a new Government comes into office, its first Budget in June 1979 was more concerned with fulfilling political commitments than with the immediate economic situation. Geoffrey Howe's first Budget was primarily concerned to switch the burden of taxation from direct to indirect taxes. The top rate of Income Tax was reduced from 83 to 60 per cent for earned income and the Standard Rate from 33 to 30 per cent. VAT was raised to a unified level of 15 per cent from its previous levels of 8 and 12.5 per cent. The tax on petrol was also increased. Planned public expenditure was to be cut by £1.5 billion. Minimum Lending Rate was raised by 2 points to 14 per cent, and a target of 7 to 11 per cent was set for the increase in the money supply.

Coming on top of the effects of the increase in oil prices, the increase in indirect taxes aggravated the wage–price spiral, by raising retail prices by 3 per cent. (The Prime Minister herself had doubts on this point and suggested that VAT should only be raised to 12.5 per cent.[12]) In the 12 months after the Budget the retail price index rose by over 20 per cent. The Government turned increasingly to monetary policy to tackle inflation. In November 1979 the Minimum Lending Rate was raised by an unprecedented 3 per cent from 14 to 17 per cent. This tightening of monetary policy came at a time when falling demand was already expected to reduce output and unemployment. The official economic forecasts in the 1979 Autumn Statement showed a fall of output of 3 per cent in 1980 and a rise in unemployment to 2 million in 1981. But in the event output fell more and unemployment rose more quickly. In 1980 the UK economy experienced its most dramatic fall in economic activity since the Great Crash in 1929. The brunt was borne by manufacturing output which fell by almost 16 per cent in 18 months, a good deal more than the 11 per cent fall between 1929 and 1931.[13] Unemployment reached 2 million in August 1981 and was standing at 2.5 million by the time of the March 1981 Budget.

In former times such a situation would have called for an expansionary Budget. But by then, the Budget was no longer recognised as an instrument for affecting demand, save in so far as the level of borrowing affected interest rates and the money supply; and then the only significant effects were seen to be on inflation rather than on output and employment. Budgetary policy was guided by the Treasury's Medium Term Financial Strategy (MTFS), (the first version of which appeared in the March 1980 Financial Statement) and was primarily aimed at reducing the PSBR without regard to the state of demand at the time. Thus in 1981 at the height of the most serious recession since the war, Geoffrey Howe introduced a budget designed to reduce the PSBR and which was deflationary rather than expansionist. The sole attempt to deal with the recession was to cut the Minimum Lending Rate from 14 to 12 per cent. Personal allowances and thresholds for Income Tax were frozen, while indirect taxes on drink, tobacco and cars were raised. The target for the PSBR was to be reduced from 4 per cent of GDP in 1980–81 to 1.5 per cent in 1983–84. The target of 7 to 11 per cent for increases in the money supply in

1979–81 was to decline 1 per cent each year to reach 4 to 8 per cent in 1983–84.

The 1981 Budget was criticised both inside and outside the cabinet by Tory 'wets';[14] and it prompted the famous letter of protest to *The Times* signed by 364 economists concerned at the prospect of a further increase in unemployment,[15] which rose to over 3 million in 1982 and remained there for over five years. If any one event had to be defined as signalling the end of postwar full employment policies, the 1981 Budget is a prime contender.

Commodity prices passed their peak in 1980 and oil prices in 1981. The rate of inflation, which had reached a peak of 22 per cent in May 1980, fell to 12 per cent in May 1981. Prices rose more slowly in 1982 and then averaged a rate of increase of around 5 per cent for the rest of the decade. Wage increases fell in a similar fashion but remained rather above the level of price increases most of the time, and the consequent increases in real wages no doubt helped to moderate wage demands. However, there can be little doubt that the major influence on both prices and wages was the unprecedented degree of deflation reflected in the continuation of unemployment at around the 3 million level until 1988.

The New Monetarist Approach

In introducing his Budgets, Geoffrey Howe consistently stated that his first priority was to 'squeeze out inflation'. In this connection, whether (as the monetarists believed) the reduction in the PSBR merely affected inflation via the money supply, or whether (as the Keynesians believed) it acted directly on demand and then on prices and wages, was of secondary importance. On either approach the measures taken acted in a deflationary direction. The Keynesians expected, however, that there would be a corresponding effect on unemployment, whereas the monetarists dismissed this as a purely temporary phenomenon. But as time went by and the Government came under increasing attack for their failure to tackle the high level of unemployment, their argument took on a new dimension: a lower PSBR would reduce the cost of government borrowing and lower interest rates.

In his 1980 Budget speech Howe said, 'Relaxed monetary

and budgetary policies might bring higher output – even higher living standards – in the very short-term, though even that is questionable, but in reality they would simply fuel inflation.' He then went on to say, 'The consequence of excessive borrowing has been high nominal interest rates, and in capital markets, the crowding out of business by the state: this has held back investment.' This marked a return to the formerly discredited interwar 'Treasury View' discussed in Chapter 2. The argument that interest rates depend on the extent of Government borrowing seems even less relevant in the 1980s when British gilts are sold in global bond markets and their prices relative to those of other major countries depend primarily on exchange rate expectations, i.e. if sterling is expected to depreciate, the rates on British bonds will be higher and vice versa. Historically, recessions lead both to higher government borrowing and lower interest rates. This assertion, however, enabled the Government to argue that cuts in the PSBR would help the economy to recover by reducing interest rates, when in practice the fiscal measures adopted were prolonging the recession.

Again in his 1982 Budget speech, the Chancellor said: 'Some argue that our fiscal policy is excessively tight, once account is taken of the effect of the recession. I do not accept this. The acid test for the PSBR is the level of interest rates at which it can be financed.' But aware of the retort that interest rates were determined on international markets, he went on to qualify this, by referring to the need to hold our interest rates 'in the lower part of the international range'.

This argument has become topical again in the EU in the mid-1990s with Finance Ministers and the European Commission advocating cuts in government deficits both to meet the Maastricht convergence criteria and as a remedy for unemployment: as in the Delors Report discussed in Chapter 10. The only validity of this proposition is that if financial markets become permeated with the view that the government is borrowing too much, the loss of confidence may drive down the price of gilts and make government borrowing more difficult. It is important therefore that governments and their central banking partners should not pour fuel on the flames and make things more difficult by themselves encouraging this misleading approach.

In defending his 1981 Budget in his memoirs a decade later, Howe writes: 'we all wanted to get interest rates down – for its own sake and because the pound was, by all practical standards, too high. If that was to happen we had to borrow less.' He believes that he had the last laugh on the 364 economists because national output stopped falling at about the time of the Budget. But the real point is that the subsequent rate of increase was too low to take up the slack in the economy in the form of unused capacity and massive unemployment. Unemployment did not come down significantly until 1988, by which time vast segments of British manufacturing industry had closed down.

One of the most disastrous consequences of the monetarist approach (combined with the effect of North Sea oil) on the balance of payments was its impact on the exchange rate. The pound appreciated by over 15 per cent in the late 1970s, weakening the competitive position of British manufacturing exports, which remained at or below their 1977 level until 1984. The depressed level of exports and the deflation of home demand had a devastating effect on manufacturing capacity and firms' readiness to invest in new plant.

THE SECOND THATCHER GOVERNMENT, 1983–7

After her second General Election victory in June 1983, Margaret Thatcher appointed Nigel Lawson as Chancellor of the Exchequer in her new Government. In the next four years he presided over what was regarded as an 'expansionary' phase; but although output expanded more rapidly, and employment increased, this was insufficient to make any impact on the level of unemployment. Employment rose by 1.5 million between 1983 and 1987, but the number of men in full-time jobs actually fell. Over a million of the jobs were for women and of these, two-thirds were for part-time employment. Unemployment only fell by 79,000, from just under 3.0 million in June 1983 to 2.9 million in June 1987. The number unemployed would, in fact, have risen but for the increasing numbers on Special Employment schemes which rose substantially over the period.

As Financial Secretary to the Treasury in the period 1979–

81 Lawson (with the help of the Treasury's new monetarist Chief Economic Adviser, Terence Burns) had been the prime architect of the Medium Term Financial Strategy (MTFS). The March 1980 Financial Statement and Budget Report laid down a series of progressively lower bands for the growth of the money stock, reducing from 7 to 11 per cent in 1980–81 to 4 to 8 per cent in 1983–84. This was allied to a series of parallel reductions in the PSBR. But as William Keegan points out, 'The Bank of England also managed to slip in a footnote that looks especially judicious with the passage of time, warning that "the way in which the money supply is defined for target purposes may need to be adjusted from time to time as circumstances change".'[16] During his Chancellorship, Lawson was progressively forced to play down the use of M3 as a target, which showed increases above the target range and proved an unreliable indicator of the degree of credit stringency. It was suspended in the autumn of 1985. So after a brief flirtation was M0.

In his first period of office, Lawson was much concerned to check the growth of public expenditure to pave the way for a general reduction (and simplification) of direct taxes. In his first March 1984 Budget he set in hand a gradual reduction from 50 per cent to 35 per cent in the rate of Corporation Tax and the phasing-out of Investment Allowances. The latter he justified on the grounds that 'with over 3 million unemployed it cannot make sense to subsidise capital so heavily at the expense of labour' – a strange claim to make when the employment-creating effects of additional industrial investment were likely to far outweigh any substitution effects. In fact the immediate effect was to stimulate investment as firms sought to invest before the Allowances were reduced. Further cuts in Income Tax followed in his next three Budgets, culminating in a 2p reduction in the basic rate in his 1987 pre-election package.

Lawson, a former financial journalist, set out his approach to economic policy in his 1984 Mais Lecture to the City University Business School.

> The conventional post-War wisdom was that unemployment was a consequence of inadequate economic growth, and economic growth was to be secured by macroeconomic policy

> – the fiscal stimulus of an enlarged Budget deficit, with monetary policy (to the extent that it could be said to exist at all) on the whole passively following fiscal policy. Inflation, by contrast, was increasingly seen as a matter to be dealt with by microeconomic policy – the panoply of controls and subsidies associated with the era of incomes policy . . . But the proper role of each is precisely the opposite . . . It is the conquest of inflation, and not the pursuit of growth and employment, which is or should be the objective of macroeconomic policy. And it is the creation of conditions conducive to growth and employment, and not the suppression of price rises, which is or should be the objective of microeconomic policy.

It was the assignment of macro-economic policy to killing inflation at all costs, with any help from incomes policy ruled out of court, rather than the relative emphasis on monetary instead of fiscal policy, that ensured a continuation of such a high level of unemployment.

Later, in his 1985 Budget, Lawson adopted a rather different approach, that of setting targets for money GDP on lines first suggested by James Meade in the 1970s. The main practical implication of this approach (see Chapter 6) meant that if prices rose more than assumed when setting the target, the rate of growth would have to be slowed down; the converse implication was that if growth was too slow and prices were on course, measures should be taken to stimulate demand. But in practice fiscal policy continued to be dominated by the desire to reduce the PSBR. The Chancellor's 'strategy for jobs' to combat what he called 'the scourge of unemployment' was directed solely at reducing labour costs. Wages Councils, which he said 'destroy jobs', were to be abolished; employers' national insurance contributions for the low-paid were reduced; and the period of employment before workers in large firms could claim 'unfair dismissal' was extended. In addition further places were to be created on the Youth Training Scheme and Community Programmes for the long-term unemployed. As unemployment failed to decrease, these Special Employment Measures were continually expanded or modified. In the following year there was a further increase to 250,000 in the number of places on Community Programmes and a New

Workers' scheme was launched giving employers a subsidy of £15 a week to employ 18–20 year olds.

Floating Rates

A key theme to emerge during the Lawson Chancellorship was the search for an appropriate exchange rate policy. The floating exchange rate regime had created new instabilities. Following its appreciation in the late 1970s the pound averaged $2.33 in 1980. Thereafter the dollar strengthened and had risen over 25 per cent by 1982 and 50 per cent in 1985.[17] The deutschmark also remained strong with only 4 per cent depreciation, but the pound fell to an average of $1.30 in 1985 after almost falling below the $1 level at the start of the year. Against all other currencies the pound had fallen by nearly 20 per cent in the first half of the 1980s, and after a time lag manufacturing exports began to rise again. This depreciation of sterling, which was primarily a function of the strength of the dollar, took place despite the fact that the balance of payments was in substantial surplus throughout the period, as the production of North Sea oil grew with net exports of oil peaking at £8 billion in 1985.

Lawson initially took the line that there was not 'in practice any half-way house between the sort of approach to the exchange rate we pursue and a fixed exchange rate'.[18] But as time went on he became increasingly involved in international efforts to stabilise exchange rates in the aftermath of the sterling crisis in January 1985. In that month the pound fell to nearly $1, and the Bank signalled an increase of 1.5 per cent in base rates, followed by another increase of 1.5 per cent a few days later and a further increase of 2 per cent at the end of the month. After the G5 meeting in January 1985, the USA agreed with the other four participants to undertake 'coordinated intervention in the markets as necessary'. This was followed by a burst of selling to keep the dollar down.[19]

Later in the year, the Plaza Agreement of September 1985, spelled the start of a period of 'managed floating', the keynote of which was 'some further orderly appreciation of the main non-dollar currencies against the dollar'. Scarred by his experience in the January crisis, the Chancellor had become convinced by then that the UK should seek stability by joining the European Monetary System. But the Prime Minister and her personal economic adviser, Alan Walters, were strongly opposed and, despite support for the proposal from other key ministers, she vetoed it in November;[20] the UK did not join for another five years. She believed strongly in floating rates and later commented: 'The Plaza Agreement gave Finance ministers – Nigel above all perhaps – the mistaken idea that they have it in their power to defy the markets indefinitely.'[21]

THATCHER AND MAJOR

Despite continued growth of demand and output, unemployment remained high. After peaking at 13 per cent in 1982, it had only fallen by 2.5 per cent by 1987. One of the most remarkable features of the Conservatives' 1987 General Election victory was that it took place (as in 1983) against the background of levels of unemployment (12 per cent in 1983 and 10.5 per cent in 1987) which in former times would have been considered politically disastrous. This must have played a considerable part, consciously or unconsciously, in encouraging the Government to continue following policies which were explicitly designed to counter inflation and paid little heed to the cost in unemployment. Indeed it must be significant that in her memoirs looking back on her 'Downing Street Years', Margaret Thatcher never refers to unemployment as one of the many critical policy problems she discussed with Ministers; it only rates a brief mention for its possible effects on public opinion, particularly at election time.

The Lawson Boom

The year 1987 was not only an election year but was the start of what came to be called the 'Lawson boom'. (It is a commentary on the British masochist approach to economic policy that whereas two Chancellors' names, Barber and Lawson, have been attached to booms, in a spirit of rebuke rather than congratulation, the Chancellors whose names were associated with recessions have not been excoriated in this way!) GDP rose sharply and unemployment began to fall more rapidly, but inflation remained below 5 per cent. Most forecasters, however, (including those in the Treasury) expected the boom to slow down. The National Institute commented in February: 'We believe that the boom is now over.' But in the event output rose rapidly again in 1988 and did not begin to slow down until 1989, finally reaching a temporary peak in the middle of 1990. Unemployment reached its low point in the same year, averaging 1.7 million in 1990, the lowest for a decade. As the boom progressed, the rate of inflation accelerated, with the retail price index showing increases of 7.8 per cent between 1988 and 1989 and 9.4 per cent between 1989 and 1990. The balance of payments deteriorated sharply. A virtually zero deficit in 1986 rose to £22.5 billion in 1989 (4.4 per cent of GDP).

The recovery in the economy boosted tax revenue and reduced the cost of unemployment pay; as a result, with the aid of privatisation receipts, the PSBR fell and in 1988–89 there was a surplus of £3 billion. Lawson proclaimed that 'Henceforth a zero PSBR will be the norm.' The Budget had been largely abandoned as a regulator of demand and when the boom led to an acceleration of inflation, monetary policy was the main instrument brought into play. Base Rate went up from 7.5 per cent in May 1988 to 15 per cent in October 1989. This and the recession after 1990 led to a sharp fall in house prices and the emerging problem of 'negative equity' i.e. house-owners with mortgages higher than the value of their house and hence unable to sell up and move.

Concern at the re-emergence of the inflationary problem fuelled discussion about joining the European Exchange Rate Mechanism (ERM). By doing so we would be entering a virtually fixed exchange rate system again, so far as relations with our European partners was concerned. Attitudes obviously depended partly on the continuing argument between the Europhiles and Eurosceptics. They also reflected predilections for floating or fixed exchange rates. The Prime Minister had long been bitterly opposed to membership on both counts. But as time wore on, an additional factor came into play: the idea that by in effect tying sterling to a non-inflationary currency like the deutschmark we should automatically be bound to achieve a correspondingly low rate of inflation. As a halfway house, from March 1987, the Chancellor (unbeknown to the Prime Minister), began to 'shadow the deutschmark'. The

Prime Minister only realised what was happening when interviewed by *Financial Times* journalists in November.

The Chancellor's policy of shadowing the deutschmark particularly riled the Prime Minister when it involved exchange rate intervention and holding down interest rates to try to keep sterling from rising appreciably above a rate of DM3 as it did in early 1988. Given the damage already done to British manufacturing industry by high exchange rates, this was a modest target. The dilemma was that interest rates could not be relied on as the sole weapon to regulate demand and inflation at home and at the same time be used to influence exchange rates. Pure monetarism was only consistent with leaving exchange rates to float freely: or, as proposed in the EMU, total economic and monetary union. The friction on this issue between the Prime Minister, relying heavily on advice from her pure monetarist adviser, Alan Walters (even though he was in Washington), and the more pragmatic Lawson, led eventually to Lawson's resignation in October 1989 on the grounds that his position had become untenable when the Prime Minister 'preferred the advice of an academic economist observing the British economy 3,000 miles away to that of her Chancellor of the Exchequer'.[22]

In and Out of the ERM

John Major succeeded Nigel Lawson as Chancellor for the remaining year of Margaret Thatcher's term of office. When Major became Prime Minister at the end of November 1990, Norman Lamont took over as Chancellor. By then economic policy was becoming increasingly focused on our relations with Europe, following the publications of the Delors Report on monetary union published in the previous year. But apart from defining our longer-term attitude to monetary union, the immediate question was whether to join the ERM. The most fundamental argument in favour of doing so was that with increasing economic integration within Europe, a system of fixed exchange rates could provide a stable basis for business decision making – such as where to invest in production facilities to supply the European market. On the other hand history had shown that fixed rates did not rule out speculative pressure on sterling; and as long as rates of inflation differed, fixed rates would have to be adjusted from time to time. The reverse of this last argument was that by accepting the 'discipline' of a fixed rate Britain would be bound to keep her rate of inflation down to the German level. This last argument was rather confused, in that its protagonists were not always clear as to whether this would happen automatically as a result of market forces or whether it was merely a device to put additional pressure on the Treasury and the Bank to follow low inflation policies. But either way, the anti-inflation argument seems to have been an important factor in the decision to join in October 1990. It may also have been a factor in going in at the excessively high rate of DM2.95. Over the three and a half years since Lawson had started to shadow the deutschmark at DM3 to the pound, prices had risen by nearly 30 per cent in Britain but by only 8 per cent in Germany. If the same real exchange rate was appropriate, the new rate should have been around DM2.50.[23] Once again Britain was impaled on an excessively high exchange rate.

The Lawson boom had reached its peak in 1990. Unemployment fell to little over 1.5 million in the summer of that year, and then began to rise rapidly reaching 3 million again at the beginning of 1993. Output stopped rising and then fell slightly: but the scope for interest rate reductions was limited by the historically high rates set by the Bundesbank following German reunification. The Government were doctrinally opposed to the use of fiscal measures to offset falling demand, particularly as the PSBR rose rapidly as tax revenue fell and the cost of social security benefits rose under the impact of the recession. Nevertheless John Major won the April 1992 General Election, albeit with a reduced majority, and a further sterling crisis came like a *deus ex machina* to release the UK economy from the ERM straitjacket.

In the earlier days of the European Monetary System there had been periodic realignments of exchange rates to adjust to changing circumstances. By the early 1990s with EMU on the horizon, the practicability of such a realignment was more difficult; by then either an upward revaluation of the deutschmark would have to have been part of a general settlement, or the franc would have to have been devalued against the mark, thus aborting years of sacrifice to maintain the *franc fort.* In the event agreement on the devaluation of the Italian lira created inevitable speculation against sterling. George Soros and others put together a 'war chest' of £10 billion to bet against continuation of the existing parity, and won.[24] On Black Wednesday (16 September 1992) a rise in interest rates to 15 per cent and massive intervention in the market by the Bank failed to hold the position, and Lamont was forced to announce our departure from the system. Sterling was floating once again.

Subsequent reductions in interest rates and the effects of the fall in the pound on exports helped to stimulate the economy, and led to a renewed rise in output and fall in unemployment. Over the next three years output rose by 9 per cent and unemployment fell from 10.5 to 8 per cent or 2.25 million. This gentle recovery did not set off any acceleration of inflation and retail prices only rose by 7.5 per cent in three years (from the fourth quarter of 1992 to the fourth quarter of 1995).

Kenneth Clarke, who succeeded Lamont in May 1993, thus found himself presiding over a period in which inflation has remained relatively low and unemployment fell. This has led to euphemistic comments about the economy being in an 'unprecedently favourable situation' – a comment which betrays a sense of values in which unemployment and its consequences are rated of little importance. The apparent conquest of inflation depends still on the economy being run with a level of unemployment between 1 and 2 million. The stark question we have to face is whether this is a 'price worth paying' for containing inflation, and if not, what is the alternative?

6 Demand Management

the tyranny of prevailing opinion. (John Stuart Mill)

THE MONETARIST LEGACY

The development of macro-economic policy during the 1980s owed much to the simplistic appeal of monetarism. The core of the monetarist approach was that inflation was purely a monetary phenomenon. The original monetarist theory as set out by Milton Friedman[1] was based on the long-standing 'quantity theory of money', and postulated that the rate of inflation depended on the rate of increase in the supply of money in the form of cash and bank credit. Thus if the growth of the money supply were properly controlled, so would be the rate of inflation. This assumption was, however, based on the faulty hypothesis that the correlation between increases in the money supply and rising prices demonstrated that the former was the cause of the latter. As is so often true in such cases, the causal sequence is not nearly so simple. The relationship depended to a large extent on the fact that the banking system is there to supply the credit needed to enable the economy to operate, and when prices rise the supply of money will automatically tend to rise in response. It is true that the availability and cost of credit affect the ease with which prices and wages can be increased, but only through their effect on business conditions, not by any automatic direct link between the quantity of money and prices.

What might be called 'pure monetarism', with its emphasis on the money supply rather than interest rates, led to the adoption of 'money targeting' by central banks: that is, setting targets for the growth of the national money supply as a means of controlling inflation. Although this is still favoured in some quarters (in particular by the Bundesbank) it can raise considerable practical difficulties: the proliferation of financial institutions taking deposits or giving credit, like building societies, raises problems about defining 'money' and the use of new means of payment, such as credit cards, alters the relationship between people's income or spending and the bank deposits they wish to hold. After struggling with a growing number of definitions of the money supply (M1, M2, M3, M4, M5, etc.) the Bank of England has given up setting any specific money supply target. Instead it now targets the inflation rate directly and the emphasis is on interest rates rather than the money supply.

The most dangerously misleading part of the original monetarist thesis was, however, that controlling the money supply would not affect unemployment, save in the short run. In their view unemployment reflected 'imperfections' in the labour market to be tackled by such measures as legislation to curb the trade unions and by abolishing or weakening machinery to regulate wages (such as Wages Councils). Short of such structural changes there was a 'natural rate of unemployment' to which the economy would eventually revert. The Thatcher experiment illustrated that this was clearly not the case. While restricting credit and raising interest rates eased the pressure to raise prices and wages, it did so only by reducing sales and output, and hence increasing unemployment. This has led to a change of emphasis, from treating the consequent unemployment as a temporary blip to regarding it as the necessary cost of keeping down inflation: 'a price worth paying', to use Norman Lamont's famous phrase when he was Chancellor of the Exchequer, an honest and accurate summary of the philosophy underlying the current approach to macro-economic policy.

It is ironic that the spread of monetarist ideas should push monetary policy to the fore just as global developments made it an increasingly inappropriate instrument for controlling demand. The supply of money in any one country or currency had become of diminishing importance when industry, and in some cases individuals, could borrow elsewhere. The development of international financial markets also meant that interest rates could no longer be determined independently in different countries. The rates in larger or stronger countries tended to set lower limits to levels of interest rates elsewhere, with differences in interest rates tending to reflect the expected movement in exchange rates. This became only too apparent in the EU where interest rates have been dominated by Germany, particularly in the case of members of the ERM.

Another damaging monetarist legacy has been the present confusion about the role of budgetary or fiscal policy in regulating demand. This is particularly untimely when the globalisation of financial markets means that there is more scope for tailoring budgetary policy to individual countries' needs than there is for monetary policy, particularly in an expansionary direction. The monetarists started the rot by alleging that budget surpluses or deficits were only of significance in so far as they affected the money supply. Budget deficits were inflationary because government borrowing increased the money supply and vice versa. By focusing attention entirely on the level of government borrowing they have also encouraged one of the most prevalent current fallacies about public finance: that purely financial transactions, such as privatisation receipts, can be viewed in the same light as measures which directly affect the demand for goods and services, such as changes in government expenditure or changes in tax rates. This is almost entirely nonsense, and a manifestation of political prejudice rather than economic reasoning, but has provided a convenient world-wide excuse for reducing the size of the state sector.

The eagerness with which the monetarist prescription was seized on in right-wing circles had little to do with economics; it was a long-awaited excuse to demolish the Keynesian consensus with its reliance on government action and sympathy for the role of the public sector in helping to stabilise demand. To the Thatcher and Reagan generation, it provided the intellectual excuse for cutting back the role of the State, a return to free market economics and a shift in power and income away from the trade unions and those they represent, all in the supposed cause of meeting the threat of inflation.

THE NEW ORTHODOXY

What is remarkable, however, is the way in which those on the centre and left of the political scene have now been infected by the monetarist virus. Just as the Keynesian revolution spread rapidly across the whole political spectrum to establish a new consensus, so today monetarist ideas have provided the basis for a new political and economic orthodoxy with differences in emphasis, rather than fundamentals, between the leadership of major political parties. On the continent, Socialist and Social Democrat parties have become prisoners of the same basic ideology as the Christian Democrats and other right-wing parties, so that while they remain concerned about the high level of unemployment they are trapped in an intellectual framework that effectively inhibits them from doing anything about it. Thus a French Socialist, Jaques Delors, has been responsible for setting an almost completely monetarist framework for the future of European integration, the full implications of which took some years to realise. In Britain, the Labour Party has been reluctant while in opposition to accept the new philosophy, but its criticisms of the government have become increasingly tactical and Tony Blair has gone out of his way to suggest that a Labour government's approach to monetary and fiscal policy would not be based on any radically different philosophy; such is the force of what John Stuart Mill called 'the tyranny of prevailing opinion'.

The New Orthodoxy may be summarised as follows:

(a) inflation should be controlled by the use of interest rates, preferably in the hands of an independent central bank;
(b) the budget should be balanced rather than used as a means of influencing demand; and
(c) unemployment should be regarded solely as a problem of the labour market.

This is in effect the doctrine now accepted by most finance ministers and their advisers, international organisations like the OECD and the European Commission, and financial commentators. While the new orthodoxy prevails, talk of any return to full employment is either hypocritical or wishful thinking, because its prescriptions are inherently deflationary and it tacitly relies on the existence of mass unemployment to lubricate the market mechanism. There is nothing new or progressive about it. It represents a regression to the ideas and social conditions which prevailed 60 to 70 years ago, the escape from which gave us full employment for a generation.

The New Orthodoxy is the public creed to which finance ministers and their advisers adhere. But in private discussion or academic publications remnants of the old Keynesian creed still appear in bastardised form. Budgetary policy (as well as monetary policy) is still acknowledged as a means of controlling demand, and demand is seen as having a direct effect on output. But the basic objective is not to maintain full employment, but to see that unemployment does not get *too low.* It is dominated by the idea that if unemployment falls below a certain level inflation will accelerate. This is not the language which is generally used in public because it gives the game away, although it sometimes peeps through with the use of such phrases as 'the sustainable rate of unemployment'.

UNEMPLOYMENT AND INFLATION

In the early postwar years some economists believed that the rate at which wages increased was directly related to the level of unemployment. This was formalised in the Phillips Curve[2] setting out the historical relation between unemployment and wage increases in the UK since 1861, which suggested that there was a fairly constant relationship between the level of unemployment and the rate of inflation – a surprising result in view of the enormous changes in labour conditions in the period considered. The Phillips Curve in effect set out the so-called 'trade-off' between unemployment and inflation.

Not surprisingly, in view of the disturbances in the world economy during the 1970s and 1980s, any simple relationship there might have been between inflation and unemployment broke down. Moreover it became increasingly evident that once inflation got under way it generated a momentum of its own and was difficult to slow down. This led to the evolution of the concept of Friedman and others of the 'natural rate of unemployment' into that of the 'non-accelerating inflation rate of unemployment' (with the ungainly acronym NAIRU). This postulated that there was a level of unemployment at which the rate of inflation would be constant (at some indeterminate level) and below which it would accelerate. Whereas the monetarist thesis left no room for traditional demand management, the NAIRU approach could be taken to imply that demand management was required, but that it should be conducted in such a way as to keep unemployment at or above the NAIRU.[3] Experience showed, however, that the implied NAIRU varies markedly over time and hence that it is not a particularly useful concept in practice. It has, however, had a baleful effect on the direction of economic policy by encouraging the idea that policy should be aimed at establishing a (high) *minimum* level of unemployment in the quest to ban inflation, and that full employment is no longer attainable. This revolution in policy objectives, however, only served to aggravate the situation by creating conditions in which higher and higher levels of unemployment were found necessary to slow down inflation.

EXPECTATIONS

Monetarists, such as Friedman, put considerable emphasis on the role of expectations in curbing inflation. His recipe was to get the government and central bank committed to some rigid rule as to the growth of the money supply. The public would then behave in a way that was consistent with stable growth and zero inflation. This suggestion was based on an unrealistic assumption about the inherent stability of the economy and the willingness and ability of governments to abdicate from any responsibility for the behaviour of the economy or the power to control it.

Later neo-classical theoreticians, such as Robert Lucas, developed the thesis that government action to affect demand was bound to be abortive because people would rationally expect it to be only short-lived. Expectations are important, but it is a mistake to assume that businessmen or trade union negotiators think or behave in the same way as people working in financial markets whose sole concern is with short-term transactions in paper assets. The fallacy in the 'rational expectations' theory is to believe that people's behaviour will not be affected by short-term government action (e.g. tax cuts) because it may later be reversed. It is, however, true that public expectations of the continuing thrust of government policy is significant. In the era of full employment, managers taking investment decisions rightly believed that they could assume that if the economy faltered the government would take steps to put it back on course. (When this expectation was falsified during the 1970s, many firms were left with over-capacity.) As we argue in Chapter 9, the re-establishment of more buoyant demand expectations is essential if investment in new capacity in the second half of the 1990s is to be adequate to enable unemployment to be reduced.

The effect of expectations on inflation, however, while frequently stressed, is not necessarily so clear or pronounced. Investment decisions have to be taken to a large extent on expectations of future sales. But decisions about changing prices largely reflect current conditions, and wage demands are still based almost entirely on the increase in prices since the last settlement rather than on any nebulous arguments about what may happen over the next 12 months. It is obviously helpful if the Government can create the expectation that inflation will be low, but not if this is done at the expense of creating the parallel expectation of continued deflation and a slow growth of demand. The desirable solution (as argued in Chapters 7 and 9) is to create an expectation of low inflation *and* buoyant demand, based on agreement that pay bargaining should be conducted in a non-inflationary manner combined with government commitment to maintain a rate of growth of demand consistent with full employment.

It is disturbing to note the apparent eagerness with which some members of the economics profession take a delight in evolving abstruse theories to prove that nothing can be done about unemployment. The practical effect on policy-makers of the protagonists of 'rational expectations' has been to inhibit the management of demand to stabilise employment. Commenting on Lucas's award of the Nobel Prize in 1995, Anatole Kaletsky writing in *The Times* described the theory as:

> a farrago of unsubstantiated conjectures and manifest nonsense. It claims to prove that every government action designed to stabilise an economy will achieve the opposite result. The economic damage done around the world by this one abstruse theory – which lies at the heart of the monetarist attack on all macro-economic policies to mitigate recessions or limit unemployment – is probably comparable to the destruction wrought by a major war.[4]

BUDGETARY POLICY

The New Orthodoxy has hopelessly confused public discussion about budgetary policy both in the UK and throughout the

EU (see Chapter 12).[5] The confusion originates with the principles that should guide government resort to borrowing. It starts from the strong presumption that governments should, if possible, not borrow at all. For example, in the UK the 1996–97 Financial Statement predicated a zero borrowing requirement before the end of the decade. On this presumption most governments, most of the time, are in forbidden territory. This is most evident in times of heavy unemployment and recession when tax revenues are depressed and the cost of unemployment pay and other social benefits is heavy.

There are two legitimate reasons for wishing to set limits to government borrowing. The first is that in certain circumstances large public deficits have been associated with runaway inflation. But that is clearly not the danger in most industrial countries today. Current budget deficits are a symptom of weak demand and depressed activity, rather than a source of excess demand. The second valid reason for limiting government borrowing is to avoid incurring an unsupportable burden of debt interest in later years. Here a distinction needs to be made first between current and capital expenditure, and then within the latter category between investment which leads to increased revenue (as in state enterprises or toll roads) and investment whose benefits (e.g. better school premises) are beneficial without producing a monetary return. As we saw in Chapters 2 and 3, the prewar Treasury actually took more heed of those distinctions than their successors do today. The reform of the government accounts now taking place reflects discussions which started seven decades ago.

Other things being equal, there is a presumption in favour of borrowing to finance investment, because its benefits are spread over a number of years. It is thus reasonable for the taxpayers enjoying its benefits at the time to pay for it, rather than for taxpayers to pay the whole cost while it is being built. But this argument is subject to the caveat that total interest charges should not rise too rapidly relative to national income or government revenue and thus become an increasing burden on the budget.

As far as revenue producing investment is concerned, public borrowing to finance it does not place a burden on subsequent budgets. Indeed in so far as there is a surplus over and above the cost of borrowing, it will help the budget balance in later years. For this reason, treating debt incurred by profitable public enterprises as on a par with other public debt is absurd, as is the consequent pressure from such bodies as the IMF for countries to privatise their public enterprises in order to reduce the ratio of national debt to national income. Such pressure has nothing to do with sound public finance, but is merely an illegitimate expression of political antagonism to public ownership irrespective of the situation or democratic decisions of the countries concerned.

We should therefore be pragmatic about the level of government borrowing. There is no justification for setting arbitrary limits to public debt, like the 60 per cent of GDP limit in the Treaty of Maastricht (see Chapter 12). The year to year budget balance (i.e. surplus or deficit) should reflect economic conditions at the time and not some predetermined formula.

MONETARY POLICY

Public discussion of monetary policy is at present dominated by the idea that changes in interest rates are the sole effective means of regulating inflation. For those who still believe that inflation is purely a monetary phenomenon there is a direct link between monetary policy and inflation. For the more sophisticated (or old-fashioned) the link is seen in terms of the effects on demand and business conditions. Interest rate policy, however, also has to take into account the fact that interest rates are a key influence on exchange rates. Since central banks are generally more concerned with keeping up, than keeping down, exchange rates, the monetary authorities tend to follow whichever of the two requirements, keeping down inflation or keeping up the exchange rates, needs the higher level of interest rates.

Monetary policy should go hand-in-hand with budgetary policy as part of a general policy for demand. The extent to which a country relies on one rather than the other will depend partly on its exchange rate policy. For example, a country striving with difficulty to maintain a given parity (e.g. France with Germany) is bound to maintain a relatively high level of interest rates, whereas a country with a floating exchange rate has more leeway. There are, however, good reasons at both national and international level for trying to keep interest rates at as low a level as possible. To do so will encourage investment, in particular, as well as stimulating demand generally. This will help to remedy the short-term lack of capacity and the long-term rate of growth. It will ease the financing of public debt in a recession. A world-wide low interest rate regime would ease the problem of the developing countries dependent on borrowing overseas and generally help to create a less deflationary international regime.

CENTRAL BANK INDEPENDENCE

One intensely undemocratic feature of the new orthodoxy is the proposition that central banks should be independent of government control and that their over-riding objective should be the pursuit of price stability. Those who favour independence do so largely because they believe that it would make central banks less subject to 'political pressures', i.e. less likely to adopt expansionary policies to combat unemployment. It is undemocratic to suggest that such a key element in economic policy should be hived off to an unelected body, which is supposed to know better what is good for us than our elected representatives. It is merely a way of imparting a further deflationary bias to the system because central bankers tend not to be much concerned with the effect of their actions on unemployment.

The other reason for not removing central banks from government control is that separating the conduct of monetary policy from that of budgetary policy would be retrograde and inefficient. Both affect the economy by regulating demand, but in different ways. Monetary policy works primarily through changes in levels of interest rates which in turn affect the exchange rate, investment and private consumption. Budgetary policy (a) directly affects demand through the level of government expenditure on goods and services or social security payments and so on and (b) indirectly affects demand through the effects of taxation on consumption and investment. Monetary and fiscal policy need to work in harmony, with common objectives and in the context of an agreed strategy.

The Maastricht recipe for an independent European Central Bank is an inevitable corollary of the monetarist philosophy underlying the Treaty and raises the fundamental issue of whether monetary union is appropriate without closer political union (which is discussed in Chapter 10). The Treaty also puts an obligation on member countries to 'start the process leading to the independence' of national central banks during the second stage of transition which started on 1 January 1994 and is due to finish in 1999.

COUNTER-CYCLICAL POLICY

One of the points affecting the relative efficacy of using monetary or fiscal policy to control demand is the speed with which each can be made effective. Changes in interest rates have the advantage that they can be made quickly (and without legislation) but their effects are difficult to predict and take some time to work their way through the system. The Bank of England is 'targeting inflation two years ahead'.[6] By contrast, changes in Income or Corporation Tax can only be made before the start of a fiscal year; and on present Budgetary procedures, these are announced in the autumn to take effect from the following April. But as far as personal taxation is concerned, the effects on consumer spending may be apparent almost as soon as the new rates become effective. Changes in indirect taxes, such as VAT, are generally announced in the November Budget and may take effect immediately, particularly if a delay would cause disruption by speculative buying in advance of an increase, or consumers holding back in anticipation of a fall.

Changes in the level of social security benefits or contributions need some warning for administrative purposes, but do not need to start at the beginning of a fiscal year. Current expenditure on such services as defence, education and health is not easily raised for counter-cyclical purposes without disrupting existing policies. There is, however, some scope for varying the timing or level of public investment in response to changes in demand. In particular at times of prolonged recession, a higher level of much-needed investment in schools, hospitals and infrastructure of various kinds should be an important element in any expansionary policy. This is especially appropriate when, as in the first half of the 1990s, the construction industry is suffering from a severe lack of demand and its capacity is shrinking drastically. What is singularly inappropriate is to counter the effects of a recession on the PSBR by cutting public investment.

There are broadly three possible responses to year to year variations in demand. The first is to raise taxes or cut expenditure when the budget deficit increases in a recession or *vice versa* in a boom. This was the conventional orthodoxy in the pre-Keynesian era, although it was not necessarily rigidly adhered to. Such policy aggravates any recession or boom by forcing the adoption of budget measures which accentuate the fall or increase in demand. Although it is clearly a nonsensical approach, long discredited, it is in fact largely implicit in most current discussion of public finance. It has become commonplace for politicians and the financial press to assume that the stronger the recovery in the economy, and hence the better the budget balance, the more the scope for cutting taxes – whereas in fact the opposite is the case.

Conversely when public investment is badly needed not only in its own right but to avoid any further contraction in the effective capacity of the building industry, the Chancellor has cut public investment in an attempt to improve the budget. This perverse reaction is entirely retrograde and has no economic justification, unless the insulting assumption that the financial community is so economically illiterate that such an approach is needed to 'maintain confidence in the markets' is to be regarded as an economic justification. In practice this approach is unlikely to be applied symmetrically. Much-needed measures to stimulate the economies in the EU have been ruled out by existing deficits, but it is unlikely that the reverse will apply and that government investment will be bolstered when the economies are stronger. The bias towards deflation always seems to be stronger than logical consistency.

The second is to make no changes in tax rates or expenditure policy where unemployment rises or falls. This means that in a recession the budget deficit will increase as (a) tax revenue falls and (b) spending on unemployment and other benefits rises. These changes in revenue and expenditure used to be referred to as 'automatic stabilisers' as they partially offset the fluctuations in demand that could otherwise have taken place. This feature was particularly valued in the US where

Congress had a major say in the Budget and the Executive was unable to make speedy changes.

The third option is to go further and cut taxes or raise government expenditure in a recession, and *vice versa* in a boom i.e. a 'counter-cyclical policy'. This means in practice basing policy each year on a judgement as to whether demand should be curbed or stimulated. This is the postwar Keynesian approach which guided Chancellors of the Exchequer until recently.

FINE-TUNING

One of the arguments against active or 'discretionary' demand management has been that macro-economic forecasting has become too inaccurate to be a reliable guide to so-called 'fine tuning' i.e. year to year demand management. In present circumstances, however, we are not talking about fine tuning but fairly coarse tuning: much of the European economy is clearly in a state of serious depression with little or no chance of unemployment declining of its own accord in the immediate future. More fundamentally, forecasting difficulties do not obviate the need for governments to make decisions on taxes and expenditure each year. So-called 'neutral' decisions rest just as much on implicit assumptions about the future of the economy as do more positive decisions. In industry managers have to make decisions on investment, manning and so on which depend on equally, or more, uncertain assumptions about the future of the economy and markets for the firm's products. Governments similarly cannot escape from this necessity.

Another invalid argument for inaction is the need for 'stable' macro-economic policies. Dissatisfaction with the drastic cyclical changes in recent years has created a demand for a more stable macro-economic climate, which in turn has been interpreted as a need for more stable macro-economic policies. It is important to be clear what this does, and does not, involve. Left to itself, the economy is not naturally stable; it may be upset either because of external shocks or because of cycles in industrial investment or consumer demand. The achievement of stable business conditions means essentially a smooth growth of demand, and this is not consistent with unchanged interest rates or fiscal 'neutrality': that is, Budgets which involve no changes in taxation or expenditure in response to current cyclical conditions. The achievement of stable conditions is bound to require appropriate adjustments in policy from time to time in the form of deliberate changes in interest rates and the balance between government expenditure and taxation (the so-called 'fiscal stance').

Every Chancellor since the War has had to face up to the need for a 'Budget judgement' on the fiscal stance for the coming financial year, i.e. the extent to which the Budget is intended to have a deflationary or expansionary effect on the economy. While the concept is still in use, its significance has become clouded. Originally the supposition was that the fiscal stance would reflect the state of the economy, and whether the Budget increased or decreased the PSBR would be a consequence of the fiscal stance. Recently it has appeared that the PSBR is determined by a desire to get it down to zero as soon as possible, and the fiscal stance is a consequence of that objective, whether or not it is appropriate for the state of the economy. For that reason, the Government markedly failed to introduce expansionary budgets during the early 1990s because they were worried about the PSBR. This aspect of the New Orthodoxy has imparted another deflationary bias to the economy.

One of the most serious threats to the sensible use of budgetary policy is confusion between the causes and effects of budget deficits or surpluses. The deterioration in budget deficits in the 1980s was caused by the high level of unemployment with its consequent costs in social security benefits and loss of tax revenue; the more buoyant budgetary position in the years of full employment reflected the converse. It is quite misleading to suggest (as some international agencies are doing)[7] that tightening budgetary policy now will reduce unemployment because last time we had full employment we had lower budget deficits. The only rationale for such a suggestion involves the quite unbelievable hypothesis that tax changes have no effect on people's expenditure – changes in government expenditure obviously do affect employment – and the equally unrealistic assertion that budget deficits determine interest rates. The sincerity of those who justify the tightening of budgetary policy on the spurious grounds that it will in due course reduce unemployment would be less in question if they were also to argue the logical converse: that when the economy requires deflationary action to combat inflation, budgetary policy should be loosened and the deficit allowed to increase! But, of course, they never do so. It is just another aspect of the deflationary bias pervading current official thinking. Reluctance to stimulate the economy by a temporary increase in the Budget deficit is a sure prescription for continued high unemployment and thus prolonging the consequential poor state of the public finances.

FATALISTIC FORECASTING

One factor contributing to the sophisticated brand of fatalism afflicting many economic observers is the increasing public attention paid to the forecasts emanating from the numerous economic modelling groups, and the manner in which these are presented. First the models are frequently based on theories about how the economy works that effectively prejudge the results. For example, some models assume that in the longer run there is a natural rate of unemployment; so that where they are used to forecast the effects of expanding demand on unemployment, they automatically give the result that any such effects are purely temporary. But these results are frequently presented as if the models were contributing fresh light on the question, rather than merely reflecting the assumptions of those who constructed them. (It often seems, moreover, that those who actually operate the models are not always aware of the rules of the game set by those who constructed them!) They thus actively hinder informed debate.

Second the economic modellers' built-in assumptions as to the way such variables as output, employment, prices and the trade balance interact, are almost inevitably determined by observation of past experience. They therefore tend to ignore institutional questions about the need to change existing relationships, such as between wage inflation and unemployment, and are not designed to provide any guidance as to how structural changes, such as the introduction of new pay bargaining arrangements, might affect the results.

Third, the forecasts rest on tacit judgements about the fiscal and monetary policies that the government will pursue in the light of the likely priority to be given to various economic objectives: in particular low inflation, full employment and a satisfactory balance of payments. Failure to make these policy assumptions explicit conceals the fact that there are government decisions to be made which may have crucial effects on the development of the economy, and a key purpose of such forecasts should be to assist in making them. But it has become the practice in forecasting in recent years to treat the level of employment not as a prime objective, but as a residual that follows from the pursuit of a low inflation rate, thus again contributing to the false impression that whatever happens to unemployment is incidental, rather than a prime concern of government policy.

POLICY OBJECTIVES

The one over-riding objective of macro-economic policy at the present time is to minimise inflation. This is underlined by the fact that one variable for which the Chancellor has an explicit target is the rate of inflation: no corresponding importance is attached to the level of unemployment, the balance of payments or the rate of growth of output per head, which are also fundamental economic variables. From a political point of view, the current obsession with minimising inflation is strange; in an era of floating exchange rates, there is little reason to think that it makes very much difference to the public or the economy whether inflation is at say, 2 per cent or 4 per cent. Just as in the 1920s and 1930s obsession with the hyper-inflation that hit Germany after the First World War inhibited any expansion of demand to counter the Slump, at a time when inflation posed no serious threat, so today the legacy of past inflation remains an incubus on present-day policy in quite different conditions. It is only when inflation begins to get to higher levels that there are real problems. Nowadays there are very few people on fixed incomes and even those with modest savings in building societies will tend to be compensated for inflation by higher interest rates. Indeed with a majority of people being borrowers, rather than lenders, the erosion of mortgage debts by inflation was very popular, even if higher interest rates were not.

The over-riding argument for minimum inflation was to maintain our competitive position in a regime of fixed exchange rates. But in a world of floating rates, where competing countries have varying inflation rates, there seems no great advantage in minimising inflation at the cost of output and jobs. Nor are there any good grounds for thinking that low inflation stimulates demand and output or encourages long-term growth. This is not to say that there is any virtue in faster inflation *per se* or that it could generate more jobs; merely that in so far as the pursuit of very low rates of inflation is leading to a sacrifice of jobs, it is not obvious that low inflation should be the only objective. The vital need is to alter the present relationship between unemployment and inflation by structural changes in the method of pay negotiation, so that much lower unemployment is consistent with low inflation.

The balance of payments has been a less explicit objective, but policy has been influenced by the fact that in the short-term holding down demand and output can be good for the current balance, mainly because it depresses imports; although, in the longer term, the effects on the industrial base, new investment and new products is likely to be adverse. This has led to a tendency to regard restrictive demand policies as a necessary means of both curbing inflation and limiting the deficit in the current balance, resulting in a very slow growth and a continued rise in unemployment.

NOMINAL DEMAND

Before leaving the subject of demand management, reference should be made to one approach to demand management and inflation put forward in recent years, namely that the growth of total demand in the economy should be set in money or 'nominal' terms at a level consistent with the long-term growth rate of the economy and a modest increase in prices.[8] This may appear to be solely a technical matter, but it has profound practical implications. The idea (in its simplest and most seductive form) is that any excessive increase in money wages and prices would automatically involve (or lead to policies which would involve) a slower growth in real demand and output; and this would then raise unemployment and exert downward pressure on the rate of increase of wages and prices.

This approach is, however, likely to be both ineffective in practice and objectionable in principle. Demand is not predetermined in money terms irrespective of how incomes increase. Indeed an acceleration of pay increases will almost certainly mean that money incomes temporarily rise faster than prices, and thus that real consumption is actually boosted. On the other hand, with fixed exchange rates, rising prices will tend to reduce exports, but there is no reason to suppose that the value of exports will automatically remain constant. Only where expenditure in the public sector is cash-limited by the Government will demand remain fixed in money terms and hence expenditure be correspondingly squeezed in real terms. Thus if nominal demand is to be kept on target when prices rise faster than the target rate, the Government would have to take positive action to reduce real demand (and *vice versa*). It is ironic that those who oppose fine-tuning of demand should put forward a system of control by target-setting that, far from acting automatically, would necessitate highly effective fine-tuning. There is a close parallel with that other example of target-setting and ineffective auto-control, money supply targets.

The approach is objectionable in principle because it does nothing to solve the problem of the wage–price spiral; it merely puts into an arithmetical formula the threat that the government will adopt deflationary measures if wages and prices rise faster than postulated. There is no reason to think that this would be any more effective than the current approach. In either event the need is to restructure the present inflationary pay bargaining system rather than to ensure that its results lead to higher unemployment.

CONCLUSION

Although demand management is currently out of fashion when discussing means of expanding the economy, it has in practice been used vigorously to hold back demand in order to restrain inflation. We have been suffering from a period of 'one-way' demand management: it has become respectable to use monetary or fiscal policy in ways that hold back demand, but not to use these same instruments as a means of increasing demand to reduce unemployment. Any such expansionary measures have become taboo for fear that they may be regarded as 'inflationary'. If we are to restore full employment, we must follow an active policy of demand management designed to secure a steady rise in demand and output which will lead to a continued reduction in unemployment to well below the levels of the last 15 years. Both monetary and fiscal policy should be directed to this end, with the balance between them depending very much on external factors. Lower interest rates in Germany and the rest of Europe would make it easier to keep them low in the UK. In addition the exchange rate regime within which we are working (see Chapter 11) will also affect our room for manoeuvre on monetary policy.

An active policy for demand management will embody a counter-cyclical element; at times the economy may need a major stimulus to achieve any expansion, and at others there may be a need to prevent such an expansion going too quickly and running into capacity or labour problems. The PSBR should be taken as a consequence of following the appropriate policies, not as a determinant of them. In the immediate future, measures such as increased public investment might increase the PSBR, but in the longer run any sustained reduction in unemployment, which is at present costing over £20 billion a year in lost revenue and additional social security payments, would revolutionise the fiscal outlook.

To be able to follow such expansionary demand policies without stimulating inflation, we must, however, at the same time reform the pay bargaining system: this is the subject of the next chapter.

7 Pay and Inflation

Adopting a pay policy is rather like jumping out of a second floor window: no one in his senses would do it unless the stairs were on fire. But in postwar Britain the stairs have always been on fire. (Denis Healey)

As we saw in Chapter 3, the possibility of wage settlements fuelling a wage–price spiral was regarded by the architects of postwar employment policies as one of the most critical problems likely to emerge with the establishment of full employment. The 1944 White Paper on Employment Policy warned that:

> it will be essential that employers and workers should exercise moderation in wages matters ... This does not mean that every wage rate must remain fixed at a particular level ... there must be opportunity for the removal of anomalies in the rate of remuneration of different grades and categories of workers, both within an industry and between different industries. The principle of stability does mean, however, that increases in the general level of wage rates must be related to increased productivity.

The tacit assumption in the White Paper and throughout the subsequent period was that the problem was essentially one of trade union power. The corollary was that this potential threat must either be curbed by voluntary restraint, or by some form of control of incomes, if full employment was to be maintained without inflation. The unacceptable (and largely unspoken) alternatives were either to abandon full employment or to reduce the bargaining power of the unions by restrictive legislation. The price for the unions maintaining their economic, social and political power was that they should only use it with restraint.

On these assumptions, the prices and incomes problem might have been assumed to be at its height in the first decades after the war, and to diminish as unemployment rose in the mid-1970s. In practice, however, it did not become most acute until full employment by postwar standards had begun to be abandoned. The period of postwar incomes policies (which lasted until 1979) fell into two distinct phases: before and after 1970. From 1946 to 1970 prices rose on average by 3.6 per cent a year and unemployment only exceeded 2.5 per cent in 1970; but from 1970 to 1979 prices went up by an average of 13 per cent a year despite higher levels of unemployment which reached over 5 per cent in the last four years.

By any subsequent yardstick the pre-1970 period was relatively successful; the problem period was the 1970s, where internal inflation was largely a result of external shocks: first the world commodity boom, then successive oil shocks. The subsequent demonology built up about the 'failure' of Keynesian demand management and incomes policies is based almost entirely on an over-simplified view of the experience of the 1970s rather than the postwar period as a whole.

LESSONS FROM THE PAST

The brief catalogue of events in Chapters 4 and 5 illustrates the precarious and temporary nature of previous attempts at maintaining an incomes policy. For 30 years there was a cycle of introduction and collapse of policies; and until Mrs Thatcher came to office, the existence or abolition of the policy depended more on the state of agreement between the government and the unions than the political philosophy of the government in power. The simplest policies, such as a complete freeze or the £6 limit, tended to be most successful (in terms of not being evaded) but were necessarily short term. They tended to leave a greater legacy of subsequent adjustments (e.g. restoration of differentials) than the more elaborate or flexible policies. There was a succession of different policy statements or stages (generally annual but sometimes more frequent) associated with each broad attempt to maintain policy. These were to some extent trying to provide room to solve the problem emerging from the previous stage; but the differences between successive stages tended to be differences across the board rather than concessions to particular groups.

There were two kinds of pressure leading to the breakdown of the policies. One was general discontent among the unions as a whole, very often associated with macro-economic developments like devaluation or the rise in import prices. The ability to maintain the necessary degree of agreement between the Government and the unions depended partly on general political leadership and the establishment of the necessary degree of sympathy between the Government and the unions, and partly on specific economic measures like tax cuts to prevent wage restraint leading to cuts in real wages.

The second cause of breakdown was the build-up of pressure from individual bargaining groups. This was partly a reaction to changes in relativities and a desire to get back to the previous place in the pecking order. It was also due to the fact that all policies had been based on rules where any exceptions were based on criteria such as fairness or labour shortages, and for obvious reasons made no overt allowance for the realities of bargaining power. Frank Blackaby underlined the ensuing tension most perceptively when he wrote: 'It is too much to expect that one can move from a world in which bargaining power is very important, to a world in which it is not important at all in one jump.'[1]

The most persistent lesson from past history is that the problem is a long-term one which needs a long-term solution. While the problems and prescriptions will vary from time to time, the machinery and procedures need to be permanent, which means that they should, so far as possible, be acceptable on a bipartisan basis, not abolished or reconstituted with every change of Government. The second lesson is that any such venture depends on securing a very wide measure of agreement from unions and employers. Parallel with this is the need for realism and flexibility: there must be some room to manoeuvre so that one insoluble conflict does not torpedo the whole policy. Finally the most inflammatory disputes tend to arise in the public sector, thus making the government's political prestige an issue; but this has remained the case even with the abolition of incomes policy.

THE FAILURE OF THE MARKET

If we are to solve the pay problems of the future without resort to mass unemployment, it is necessary both to take into account the lessons of the past and also to re-evaluate the nature of the problems to be tackled in the light of changing circumstances. The experience of the UK in the 1980s made it clear that the problem is not simply a reflection of potential union power in conditions of high employment. The wage–price spiral reflects the fact that although the myriad of wage bargains struck each year may in each case represent a rational market decision from the point of view of each individual firm and bargaining group, for employers and workers as a whole the resultant increases in money wages do not necessarily represent a rational result. If the average increase in money wages is appreciably greater than the average rise in productivity, inflation is the inevitable outcome, and this is against the general interest. In other words contrary to classical economic theory, the market does not produce an ideal solution: the collective interests of employers and employees do not accord with the sum of individual interests, because each bargaining unit ignores the fact that one trade unionist's wage increase may be another's price increase. Moreover the supposition that market forces at least solve the problem of changing relativities in a dynamic economy is also wide of the mark. Part of the inflationary pressure stems from continual leapfrogging as workers try to restore relativities or differentials which have changed to their disadvantage. Relative pay is never in equilibrium.

Free market theorists have treated the wage–price spiral problem as necessitating a 'reform' of labour markets, by which they mean essentially measures to weaken the power of the trade unions and wage-earners generally. This attack on the problem has taken two forms: in the government's case, legislation dealing with such matters as picketing, sympathetic industrial action and strike ballots; in the employers' case, moves to decentralise bargaining procedures, ostensibly to provide greater flexibility but often strongly motivated by a feeling that replacing national with local negotiations tends to weaken the unions. The main argument adduced in favour of plant level bargaining has been that it facilitated management's efforts to achieve higher productivity by buying out restrictive practices or giving employees special incentives to introduce new methods of working. We should, however, be wary of accepting as a norm (to put it crudely), the concept of management locked in perpetual conflict with its workforce and compelled to bribe its employees every time it wishes to introduce some improved method of working. Even though this may still be realistic in some firms, it is an out-of-date recipe for industrial success. Rather the norm which we should seek to establish is one of more settled pay structures with management relying on the positive cooperation of workers in devising and implementing new methods as a normal (and worthwhile) part of their jobs. It is clear which approach our most successful competitors are adopting.

The emphasis on productivity bargaining encourages firms in industries where productivity is growing rapidly to give high wage increases, which are then quickly matched by similar increases throughout the economy. Individual firms follow the trend because they feel vulnerable to the threat of industrial action if they believe their competitors will not resist union pressure. The firm-by-firm approach to pay also encourages firms to poach skilled workers rather than to train them. The idea that this approach would discourage workers from demanding high pay increases for fear of reducing their own firm's competitiveness seems to have had little practical effect.

There are thus strong *a priori* arguments why decentralisation of pay bargaining will not solve the problem of inflation, unless accompanied by a high level of unemployment. The experience of other countries tends to show that some form of centralisation[2] is the key to taking into account broader considerations, such as the impact on inflation, in the bargaining process. The statistical evidence is mixed because so many other factors – economic, political and cultural – are involved.[3] Calmfors and Driffil[4] developed the thesis that either highly centralised systems or highly decentralised systems do well, but that those in the middle, like the UK, do badly. This thesis has been taken as a basis for arguing in favour of further decentralisation and wage flexibility. But Calmfors and Driffil's two major examples of highly decentralised systems were Japan and the United States: Japan is culturally unique and has in most respects a highly centralised economic system; and the US has a comparatively weak union structure. It is difficult to resist the belief that the advocates of further decentralisation are at heart more interested in achieving a situation where the trade unions play a lesser role in wage setting, than in whether or not it will cure the problem of inflation.

One of the dangers of decentralised bargaining is that it

encourages the mistaken belief that the workers in any one firm are entitled to wage increases to match the increase in productivity in that firm. But to keep inflation within acceptable levels wage increases on average across the whole economy must not greatly exceed the *average* increase in productivity in the economy. If, however, workers in manufacturing firms (say, in the motor industry) with high productivity gains get large increases in money wages, everybody else will try to follow. The result will be a combination of unacceptably high inflation and mounting injustice to workers in such sectors as health and education, where the potential for measurable productivity gains is strictly limited, and their wages inevitably fail to keep up. Pay for similar skills in different industries should rise broadly in line. This means that to keep down the rate of inflation, there must be price reductions (or relatively small increases) in sectors where high productivity gains are possible in order to offset price increases in sectors where the potential for improving productivity is more limited.

MEETING THE CHALLENGE

It should be clear by now that decentralising pay bargaining is not a remedy for inflation unless accompanied by heavy unemployment. A fragmented wage bargaining structure leads to an ultimately irrational position, by disregarding the common objective of avoiding inflation. The question is how to alter the system so that the common objective of limiting the average increase in money wages can be given sufficient weight in the process of settling pay. An essential prerequisite is to change the climate of opinion. No form of incomes policy can succeed without a very wide measure of popular support, or at least acceptance.

The first need therefore is to counter the view that the changes in the structure of pay bargaining and the decline in union membership in recent years now rule out any effective new incomes policy.[5] It is important here to distinguish between the political and economic efficacy of any policy, as attitudes to past policies have been dominated by the associated political crises rather than any assessment of their economic impact. In many respects the present bargaining structure makes a Government's task easier. The fact that there are not so many major national agreements as there used to be should ease the political difficulties of embarking on any new policy as they lessen the danger of the Government becoming involved in politically damaging pay disputes.

As regards the potential economic efficacy of any new policy, in so far as a higher number of national agreements and greater trade union involvement helped in the past to keep pay increases within or near to the official guidelines, recent changes make any policy more difficult to police. They have also made pay more sensitive to market forces, so that any strengthening of the demand for labour may have a greater effect on pay than it would in the past. On the other hand there is less danger of spectacular high settlements setting the pace in breaching the guidelines. It must also be remembered that trade union membership is not necessarily a reliable measure of the effect of union agreements in affecting increases. Many small organisations, with little or no union membership, take union rates or changes in union rates for guidance, for lack of any other starting point. It seems improbable that any general pay agreement will be torpedoed by masses of small employers giving their employees higher pay increases than their larger competitors who are following the agreed guidelines. It still seems likely that, as in the past, any major attack will come from the big battalions, and the fact that the big battalions are now fewer and weaker should make any policy less vulnerable.

RESTRAINT OR STRATEGY?

There is little disagreement with the idea that 'wage restraint' is vital if inflation is to be avoided. But what is the difference (if any) between 'wage restraint' and having a 'pay strategy' or 'incomes policy'? There are in fact a number of important differences. The idea of wage 'restraint', without any agreed policy on incomes, suffers from the weakness that any one bargaining group that exercises restraint has no guarantee that other groups will do the same. Thus though at least some other groups may in the event hold back, each group may justifiably feel that they are being asked to sacrifice real income by exercising restraint, because the prices of what they consume will not be affected. This is, in a less extreme form, the problem which Keynes highlighted in relation to cuts in miners' pay in the 1920s (see Chapter 2). On the other hand, if there is a general agreement (or policy) covering all bargaining groups, 'restraint' is clearly aimed at keeping down the prices of what people buy as well as the amount they earn. Moreover agreement on a 'going rate' or 'norm' establishes a yardstick which enables different groups to feel they are being treated in a fair or comparable way.

The second difference between calls for unstructured wage restraint and an agreed pay strategy is that a long-term policy should be aimed at solving, or at least ameliorating, a number of related problems. It must tackle the problem of workers' conflicting views on relative pay, and hence reduce the continual tendency to leapfrog which is one of the causes of inflation. It must also recognise the fact that the vast majority of the public want to see better methods of resolving industrial disputes, particularly in essential services, than resort to industrial action and strikes. Thus a key objective in any strategy should be to improve the machinery for resolving pay disputes.

A TRIPARTITE APPROACH

In the past the key role in pay policy in the UK rested with government. This has been for the obvious reason that the government's economic policy responsibilities have led it to introduce various forms of policy to deal with the problems of inflation and the balance of payments. As we have seen in previous chapters, for many years, governments of both parties took the lead in negotiating agreement with the employers' organisations and the unions, in setting up machinery to issue advice or adjudicate on individual bargains, and in some instances introduced legislation to enforce such policies. One of the results of this has been that the government of the day has attracted most of the unpopularity and opprobrium connected with such policies, rather than the TUC and CBI. This has been reinforced by the tendency of both major political parties when in opposition to exploit incomes policy disputes for short-term political advantage (the Jekyll and Hyde syndrome), as during the miners' strike during the Heath government and the 'winter of discontent' during the Callaghan government. This experience accounts for the suggestion that if there is to be any form of coordinated wage bargaining the government should not be involved in any new incomes policy: it should be left to the employers and unions to sort out at a national level.

While there are apparent examples of such a purely bilateral approach being successful in other countries, it is easy to ignore some of the pitfalls that this would involve in our present circumstances. One of these (which no doubt makes it attractive to politicians) is that any unpopularity involved could accrue to the employers' associations and trade unions rather than the government. But are they in a position to take such a strain? It is one thing for the CBI or TUC to agree a potentially unpopular policy at the government's behest, with the government there to take the blame when particular disputes evolve; it is quite another for the CBI or TUC to hold the line on their own. The public would quite rightly expect the government to accept responsibility for such a central aspect of national economic policy. Moreover the government, both as the largest employer and as responsible for macro-economic policy, is in no position merely to stand on the sidelines. This has the further implication that if there is to be any long-term solution to the problem, some degree of political consensus is also highly desirable, so that incomes policies do not again become a political football.

Some of those who have studied experience abroad emphasise the role of employer coordination in keeping down the level of pay increases. Soskice,[6] for example, concludes his analysis of foreign experience with the suggestion that the fundamental problem is how to develop effective coordination between employers. But the fact that employer coordination has become increasingly important in some countries as trade union power has weakened does not necessarily mean that this is the most practical way forward for the UK. It would seem unlikely that the CBI would be predisposed to take any initiative on its own, or that the TUC would be content to play second fiddle to the employers in the evolution of a national pay strategy. Both need to be involved.

The first step in instituting any new policy must be for the government to reach agreement with representatives of employers and the unions on a general policy for pay bargaining not just for one year ahead, but if possible for a longer period. Failure to agree by any one of these three parties dooms the initiative from the start. Any attempt by the government to impose a policy without agreement with the unions will inevitably lead to damaging conflict, with the government becoming involved directly in a series of major disputes. The employers' agreement is also essential, since at the end of the day their willingness to resist demands which are out of line with the policy is necessary to make it effective.

Central talks do, however, necessitate both employers and workers being organised in such a way that their representatives at national level can commit their constituent organisations, and members, to a significant extent. The unions are probably still capable of doing so. But with the decline of industry-wide bargaining and employers' organisations, the CBI may have to strengthen its organisation to deliver an effective commitment by employers as a whole.

A LONG-TERM ECONOMIC STRATEGY

Any such exercise must start from an objective assessment of the problem, in particular the general magnitude of pay and price increases that are compatible with our economic position. But it would be a mistake to conceive of the assessment solely as a text for discussions on the problem of wage inflation. All the major issues of economic policy are interrelated: employment growth, investment, public expenditure, taxation, training, regional policy, balance of payments, European integration, as well as pay and inflation. Moreover they all need to be considered against a longer horizon than the forthcoming financial year or the next wage round. There is thus a need for a wide-ranging economic strategy document covering a four or five year period to serve as a framework for more detailed consideration of other issues. This would both cover the government's own programmes and constitute a general review of economic policy. Key elements would be: a commitment to expansionary demand policies; supply-side measures to encourage the build-up of capacity and skills and to stimulate regional development; and an agreement on pay bargaining. It should have the longer-term objective of reducing unemployment to permanently lower levels. The development of such a strategy, with as wide a level of consultation and support as possible, would demonstrate clarity of purpose and encourage the industrial confidence needed to fulfil it.

A POLICY FOR PAY

It is sometimes said that any new attempt to moderate pay increases should not involve anything in the nature of 'Norms' or 'Guidelines', simply because previous incomes policies have done so. This is really just playing with words. If there are to be central talks about pay, they must obviously deal in figures. Any agreement must spell out a level or range of pay increases that is compatible with maintaining a low rate of inflation. Any agreement without figures would be meaningless. Indeed the existing concept of a 'going rate' for wage increases is the most obvious starting-point for giving any general agreement on restraint some quantitative reality.

The key principle must be that increases in real wages should be geared to the rate of growth of productivity across the economy as a whole, rather than productivity improvements in particular firms or industries. Only in this way will the pay of people with the same (or similar) skills, working in different firms, remain in line – a natural concomitant of a free labour market. The corollary is that starting from a low and acceptable level of inflation, the general rate for pay settlements in the next year consistent with inflation continuing at that rate should be no higher than the rise in the cost of living since the last settlement *plus* the rate of overall improvement in productivity.

It is, however, essential to avoid any excessively mechanical formula for percentage or absolute increases for workers in every sector which fails to leave room for adjustments in differentials and relativities: this, of course, is the danger in concentrating on short-term expedients. Any long-term arrangements must provide for such adjustments. Because most groups of workers feel they are a special case, any national discussions are bound to lead into the question of what circumstances justify larger (or smaller) increases than average. It thus seems inevitable that such talks will be concerned both with the magnitude of the 'going rate' and the circumstances justifying exceptional increases, but obviously the formulae adopted must not be so elastic as to make any general agreement valueless.

PUBLIC SECTOR PAY

Public sector pay negotiations always tends to hold the centre of the stage when pay is in the spotlight. There are a number of reasons for this: the government as an employer (either at first- or second-hand) tends to follow any guidelines more rigorously than the private sector may; large numbers of high profile employees are involved (e.g. civil servants, nurses, teachers); any dispute may threaten a vital service, such as the ambulance or fire service; and the political dimension ensures that the dis-pute is fully covered in the media. It is thus no coincidence that the most traumatic disputes associated with the breakdown of pay policies have been in the public sector. But disputes of this nature are not confined to governments trying to implement a general incomes policy; they can also arise from any attempt to hold the line on public sector pay awards, irrespective of whether a general incomes policy is in force. There is, moreover, an irony in the amount of emphasis placed on public sector pay awards, in that they tend to follow, or lag behind, private sector increases and are not for the most part a major culprit in any inflationary outbreak. Nor, of course, do they directly affect the prices of exports or goods in the shops.

Nevertheless public sector pay determination inevitably plays a key role in any pay strategy, since the government's responsibilities as employer, for public expenditure and for combating inflation all combine to make public sector pay a sensitive area. In recent years public sector pay policy has been primarily determined by the desire to limit public expenditure. This has reflected a basically negative attitude to public provision of services such as education and health, and has resulted in an implicit policy of paying as little as could be got away with, and not, for example, approaching teachers' pay as a means of raising their status as part of an endeavour to improve the quality of education. Only those groups with considerable social or moral clout, such as the doctors and nurses, have from time to time succeeded in bucking this trend. Moreover relative pay within the public sector has reflected the general trends within the economy as a whole, with the low-paid and unskilled doing less well than professional and higher paid workers. When pay in public services lags behind that in the private sector for some time, sooner or later this will create a difficult 'catching-up' problem.

There are then two problems: the short-term one of bringing public sector pay more nearly into line with the private sector in certain fields; and the longer-term one of avoiding the cycle of relative decline and catching-up which has plagued the public sector for the last two decades. The second problem is not so much one of pay policy as such, but rather a reflection of public expenditure policy, with the introduction of cash limits combined with over-optimistic and unrealistic assumptions about inflation and wage increases. This system (if it can be dignified as such) has played a key part in keeping down public sector pay and squeezing the resources available for health, education and other public services. The extent of this squeeze is hidden by the misleading definition of increases in expenditure in 'real terms', as increases over and above the increase in inflation in general, rather than costs in the particular service in question. Given that costs in labour-intensive fields like health and education will inevitably rise faster than those of factory-made goods, this method of presentation has consistently misrepresented the real changes in resources employed in these services.

Public sector pay assumptions in the annual public expenditure exercise need to be put on a realistic footing *vis-à-vis* what is likely to happen in the rest of the economy. If this is to be done without stimulating further inflation, public sector pay assumptions should be in line with agreed assumptions or guidelines for the economy as a whole. There must be a shift of emphasis away from that of making public sector settlements test cases for implementing any economy-wide guidelines and hence a battle ground for any disputes linked to incomes policy. Regarding incomes policy as something to be started, and held to rigorously in the public sector in the hope that the private sector will follow, is unlikely to be successful and will lead to continued erosion of public sector pay. The approach must be first to seek agreement on general guidelines and then to implement them in public sector negotiations. The question of 'catching-up' increases then becomes part of the general problem of 'exceptional' increases. The background investigations and data for settling these problems could be the task of a new advisory body but, as indicated below, such a body should play a role in both the private and public sectors.

MINIMUM WAGE

The introduction of a national minimum wage, and a commission or review body to set it, would be a further factor involving the government in pay questions. The initial setting of a minimum wage could have knock-on effects unless there is a general agreement that its impact in helping low earners must not be eroded by corresponding increases for those better paid. Year to year changes in the minimum wage could be a significant factor in determining the going rate. Indeed the general level of pay increases needs to be agreed before, or at the same time, as setting a new level for the national minimum wage. In this connection there is one particular pitfall that needs to be watched. This could occur if, for what might be good reasons taken in isolation, the minimum wage was initially set rather low with a view to raising it gradually in relation to average wages over, say, a five year period. The danger could be that the relatively high rate of increase of the minimum wage each year might then be taken as a going rate, unless there was clear agreement to the contrary right from the start.

SYNCHRONISATION

One proposal for making unions and employers more aware of the effect of their settlements is that negotiations should be 'synchronised' i.e. all take place in the same part of the year. The advantages of such a system would be that it would be more difficult to accept a series of high settlements as special cases, and the inflationary impact of the emergence of a high 'going rate' would be more speedily apparent. Moreover it would lessen the danger of those at the end of the pay round taking the level of previous settlements as a minimum to be exceeded. Two prominent trade union leaders, John Edmonds and Alan Tuffin, made proposals along these lines in 1990.[7] They suggested that all major negotiations should take place in the first three months of the year, following a public discussion between the government, CBI and TUC of Britain's economic prospects. But there are also dangers in synchronisation. Any dispute in one part of the public sector would quickly spread to the whole of the sector; and similarly, though possibly to a lesser extent, any strikes in the private sector could be more widespread. (On the other hand, the same factors could make any disputes more costly for the unions, which might have a restraining effect.)

DURATION OF SETTLEMENTS

One of the contributory factors to the present problem is the universal assumption that there must be annual pay increases. Given that there is a certain minimum increase in money or percentage terms which seems worthwhile, the annual pay round makes it difficult to keep down the rate of increase of money wages to a reasonable level. Now that inflation has slowed down, serious attention should be given to the possibility of increasing the time which elapses between successive pay increases.

Longer-term settlements do not necessarily mean that there should be no increases in the interim: they can embody interim increases on some predetermined formula. Starting from a position of low inflation, such increases could in normal times be linked to increases in the cost of living; but as the experience of the early 1970s shows, such indexing can be dangerous if an unforeseen external shock leads to an acceleration in inflation. The safest solution is probably to base such interim increases on a conservative view of the annual increase in overall productivity, say 2 per cent a year. Any such arrangements need, however, to be constructed in such a way as to leave room to negotiate a worthwhile increase at the end of the two or three year agreement, otherwise they will be more, rather than less, inflationary than annual agreements.

IMPLEMENTING A PAY AGREEMENT

Granted the need for some form of coordinated wage bargaining or general agreement on pay policy, how can such an agreement be made effective, particularly in the face of the increasing fragmentation of wage bargaining? The problem must be solved without any return to a regime of statutory compulsion, which has come into disrepute for a number of reasons. There is first the underlying constitutional objection that statutory compulsion can translate a strike against an employer into a strike against the government or the law, and the usual processes of compromise needed to end serious industrial disputes could be hampered if they effectively run up against the law. Compulsion also tends to lead to bureaucracy and rigidity; though again the degree of rigidity depends on the nature of the policy being pursued. A further basic weakness arises from the inequity arising from the limited coverage of any policy. The incomes of the self-employed are necessarily excluded; so too in practice are large numbers of employees in smaller firms, together with managers whose pay is not determined by collective bargaining. In finding a long-term solution to the pay problem, statutory control on the lines of earlier incomes policies is thus neither desirable nor practical. This does not, however, mean that nothing should be done to persuade, encourage or pressurise bargainers to settle within the terms of a nationally agreed policy. For the essence of such an agreement is that individual bargaining units are prepared to hold back because they are confident that others will also do so; such confidence that the policy will be effective is basic to the whole exercise.

How far then should we go in setting up any formal means of making it effective? In devising any new institutional machinery, there are three possible functions to consider: (a) monitoring *per se* i.e. compiling information on claims and settlements; (b) considering the claims or settlements in relation to the policy guidelines; and (c) settling unresolved disputes. As a minimum, there is a strong case for monitoring what is going on. No doubt each of the bodies involved, the CBI, the TUC and the government will keep a watch on the situation; but there is a need for some independent central body to monitor claims and settlements.

PAY ADVISORY COMMISSION

The job of monitoring claims and settlements might be undertaken by a new advisory body, which might be called the Pay Advisory Commission, set up with powers to gather information on pay negotiations. Such an organisation should cover both the public and private sectors. There is in addition a strong case for making it responsible for commenting on individual proposals in relation to the policy agreed. To do so it would need the authority to make representations to both parties in any pay negotiations in either the public or private sector, and to give advice during any recourse to conciliation. The Commission would have a particularly important role in providing independent advice in public sector pay negotiations and to the Pay Review bodies, which should be amalgamated.

The Commission should not, however, have any statutory power to impose settlements or act as final adjudicator. But as a last resort there is a case for giving the Commission the power to refer a negotiation to compulsory arbitration. Any such references to compulsory arbitration would, however, have to be confined to exceptional cases and used as rarely as possible. Such arbitration would differ from the traditional process in that it would be specifically conducted against the guidelines of the agreed policy, and with the advice of the Commission.

Under such an arrangement, the Commission would not be faced with the position of its predecessors which had to lay down final settlements. Moreover, there is a deliberate distinction in making the final process one of 'arbitration' rather than 'adjudication'. This would facilitate the use of the inevitable 'grey area' in many such cases to provide enough flexibility to enable the arbitration process not only to uphold the agreed policy but also to settle the dispute in a realistic manner, taking into account such factors as the balance of power and the climate of public opinion, which would come into play in a purely negotiating process: what George Woodcock, the TUC General Secretary, once called 'those shoddy, shabby, dirty compromises which are the essence of practical people trying to do a job!' In other words the objective would be to achieve a better result with less conflict than would be achieved by unfettered negotiations and industrial action.

Under such arrangements the question of who should have the power to refer disputes to arbitration is an important and delicate one: in particular, should either of the parties to a dispute have the right to have it referred to arbitration if the other party does not agree? Whilst such an arrangement might seem reasonable at first sight, it would create a danger of inhibiting the normal negotiating process and placing an excessive load on the arbitration machinery. Where, however, both parties agreed to go to arbitration, it would seem sensible that the Commission should go along with this procedure. Further consideration would be needed of the changes to the present arbitration machinery to enable it to proceed in this formal way and to establish a consistent approach to the arbitrators' task.

Greater use of arbitration to avoid industrial action (either on these or similar lines) would command considerable public support. In considering new ways of tackling the problem in the 1990s, we should therefore take the opportunity to make a combined attack on both the two major unresolved problems of pay bargaining: how to safeguard the national interest in avoiding inflation, and how to resolve disputes without industrial action, with their damaging effects not only on the parties directly involved but also on the public at large.

TAX-BASED POLICIES

To avoid the need for any such institutional machinery, it has sometimes been suggested that the tax system should be used to police any national pay agreement. There are, however, a number of overwhelming difficulties in such an approach. It could only be based on a simple uniform norm with no provision for flexibility – an impossible condition for any long-term policy. The detailed provisions of tax law needed to administer such a tax in any reasonable and acceptable manner would be extremely complicated. Taxing company profits would not meet the point that breaches in the policy guidelines generally occur despite strong resistance from the employer. On the other hand, penal taxes on individuals whose rises breached the guidelines would make the rumpus over the poll tax look like a storm in a tea cup. Of all approaches this would be the most rigid: see Appendix 2 for a fuller discussion.

PRICES POLICY

One of the hurdles to be overcome in reaching agreement on a pay strategy is to make it clear that such a strategy does not involve a return to a regime of price control. For (as we saw in Chapters 4 and 5) in the past, incomes policies have nearly always been accompanied by prices policies. This association has come about in three main ways. The first was that since an incomes policy was not an end in itself but intended to affect the price level, analysis and discussion was bound to encompass prices as well as incomes. The second was that since the object was to keep prices down, price control was seen as the most direct way of tackling the problem. The third was that when there was a statutory control of incomes, price control was seen as a way of preventing employers from making excessively high profits as a consequence.

If, however, the problem is one of cost inflation, and profit margins are not seen as excessive, there is no economic case for accompanying incomes policy by any parallel action on prices. Any pressure to do so would seem to be a purely political one based on a false symmetry. Because of the variety of products involved price control is inevitably highly detailed and bureaucratic; it cannot prevent inflation arising from the wage–price spiral. Moreover, price controls would discourage inward foreign investment; and run counter to all attempts to encourage industrial development.

There may be a case for more active investigations by the Monopolies and Mergers Commission (possibly with wider terms of reference) into problems in particular areas. The regulation of public utility prices will also come into the picture because of their high profile and essential nature of the services they provide. But it is important to distinguish between any action required to tackle high prices due to restrictive practices, or special institutional or economic conditions in particular fields, on the one hand, and any idea of imposing general price controls on the other. There can be no question of any reimposition of price control.

EMPLOYERS' AND TRADE UNIONS' ATTITUDES

Employers, particularly in manufacturing industry, have a great deal to gain from an effective pay policy, which would make it possible to allow demand to expand more rapidly without accelerating inflation. On the other hand, management has a natural distaste for any further public interference or constraints; and it perceives (correctly) that agreement on a more collective approach to pay will in the longer run strengthen the trade union movement at a national level. It would also, of course, require a strengthening of the CBI. The management of many of the larger, and more stable, industrial companies realise, however, that the 'anti-corporatist' atmosphere of recent years has not served industry well. Legitimate lobbying for collective industrial interests has increasingly given way to lobbying by particular firms for special favours, in a manner which has sometimes bordered on the scandalous.

Trade union reluctance to participate in a pay policy is frequently based on the fear that it would involve a sacrifice, in the sense that their members' real wages would be lower than would otherwise have been the case. It is not, however, the objective of a counter-inflationary incomes policy to lower real wages, or the rate at which they increase – although in certain circumstances this may be inevitable, with or without an incomes policy e.g. in the face of a sharp rise in import prices. The objective is rather to avoid self-defeating increases in money wages and prices that cancel each other out. Real wages depend basically on the growth of efficiency and the cost of what we buy from abroad, although in the short-term they may show gains and losses when money incomes temporarily rise faster or slower than prices. An incomes policy may, however, affect the relative position of different groups of workers, in particular those least powerful in relation to those with the most clout.

The idea that pay policy involves cuts in real wages has arisen partly from the problems of introducing an incomes policy when prices are rising sharply: naturally enough, the circumstances in which such policies have been most frequently introduced. If, for example, prices have been rising at an annual rate of 10 per cent and in an attempt to slow down inflation it is agreed that money wages in the next round should only rise by say, 6 per cent, wage earners will not be fully compensated for the rise in prices in the last 12 months. In this sense 'real wages will have been cut', relative to where they were 12 months ago.[8] But holding increases in money wages temporarily below past price increases is generally an inescapable condition for slowing down a rapid wage–price spiral, whether it is done by means of pay policy *per se*, or by deflation. Indeed it is the difficulty of slowing down money wage increases in such circumstances that makes inflation once started, so difficult to halt. The moral is that the time to get an incomes policy established is before wage increases start to accelerate: that is before it appears to be necessary, not after.

THE FUTURE FOR THE UNIONS

The rate of increase in money wages must be kept at moderate levels by one means or another, but the route by which this end is achieved will be crucial to the future of the trade union movement. It is the great paradox of any move towards agreement on a national pay policy that while at first sight it appears as a major curb on the freedom of the trade unions, in the longer run the trade union movement has so much to gain from such an approach. It was because they realised this that the Thatcher government was so strongly opposed to a move in this direction. The reliance on deflation and unemployment to curb wage increases over the last decade reflected the climate of hostility to the unions and general attempts to reduce their power and influence. The Thatcher administration made a deliberate point of cutting down consultation with the TUC and the unions to the absolute minimum. The trend towards employee representation, which reached an apogee with the report of the Bullock Committee, was reversed, and the European Community's Social Charter was treated with official hostility.

The eventual consequence of such a trend would be to encourage the development of 'business unions' solely devoted to promoting the sectional interests of their own members and a weakening of the ties of common interest and mutual concern expressed in organisational terms in their affiliation to the TUC. There are some who think that such a development is desirable and should be encouraged, either on industrial grounds or in the belief that this would weaken the Labour Party in its historical form. It would, however, create very serious dangers both to our social structure and to our economic efficiency. Narrowly focused unions are often the most prone to restrictive practices. They are most liable to push the interests of the hard-core workers in the areas in which they are recognised at the expense of those outside the magic circle. The more the trade unions operate in a sectional manner, the greater the danger of wage leapfrogging and the greater the difficulty of any concerted action to avoid inflation.

The trade union movement is at a cross-roads. If the unions are pushed further down the road they travelled in the 1980s, they will pay increasingly less attention to issues which affect workers and their families as a whole, and more and more to the narrower interests of their own particular members. The interests of the skilled and more highly paid will take increasing precedence over the less skilled and less specialised. Social justice will go off the trade union agenda. The alternative is to demonstrate that the trade union movement as a whole is acutely aware of the dangers of a continuation of a free-for-all in wage bargaining and that it has the will to do something about it. The union movement is the natural body to take such an initiative because its whole tradition and ethos is based on collective action. At a point in our political and economic history where the move towards mainly self-centred action threatens the stability of our society, the trade union movement would be a natural body to reassert the need for a more collective approach to the problem of pay bargaining.

A RETURN TO 'CORPORATISM'?

The word 'corporatism' has been used loosely in recent years, in a derogatory way, to decry the type of arrangements under which the government consulted such organisations as the CBI and TUC as part of the customary process of policy making: a process formalised with the creation of the National Economic Development Council by Harold Macmillan's Chancellor, Selwyn Lloyd, in 1961. The Thatcher credo that 'there is no such thing as society' has been strongly anti-corporatist. One result of this has been to enhance the importance of the

City and financial institutions relative to industry: the City is more concentrated and has stronger natural links with a Conservative Cabinet than the general run of industry which is more dependent on organised representation. Moreover, fear of financial markets makes maintaining the confidence of the City appear much more important than that of maintaining the confidence of industry.

The Thatcherite drive to lessen the power of the trade unions cannot be justified on the ground that their actions to protect their members were sometimes restrictive. It was fortunate for her, and unfortunate for the unions, that the most notorious, and untypical case, was the newspaper industry, because the restrictive practices there have led many journalists and commentators to react as if they were typical of industry as a whole. They were not. If occasional resort to inefficient or restrictive practices were to be taken as a cause for elimination, the unions would not be the only part of industry to perish. Mrs Thatcher's desire to smash the power of the unions, in particular the mineworkers, was not based on efficiency, but on the desire to reassert the power of one section of the community relative to the others. Macmillan, an ex-guards officer himself, once referred to the National Union of Mineworkers as the 'Brigade of Guards of the Labour Movement'. He saw it as a proud institution woven into the fabric of British society, to be worked with (or sometimes against), but not as something to be destroyed.

A strong theme in virtually every recent critique of the Thatcher years (not only from the left) has been the need to move towards a more collective (if you will, 'corporatist') approach to industrial problems: for example, by David Marquand, with his evocation of the 'developmental State',[9] and by Will Hutton with the case for 'stakeholder capitalism'.[10] Cries about a return to 'corporatism' should not deter us from redressing the balance. Formal and informal consultation with organised interest groups has an important role to play in democratic government. Margaret Thatcher's tendency to spurn such consultation was part and parcel of her over-bearing contempt for anything smacking of consensus. Yet our industrial success is highly dependent on consensus at every level: ranging from consensus between management and employees within the firm to achieve common objectives, to consensus between employees and unions at national level on a pay policy to avoid inflation.

The recent tendency to use the term 'corporatism' as a means of disparaging any such tripartite arrangements shows a failure to distinguish between the distortion of democratic government by paying excessive attention to the special interests of powerful corporate bodies, and the strengthening of democratic government by the widest possible consultation and participation in devising economic policies.

REFORM BY CONSENT

The two essential features of any new arrangements are first that bargaining over individual claims should be preceded by a national agreement over the general magnitude of such increases and the principles to be applied, and second, that unions and employers should be confident that if they adhere to such an agreement others would do likewise. The roles of existing or new institutions in reaching an agreement or implementing it will inevitably require discussion and negotiation, but in the end the precise machinery is of less importance than a resolution to tackle the problem.

There would be considerable tactical advantages in establishing an incomes policy when inflation is low. It would be much more difficult to start such policies when inflation was rising again and unions might have to be asked to agree on a rate of money wage increases below the rate of inflation. With inflation at around 2 to 4 per cent, a satisfactory wage round under a new pay policy need not involve wage settlements below the past rate of inflation. This would considerably ease the whole process of getting agreement on a new approach. Such an initiative would inoculate the economy in advance against the onset of inflation when there was a sudden change in economic circumstances.

The possibility of establishing a successful agreement on pay is regarded with scepticism in some quarters after the traumas of the 'Winter of Discontent'. But the true lesson of past experience is not that any such agreement is bound to fail, but that to be effective it must be realistic and based on a wide measure of public support. More broadly, British economic policy is in danger of becoming paralysed by the fact that all the major tools of economic management have come to grief at one time or another. It is fallacious to conclude that because of past failures we should never use fiscal or monetary policy again. The same applies to pay policy. To take an industrial analogy, it would be as though a firm with a marketing disaster or a technical failure were to believe that the answer were to drop marketing or abolish its technical department. This would clearly be nonsense. The challenge is to see where mistakes were made and use the available instruments of policy more effectively.

An agreement on pay must be seen as an essential contribution to a Government commitment to an expansionary strategy to achieve full employment. To be realistic it should be directed towards an attainable target, not a theoretical one calculated to yield zero inflation if it were perfectly effective. Above all the aim should be to establish a lasting, long-term agreement rather than a temporary expedient; which in the end means achieving some degree of consensus between political parties to prevent pay policy once again becoming a political football. Pay policy differs in kind from most other types of policy in that the problem is to a large extent one of influencing public attitudes rather than detailed machinery or policy statements, necessary as these may be. It seems unlikely that any new consensus will be reached either in the union movement or elsewhere without strong political leadership.

8 Jobs and People

The predominance of monetarist thinking in recent years has been associated with a revival of the prewar view that the cure for unemployment lies in 'the labour market', rather than in strengthening the demand for goods and services. The phrase 'the labour market' often seems one of the economic profession's more unhappy pieces of jargon. It conjures up visions of people being auctioned like cattle, or of agricultural workers in the nineteenth century coming to the County Town for the Michaelmas hiring, and in doing so suggests that, if the price for their labour was right, everyone would get a job. But as we saw earlier, the supply and demand for labour is different from that for anything else, in that the receipts from selling labour (i.e. wages and salaries) are a major component of the demand for it (or the goods that labour is needed to produce).

LABOUR MARKET FALLACIES

The misleading thesis that unemployment reflects an imbalance between the supply and demand for labour that can be remedied by adjusting the price still, however, underlies a variety of current proposals for tackling unemployment, most of which have in common the fact that they would worsen the lot of the unemployed and the ordinary wage earner. The simple version is that cutting wages will reduce unemployment. The more sophisticated variant is that while lower real wages will not in themselves lead to higher employment, they are a necessary consequence of it. (Keynes originally made this assumption in the *General Theory*, but later modified his views.)[1] In each case the proposition rests on the fallacious assumption that the average productivity of labour falls as output and employment increase. This assumption, so basic to nineteenth-century economic theory, may have some validity in agriculture, assuming that successively less productive land is brought into production as demand increases (as in Ricardo's theory of rent); but it bears little relation to the facts of modern industrial life.

The classical economists were wedded to the idea that average costs would rise, rather than fall, as output expanded, because it was a necessary concomitant of their theory of 'perfect competition' which assumed that a firm could sell as much as it wished of its product at the existing market price: for if a firm's average costs did not rise with increasing output, there would be no limit to how much it could produce or sell. But in reality the market for any one firm's products is finite and depends on their quality, brand image, service, local connections and so on: although a firm's costs may decline when it produces and sells more, its ability to do so is (as we all know) limited by market factors, and at some point cutting prices to expand sales will bring prices below costs.[2] In the real world competition is not perfect and costs do not increase as output expands.

PRODUCTIVITY, COSTS AND OUTPUT

In industry today the two key issues are: (a) how is productivity related to output within a plant; and (b) how does average productivity compare in different plants which only come into (or out of) use as output rises (or falls)? In general, average productivity rises with output in a under-used plant: not because the marginal productivity of successive new workers increases, but because additional operatives (each with more or less the same productivity) dilute the overhead costs of managers, and so on. This is, of course, why it is worthwhile for firms to pay premium rates for overtime or night and weekend working. This effect usually more than compensates for any question as to whether the new recruits are less able or well-trained than those already on the job. The one situation where increasing output may lead to a fall in productivity is where the plant is already working virtually at full capacity and inefficient methods of working have to be adopted to squeeze out the extra output.

As far as successive plants are concerned, the position is not symmetrical between closing a succession of plants in a recession and opening new plants in a recovery – assuming that the closed plants are closed for good, which is generally the case. When plants are closed, the least efficient are closed first; so that cutting output reduces costs. But when successive new plants are brought in over a period of recovery, they should each be more efficient and lower in cost than their predecessors; so that expanding output by expanding capacity results in lower costs.

In considering therefore the implications for real wages of expanding demand and output, the most realistic general assumption is that average productivity will improve rather than decline. These facts are widely known to those who work in industry, and were recognised by many economists 60 or 70 years ago.[3] Roy Harrod wrote in 1967:

> During the 'twenties many of us were deeply interested in Keynes's advocacy of measures to promote fuller employment. According to the traditional theory, success in this would entail higher marginal costs and lower real wages. And yet there was a great paradox. If an academic economist left his ivory tower and mingled a little with industrialists in the field, he could not help being impressed with the fact that the great majority of these industrialists affirmed that they could produce at lower cost, both in the long *and* in the short period, if only they had a bigger demand to satisfy. There seemed to be a stark contradiction between the views of the industrialists and the theory of perfect competition. And, of course, if the industrialists were right, this would be helpful for Keynesian policy.[4]

Most of the current discussion of unemployment, together with much modern economic theory, still implicitly assumes, however, that lower real wages or labour costs are needed to increase employment: for example, proposals to deregulate the labour market, reduce taxes on employment or subsidise the employment of certain types of worker. Common observation suggests the reverse: that where current output is economic, additional output at today's prices and wages will almost always be equally, or more, profitable.[5] It is lack of demand, not the need to cut the price of labour, that holds back output and employment.

It is well nigh incredible that one of the most important basic assumptions of neo-classical economics has no empirical foundation and receives so little critical comment. But then, as Galbraith has said:

> reputable or, as it is often called, mainstream economics has for some centuries given grace and acceptability to convenient belief – to what the socially and economically favoured most wish or need to have believed . . . To serve these ends, it must be emphasised, the required doctrine need not be subject to serious empirical proof.[6]

Thus the doctrine of diminishing returns led to the convenient conclusion that those who were out of work were there through their own fault in demanding too high a price for their labour; and hence reducing wages would benefit both employers of labour and the unemployed.

One of the consequences of the common but erroneous assumption that lower real wages are necessary to reduce unemployment is to build up a quite misleading picture of the 'cost' of achieving full employment. The first point is that in any event reducing unemployment means that more goods and services are produced and the community is that much better off. Second, if the additional workers do not reduce the average level of productivity, their pay packets can be as high as those of people already in work without presenting problems either of profitability to the employer or of excessive demand on the additional resources. There is not therefore a problem of 'insiders' and 'outsiders' with the marginal workers needing to be worse paid if they are to be employed at all: as, for example, James Meade suggested in his final work, *Full Employment Regained?*, which was much concerned with the redistribution effects of the 'relatively low real wage rates needed to maintain Full Employment'.

Reducing wages is neither a necessary nor an effective solution to unemployment. It is true that keeping down real wages and other costs relative to our competitors can improve one country's competitive position and thus increase its employment at the expense of others. But in a situation where virtually all industrial countries are suffering from heavy unemployment (partly hidden rather than apparent in the case of Japan), such beggar-my-neighbour policies merely shift unemployment from one country to another and do not represent an acceptable solution. Adjustments in relative costs between countries are better handled by exchange rate policy than by trying to cut wages to this end (as we saw in Chapter 2); and exchange rate adjustments should be limited to the needs of the balance of payments and not regarded as a means of exporting unemployment.

INTENSIFYING THE SEARCH FOR JOBS

There is, however, another set of labour market proposals which do not depend on assuming that productivity falls as employment increases. The theoretical justification for these is that by intensifying the search for jobs, wages will rise more slowly and unemployment can be kept lower without inflation i.e. the NAIRU will be reduced. Such proposals concentrate on getting particular sections of the unemployed back into work. Three groups attract particular attention: those who are alleged to prefer to remain unemployed, the long-term unemployed and school leavers. In all three cases, however, there seems no reason why such action should in itself increase the total number of jobs available.

As far as the first category is concerned, while there may be a small minority of people who are not actively seeking employment because they feel they are better off unemployed – either because they are in a benefit trap, or have given up hope of a job – there is no reason why making life on the dole more unpleasant for them (or lessening the reduction in benefits if they get work) should increase the total number of jobs; and it seems doubtful whether such measures would have any significant effect on wage demands. But in their popular text book on unemployment, Layard, Nickell and Jackman go so far as to maintain that 'The unconditional payment of benefits for an indefinite period is clearly a major cause of high European unemployment.'[7] We should be worrying more about the effects of the continual erosion of benefits on the plight of the vast majority of those who are desperate for work rather than the small minority who are out to beat the system. Experience shows that if demand is strong enough and jobs become available, there is no problem of people preferring to live on benefit. The idea that over-generous benefits are keeping up the number of unemployed at a time when there is a widespread shortage of jobs is both cruel and mischievous.

This type of thinking, combined with the desire to keep

down the cost of social security benefits, has provided a pretext for a series of measures to restrict the value of the benefits available to the unemployed and aggravate their financial plight. Whereas in 1978/9, on average the unemployed received from benefits 55 per cent of their former income from work, by 1987 this ratio had fallen to 39 per cent.[8] In 1987, for about 70 per cent of those unemployed, unemployment-related benefits replaced less than half their previous earnings.[9] Another and more recent measure of increasing financial hardship among the unemployed is available from the Department of Social Security (DSS) report on *Households below Average Income.*[10] In 1992/3, 75 per cent of families suffering from unemployment had an income less than half average income, as compared with 58 per cent in 1979 (in both cases after allowing for housing costs). The number of children in families with incomes less than half the national average had risen from 1.4 million to 4.3 million. The policy followed since 1984 of linking benefits to prices rather than earnings has meant that the erosion of the value of benefits is still continuing. Such harsh restrictions not only cause severe financial hardship, but serious stress and worry.

ETHNIC MINORITIES

Ethnic minorities have been particularly badly hit by unemployment. The Labour Force Survey for Spring 1995 showed that while the (ILO) unemployment rate (see Appendix 1) was 8 per cent for white workers, it was 19 per cent for non-whites. Pakistani/Bangladeshi workers had the highest rate of 27 per cent, with Afro-Caribbeans at 24 per cent. In Greater London 11 per cent of whites were unemployed but 24 per cent of non-whites. Black workers were also likely to be unemployed for longer than whites: 60 per cent of Afro-Caribbean workers unemployed in the Spring of 1994 had been without work for over one year compared to 44 per cent of unemployed white workers.[11]

Racial discrimination in one form or another must be a factor in this situation. The percentage of highly qualified non-whites unemployed (6.9 per cent) was more than double the rate (3.1 per cent) for highly qualified white people. The situation tends to be prolonged by the fact that the jobs that non-white workers do get are often those most vulnerable to redundancy.

LONG-TERM UNEMPLOYMENT

Long-term unemployment has become an increasing problem as unemployment has risen and jobs have been harder to get. In the summer of 1995, 1.0 million people claiming unemployment benefit had been out of work for over a year. It is obviously important to help those concerned get back into employment. The main problem facing the long-term unemployed is probably not, as is generally suggested, that their skills have become rusty or their work experience out of date, but that many employers are reluctant to recruit them; this reflects a more general tendency for employers to favour those already in work over those who are unemployed. The reason for this is simple. When making people redundant, managers try so far as possible to keep those workers that they consider the best and get rid of those that they consider less competent. Thus when they come to recruit again, they assume that other employers have been behaving in the same way. (Even university appointment boards work on this assumption.) Similarly, the longer people have been out of work, the more likely managers are to assume that the fact that they have failed to impress other recruiters must mean that they are not strong candidates. This factor obviously has less force in depressed areas where unemployment has been consistently high for some time. But the higher unemployment has become and the greater the number of people who apply for any particular job, the more likely are recruiters to fall back on general criteria such as age, or whether the applicants have been out of work for long, when they have to sift through numerous candidates.

The long-term unemployed therefore need particular help to overcome their perceived lack of ability, whether or not this perception is justified. The fallacy, however, is to assume that reducing the numbers of long-term unemployed will in itself have any significant effect in reducing total unemployment. Subsidising employers who take on the long-term unemployed (or unemployed young people) will generally mean that they will employ such people instead of someone else, not that they will increase their labour force. This is borne out by a study of the effects of the Government's Pilot Workstart Schemes made by the Institute of Employment Studies.[12] This scheme offered employers a subsidy of £60 a week for 26 weeks and then £30 a week for 26 weeks for each full-time recruit who had been continuously unemployed for two years (four years in London). Whereas the study found that the subsidy had been effective in getting employers to take on the very long-term unemployed, the scheme did not appear to have had much effect on total employment. In only 17 per cent of cases were jobs created as a result of the subsidy where there would otherwise have been no vacancy; and there is no evidence that these represented any increase in total employment. If a garage or dry cleaner in the scheme took on an extra person and got more work, its competitor elsewhere may have had to make someone redundant.

YOUTH UNEMPLOYMENT

The age group worst hit by unemployment (with some of the most serious consequences) is the under-twenties. In the summer of 1995 over 20 per cent of 16- to 19-year-olds who had left school were unemployed. There are powerful reasons for providing special assistance to young people who are unemployed, particularly in areas of persistently high unemployment; but the most effective way to help young people is to strengthen the general demand for labour. Special measures to help them or any other particular groups of unemployed people are of only limited benefit when there is a general shortage of jobs, and should not be regarded as a means of reducing total unemployment.

Similar considerations apply to regional measures, of which little has been heard in recent years, partly because the experience of different areas of the country has been less varied than in the past. While in October 1995 unemployment in Northern Ireland and the Northern Region was over 10 per cent, Greater London was almost as bad with 9.6 per cent. If, however, the general level of unemployment were to fall appreciably, there would once again be more conspicuous differences between areas. There would then be considerable scope for assisting such areas by special incentives for industrial development or additional investment in infrastructure.

THE CHANGING LABOUR MARKET

One source of confusion in discussing the causes of, and remedies for, mass unemployment is the effect of certain structural changes in the labour market, many of them predating the abandonment of full employment. Perhaps the most dramatic of these is the increase in the number of women in, or seeking, employment. In 1971, only 57 per cent of women of working age were in the labour force; 20 years later the proportion had risen to 71 per cent. The increase was most marked in the 25–34-year-old group where the participation rate rose from 45 per cent to 70 per cent as more women with school-aged children remained at work.[13] Approaching half of women's jobs were part-time, which can take a variety of forms.

> 'Part-time' employment includes the clerical worker on a regular, 24-hour-a-week contract; the DIY sales operator working a 3-day 'weekend' for full-time wages; the local authority job-sharer on 17 hours per week with membership of a pension scheme; the shop assistant whose hours vary each week; the cleaner who works for 3 hours per week, and the production-line operator on a zero hours contract.[14]

Over the same period, 1971–91, the participation rate for men of working age fell slightly from 91 per cent to 88 per cent as the demand for labour weakened. The change was noticeable among older men: in 1991 less than half men aged between 60 and 64 were in work. There seems little doubt that if the demand for labour were stronger, both more men and more women would enter or remain in the labour force who today form part of the one million 'hidden' unemployed.

The increase in the number of women working has led to a consequential increase in the number of households with two earners, while at the same time higher unemployment has increased the number of households with no earners. Between

1975 and 1990 the proportion of households with two adults of working age where both worked rose from 51 to 60 per cent, but the proportion with no earner rose from 3 to 11 per cent.[15]

A return to full employment in the 1990s would mean a higher proportion of part-time jobs for women than it did in the 1960s. But there is no reason to suppose that if the demand for labour were stronger there would be any mismatch between the demand and supply of full-time versus part-time jobs. Most employers have considerable scope for flexibility in deciding whether to employ full-timers or part-timers according to the wishes of their potential employees. The key point about the relation of full employment to the revolution in women's working patterns and family life is that it would shift the balance of choice from the employer to their employees. 'Flexibility' in conditions of work is desirable if it means that women (and men) can adjust their working pattern to the needs of family life (and other personal circumstances, such as studying for additional qualifications). 'Flexibility' is much less desirable, where as now, it is synonymous with insecurity and means that people can be laid off at short notice or expected to work unreasonable hours. In most EU countries, minimum wages, working conditions and social security contributions apply regardless of hours; in the UK, no such principle of 'equal treatment' applies, and both employment legislation and the structure of national insurance contributions create important incentives towards part-time employment.[16] In times of buoyant demand the good employer will reach an appropriate *modus vivendi* with his or her staff that can be beneficial to them both.

The number of men and women remaining at work over the age of 60 would seem likely to increase substantially if the demand for labour were stronger. Many of those dropping out of the labour force at the present time do so not from choice. Indeed with improved health and longer life expectation, more people than in the past will want to continue working after the age of 65, in some cases part-time rather than full-time. With a stronger demand for labour there will be more scope for them to do so. Compulsory retiring ages will at the same point become an anachronism. The only potential factor working the other way is that, among higher income groups, people may find it easier to accumulate the financial resources needed for earlier retirement, but only by accepting a greater drop in their standard of living than if they had retired later. Full employment could revolutionise the whole problem of the so-called 'demographic time bomb' by raising the proportion of older people at work. This is just one facet of the fact that any return to full employment would be that many people not now seeking jobs – the so-called 'economically inactive' – would return to the labour market.

HIDDEN UNEMPLOYMENT

The official unemployment figures show the number of people claiming unemployment (or unemployment-related) benefits on a particular day in the month. Continual changes in the rules governing eligibility for such benefits have tended to reduce the figures and cast doubt on their validity as an indicator of the 'true' unemployment (see Appendix 1). Both the Royal Statistical Society[17] and the House of Commons Employment Committee[18] have suggested that the present situation is unsatisfactory and that more use should be made of the information obtained in the regular Labour Force Surveys based on questioning households.

The Surveys show that there are around a further one million people not claiming unemployment benefit, but actively seeking work: the 'hidden unemployed'. This applies particularly to the large numbers of women who want a job but who are not eligible for unemployment pay or actively seeking work, and to older men. The Unemployment Unit publish a regular series of estimates of 'broad' unemployment based on the Labour Force Surveys. These include people who want work, and are available to start in two weeks but have not been looking for work. In the summer of 1995 when the claimant count averaged 2.3 million, their figure for 'broad unemployment' was 3.5 million.[19]

The extent of 'hidden' unemployment varies according to how strict a definition of seeking work is adopted. John Wells has produced a similar estimate (on a slightly different basis), raising the official total of 2.81 million unemployed in the summer of 1993 to an alternative figure of 4.07 million.[20]

The importance of these estimates lies not so much in the exact figures as the evidence that there are many people not counted in the official unemployment statistics who would take jobs if the demand for labour were stronger. Hence to reduce the number of those officially unemployed by, say, one million, would require considerably more than one million new jobs as some of the hidden unemployed or economically 'inactive' came back into the labour market.

WORK-SHARING

The idea of 'work-sharing' (i.e. spreading the available work more widely) has obvious attractions at a time of heavy unemployment. But it is a dangerous fallacy to think that there is a pre-determined demand for labour or fixed amount of work to go round. (Indeed on present policies if unemployment were appreciably decreased in this way, the Treasury and the Bank might well be seeking to restrict demand for fear of inflation.) It is, however, absurd and anti-social when work is scarce, that many men (in particular) are forced by their employers to work excessively long hours for fear of losing their jobs. Britain's failure to ratify the Social Chapter aggravates this situation. In many other EU countries standard weekly working hours are set by law. Thus one positive response to the 'work-sharing' approach is that it provides an additional argument for limiting hours worked where they could otherwise be excessive on social grounds.

Where the concept of work-sharing does seem appropriate is in employers' response to temporary recessions in demand. As we shall discuss in the next chapter, one of the problems of returning to full employment is to rebuild our capacity – in the widest sense, not just of plant – and maintain it at a level compatible with full employment during any temporary recessions. Part of such a process must be to keep a firm's labour force as far as possible intact during recession by reducing hours rather than numbers. This accords with Japanese and German practice, but is increasingly difficult where industrial decisions are dominated by the myopic reaction of city financial analysts. Whereas in the past, managers who could not sustain or expand their business enough to employ their existing workforce were regarded as having failed, today, 'down-sizing' the workforce is applauded as a sign of management virility.

IS THERE A SHORTAGE OF UNSKILLED JOBS?

Another fashionable labour market theory is the so-called 'shortage of unskilled jobs'. But most of what has been written about the problem of unemployment among the unskilled is based on the inaccurate assumption that the 'demand for unskilled labour', in the sense of the number of jobs that the unskilled succeed in getting, is a direct reflection of the type of jobs available. It clearly is not. If an unemployed university graduate replaces someone with no qualifications in a job stocking the shelves in the local supermarket, there has in this sense been a decline in 'the demand for unskilled labour' but not a loss in unskilled jobs. Any statistical analysis of job losses based on the educational qualifications of those in or out of work must be regarded in this light. Most of the statistics purporting to prove that the industrial countries are suffering 'from a loss of unskilled jobs' can equally well be interpreted as demonstrating that the unskilled are the least effective competitors in the competition for the available jobs.

While the detailed statistical analyses show that the unskilled have the highest incidence of unemployment, relative changes in recent years do not fall in any simple pattern or support any general thesis about unskilled jobs. Nickell and Bell have analysed the disparate movements of unemployment among the skilled and unskilled in a number of OECD countries.[21] They treat as 'skilled' those with a high educational qualification e.g. in the UK: A levels, or a professional qualification or a degree. The 'unskilled' are defined as those who leave school with no qualifications. This leaves, of course, a middle group accounting for about one-third of the male working population. (The figures refer only to men on the grounds that factors other than education are more important in determining the cause of female unemployment.) Nickell and Bell distinguish two phases over the last 20 years or so. In the period from the early or mid-1970s to the late 1980s the countries where data is available fall into two groups. The first group, consisting of the US, Japan, Norway and Sweden, experienced small increases in unemployment and the increase was concentrated on the unskilled. The second group, consisting of Germany, the Netherlands, Spain, the UK and Canada, experienced larger rises in unemployment with a significant rise in unemployment among those who had been through higher education. In the subsequent sharp recession in the early 1990s, the further rise in unemployment involved substantial increases in unemployment among both skilled and unskilled.

The emphasis on skilled as against unskilled jobs in this and other studies rests on the unrealistic assumption that there are two (or more) groups of jobs with a corresponding number of classes of potential workers, and that Group 1 jobs can only be filled by Group 1 people. In real life there are relatively few jobs, particularly in industry, which can only be filled by people with specific qualifications. Where the restriction is most highly specified it is generally a question of public safety (e.g. doctors or electricians) or semi-restrictive practices (e.g. lawyers and accountants); and many of these jobs are in non-industrial sectors. In industry, most former demarcations covering skilled jobs for time-served apprentices have gone by the board. It is strange that the concept of a sharp division between skilled and unskilled should suddenly come to the fore at a time when the old distinctions between skilled craftsmen and unskilled labourers is no longer so important, and the workforce has a much more closely graduated spectrum of skills, training and ability.

In practice there is a range of people of varying degrees of ability, experience and qualifications that can fill a vacant post, and employers try to get the best person they can. When demand for labour is strong, employers have to be content with people at the bottom of the range of available skills, education or ability. But when demand is weak, employers can be more selective and posts tend to be filled by people at the top of the ability range. The knock-on effect is that the less skilled or less able fall off the bottom of the jobs ladder. In other words, the fact that a higher proportion of the less skilled and less educated may be unemployed reflects the fact that they lose out in the battle for jobs, rather than the nature of the jobs available. This is particularly true in the service trades where the 'better educated' tend to get the available jobs, and may in many cases be heavily over-qualified for the work in hand:

for example, university graduates are taking lower-grade jobs. Hence as unemployment rises it tends to be concentrated on those at the bottom of the hierarchy of skills and ability. This also helps to explain why higher unemployment is associated with growing inequality of earnings, as the less well-placed have to compete most fiercely for jobs.

Is this then a justification for arguing that those out of work can only command lower wages than those at work? The answer is 'No' because, for the reasons discussed earlier, costs tend to decline as output increases irrespective of any minor difference in the ability or productivity of the people employed. Take a hotel, for example: if its room occupancy increases and an extra chambermaid has to be employed at the same rate of pay as the others, its profitability will rise whether or not she is just as efficient. Postwar experience suggests that it is only when unemployment is very low, and then only to a limited extent, that those unemployed may differ markedly in efficiency from those in work.

None of this is to deny the merits of more and better education and training. But it does suggest that we should not try to create more unskilled jobs by further cheapening the cost of unskilled labour or other means. If there are enough jobs in total to go round, all the evidence of wartime and postwar history is that few people will be excluded from work because the jobs are too skilled or the workforce too unskilled.

NORTH–SOUTH

The emphasis on unemployment among the unskilled has encouraged the popular thesis that unemployment in the more highly industrialised countries reflects increased competition from developing countries with a very low cost of unskilled labour. This thesis has been developed in most detail by Adrian Wood in his study on North–South Trade.[22] But the fact that competition may be most acute in such industries does not mean that the remedy is to reduce wages for the unskilled workers in Europe, or that we have to beat such competition to ensure full employment. This point will be discussed in more detail in Chapter 10 in the context of the Delors White Paper on Unemployment. Europe's competitive strength lies in developing the more advanced industries and in effect creating more 'skilled' jobs.

Wood argues that even if the trade effects balance out, the industrial countries require less labour to make an equivalent value of relatively high technology machinery to export to the developing countries than the jobs we lose by importing an equivalent value of labour-intensive products, such as textiles. It may (to take imaginary figures) only need 70 British workers to produce the machinery needed to buy the textiles from China that previously needed 100 British workers to produce, so 30 jobs have been 'lost'; but this merely means that we can have a satisfactory balance of payments and employ more labour to meet our own needs. Whether or not we have full employment in such a situation is a matter of the level of demand in the UK. Competition from the developing world is not an argument against following more expansionary policies in the industrialised countries. It is the developing world that has a balance of payments problem, rather than the industrial countries taken as a whole. The correct policy is to expand demand in the industrial countries to reduce unemployment, and broadly speaking leave market forces to determine the long-term pattern of the industrial structure.

The real problem for the industrial countries is not the threat of cheap imports of labour-intensive products, but the difficulties of adjusting to a changing industrial structure: as, for example, in the case of localities strongly dependent on steel or shipbuilding where production has been shifting away from the older industrial countries. The problem of such adjustments is most acute when unemployment is generally high. Where there is a strong demand for labour, the creation of new industries and jobs in declining areas is very much easier; as was apparent in the massive restructuring of the British steel industry in the 1970s with extensive plant closures in towns highly dependent on the industry.

SKILLS AND TRAINING

Peter Robinson has examined the relationship between unemployment and skills or qualifications using some of the same data as Nickell and Bell. He, however, draws a distinction between 'skills', covering literacy, numeracy, personal and job-specific skills, and formal 'qualifications' such as A levels.[23] Where employers reported recruitment difficulties they attributed them to lack of 'skills' rather than 'qualifications'. But there is little or no statistical evidence about skills in this broad sense, as there is about educational qualifications. Robinson points out that the proportion of the unemployed who are unqualified has been declining significantly. Although the less qualified are most easily pushed off the jobs ladder, a large number of the unemployed are well qualified. By 1994, 40 per cent of unemployed men had A level or equivalent qualifications or some form of higher education, and only 30 per cent had no formal qualifications; whereas in 1979, 70 per cent of unemployed men had no formal qualifications. This reflects both the tendency for more qualified people to become unemployed as total unemployment rises and the fact that the proportion of the workforce with educational qualifications has risen sharply in recent years: between 1984 and 1994 the proportion with higher educational qualifications rose from 12 per cent to 19 per cent. Robinson concludes that it is 'misleading to paint a portrait of the unemployed in the mid 1990s as being primarily unqualified.'

The two questions that need to be asked about training programmes for the unemployed are (a) whether they will reduce unemployment in total and (b) whether they will help those concerned to get jobs. There is no reason to think that such programmes by themselves will lead to any increase in jobs. As to the effects on individuals, Robinson finds no evidence in the US or Europe that large-scale training programmes positively help the individuals concerned. While some forms of education and training, or special schemes for young people and the long-term unemployed, may help particular individuals or groups to compete in the jobs market, they will not in themselves create more jobs. Such schemes may form a useful part of an overall strategy for full employment (as in Sweden), and better education and training can be valuable in improving industrial efficiency, but it is misleading to regard them as a significant instrument for reducing unemployment on their own. Any political platform to reduce unemployment based solely on such measures is guilty of offering a false prospectus.

THE GROWTH OF INEQUALITY

The weakening in the demand for labour since the end of the 1970s has been a major factor in the striking growth of inequality in the UK in this period: it has both widened the disparity of earnings and added large numbers of unemployed to the pool of low-income families. The Rowntree Report on Income and Wealth[24] concluded that:

> Internationally the UK was exceptional in the pace and extent of the increase in inequality in the 1980s . . . The speed with which inequality increased in the UK between 1977 and 1990 was faster than in any of the other countries listed with the exception of New Zealand over the four years to 1989.

The Report found that 'Since 1979 the lowest income groups have not benefitted from economic growth.' DSS figures for 1992/3[25] show that, after allowing for housing costs, the real income of the poorest 10 per cent had fallen by 17 per cent since 1979, and the real income of the next lowest 10 per cent has remained virtually unchanged. The number of families with less than half the average income had risen from 4.4 million to 11.5 million within the same period. Apart from the growth in the number of unemployed, the situation has been aggravated by the policy of freezing unemployment and other benefits in real terms whilst wages and salaries have continued to show real increases.

A further source of growing inequality has been the fact that the pay of the higher paid has risen more rapidly than that of the lower paid. The Rowntree Report found that after 1978, the real wages of the lowest paid third of male workers showed little change and were actually lower in 1992 than 1975; but real wages in the middle third rose by 35 per cent, and in the top third by 50 per cent. Women's wages showed a similar trend. We should be suspicious of any measures which could make this trend worse under the pretext of cutting unemployment.

It is noteworthy that the 'labour market' approaches to curing unemployment would tend to worsen still further the position of the less well-paid wage earner. Just as readiness to sacrifice jobs to control inflation reflects a particular set of political and social values, so too does the idea of reducing wages still further for those who are already worst paid. As we have already shown, any intellectual justification for them rests on the erroneous assumption of 'decreasing returns', i.e. that higher production is uneconomic without lower wages. Moreover, there is clearly no historical justification for thinking that greater inequality and a weakening in the protection of labour are a precondition for a return to full employment. On the contrary, low pay and insecurity are not a recipe for full employment, but a consequence of a weak demand for labour. The period of full employment was one where labour was stronger and society more egalitarian. For this reason many of those who press strongly for labour market measures to weaken the position of employees have no real desire to return to a state of full employment. Those who do should not follow their lead. The re-emergence of mass unemployment has already taken sufficient toll in terms of increased poverty and growing inequality without deliberately aggravating it by further measures to deregulate the labour market or depress the wages of the unskilled.

9 The Capacity Problem

One of the problems of restoring full employment today is the effect on industrial capacity of so many years of heavy unemployment. In the 1980s levels of capacity throughout the EU were eroded by closures and inhibitions on investment in additional capacity. As a result, we no longer have adequate capacity to employ the potential workforce fully, even if demand were adequate. Capacity will need to be built up in line with increasing demand, if unemployment is to be reduced without pressure on capacity and consequent price increases stimulating inflation *en route*. The problem is, however, that it is easier to reduce capacity by depressing demand than to increase it by expanding demand. The desire to avoid inflation makes it impractical to increase capacity simply by expanding demand to the point where there are shortages and then waiting for capacity to expand to satisfy them.

The Treasury and the Bank are legitimately concerned that the economy will run into capacity limitations and price increases will accelerate; but the imminence of capacity shortages may be exaggerated. In 1995 output in manufacturing, the sector where the concept of capacity limitations is most meaningful, was only just returning to its pre-recession peak reached five years earlier. How close output is to current capacity limitations at any one time is difficult to determine. For a concept whose supposed magnitude is having such a powerful influence on budgetary and monetary policy, there is surprisingly little hard information to go on. (The CBI and Chambers of Commerce regular industrial inquiries give some indications of changes in pressure on capacity but do not purport to give any absolute measure of potential output, and hence how far we are away from any capacity limits.) Moreover, with the shift in emphasis away from traditional manufacturing industries, what constitutes 'capacity' needs examining much more broadly.

To establish clearly the interrelationship between capacity, unemployment and inflation in the 1990s, we must first get away from the NAIRU concept, i.e. that there must be a given minimum level of unemployment to avoid inflation accelerating.

As we saw in Chapter 6, experience denies this. The more recent tendency to discuss the problem of inflation in terms of the so-called 'output gap' is a step forward: at least it takes into account the effect of the reduction in effective capacity following long periods of relatively low demand and high unemployment. But the concept fails to distinguish two distinct factors: (a) the gap between output and effective capacity i.e. the rate of capacity utilisation; and (b) the propensity to inflation at any given rate of capacity utilisation. Because the second factor varies with time and circumstance, the physical output gap needed to avoid inflation may also vary considerably, as did the NAIRU. Just as there is no fixed level of unemployment at which the economy will operate to keep within a given level of inflation, neither is there any fixed gap between actual and potential output.

It may be correct to think that, in the short term, keeping demand well in check will lead to a low rate of inflation; but in the longer term the effect of such a policy in limiting the rate of growth of capacity accentuates the danger of inflation. Keeping down the growth of capacity not only perpetuates high unemployment, but also the vulnerability of the economy to upturns in demand, even if (as in the so-called 'Lawson boom') the economy is still operating way below full employment levels. Indeed setting tighter and tighter inflation targets may ironically enough be a recipe for making the economy more susceptible to inflation through lack of capacity, and thus having to operate the economy at higher and higher levels of unemployment. There is no convincing reason for the popular political shibboleth that low inflation will stimulate growth. Indeed if it is the Government's view that industry should be working at less than *x* per cent of capacity to keep down inflation, but industry finds it most profitable and safer to operate at over *x* per cent of capacity, the result can be a vicious downward spiral as firms try to cut capacity to secure higher utilisation and maximum profitability. This is what appears to have been happening to manufacturing industry in the 1980s.

There are thus two related and complementary approaches to solving this problem. One is to encourage the expansion of capacity. The other is to take measures to reduce the tendency to inflation at any given level of capacity utilisation (e.g. by the reform of pay bargaining) so that the government is less concerned to hold down demand.

DEMAND EXPECTATIONS

Since firms' decisions to expand capacity are based to a large extent on their assessment of their future sales, the first question is what, if anything, can government do to reinforce confidence in future expansion? Expectations depend in part on the public understanding as to government policy and objectives and in part on an assessment of how it will turn out in practice. At present Government policy is expressed entirely in terms of keeping down inflation, and there is no suggestion that in doing so they will be inhibited by the level of unemployment. They are therefore setting up a vicious circle by effectively creating low growth expectations. For the government merely to have a short-term target for inflation is inadequate. It is necessary to think again about the way in which macroeconomic policy is conceived and expressed. As a start it should embody objectives for the growth of output and capacity as well as rates of inflation. For example the annual Budget 'Red Book' should not treat the figures for output and unemployment as forecasts on some unstated policy assumptions about the relation between demand and inflation, but as an inherent part of a longer-term strategy.

Any government that is serious about achieving a long-term reduction in unemployment will have to find means of convincing industry that demand will increase enough to justify the extra capacity needed for higher employment. There are bound, of course, still to be periodic fluctuations in demand and output, but the need is to establish a longer-term trend consistent with a gradual reduction in the level of unemployment. Successive Budget Red Books have made it clear that this has not been the Treasury's present intention. They assume that in the next five years output would only increase fast enough to get back on to its previous trend, which would leave unemployment at the high average levels of the last decade.

Firms need to be confident that demand will grow at such a rate as to validate any expansion of their capacity. But in so far as experience is the greatest determinant of expectations, we start from a very difficult point. Experience in recent years had made managers naturally cautious about over-estimating future sales as the penalties for doing so tend to be much greater than for losing potential business by failing to expand capacity. To re-establish such confidence will be difficult, and will require a major change in the whole tenor of economic policy.

EXPANSION AND RISK

Bound up with the question of demand expectations is firms' perception of risk. The characteristic of marginal additions to capacity is not that the real cost of their output is higher, as the classicists suggest: on the contrary (as was argued in the last chapter) it is lower. Labour costs should be lower; so too should capital costs, save to the extent that lower returns are acceptable on existing or sunk capital than new capital. The critical problem is the extra risk involved, because demand may not expand sufficiently to validate such expansion. A key question therefore is how can this risk be reduced and made less inhibiting? There are two problems: to reduce the actual risk and to make firms more willing to take it. The latter point may turn out to be a crucial one in the next decade. The generation now reaching top management posts have lived through a period in which their more adventurous and expansionist contemporaries have often had their judgement faulted and lost their jobs, or if they ran their own businesses lost their livelihood and their home. This is bound to have an inhibiting effect on decision making, just as many of the generation who lived through the 1930s often seemed over-cautious in the postwar years in the face of the buoyant level of demand then prevailing.

The risks of investing in capacity, which is in the event not fully utilised, depends on two main factors: the magnitude of the losses, or shortfall in profits, and the ability of the company to absorb them. In so far as the costs of expanding capacity are capital costs, the key factors are first the cost of financing it, and then the ability to cut dividends temporarily, or pay them out of reserves, in so far as the capital is in the form of equity. Whatever the opportunity cost of capital, the use of a company's own reserves, rather than raising new capital, makes a temporary failure to achieve the expected returns less dangerous. In either case, however, the attitudes of financial institutions and commentators are of crucial importance. Willingness to take a long-term view is vital.

In the UK a number of institutional factors militate against risk-taking. In the case of smaller firms, their dependence on bank loans and the shortage of risk capital makes them particularly vulnerable when profits are squeezed. With larger businesses, the problem is not so much the supply of equity, but the pressure of the market for short-term results in terms of share prices rather than the long-term profitability of the business. Their access to our highly developed stock market is a mixed blessing. The stock market is inherently short-term in outlook. Fund managers are constantly being judged on their monthly, quarterly or annual performance. If a firm keeps on plant or labour which is temporarily underemployed in a recession, financial analysts criticise them and implicitly assume that capacity should automatically be trimmed in line with any fall in demand. As Will Hutton has argued very persuasively, the whole British financial system operates in a way which aggravates this problem.[1]

With the development of service industries, the concept of 'capacity' is increasingly less dependent on physical capacity and more dependent on people: managerial organisation, trained and experienced staff, sales agents, and so on. The dilemma here is that the easier it is to hire and fire people, the less the apparent risk of taking on more staff either to work new plant or in service industries as additional 'capacity' in themselves. On the other hand, in the longer term the efficiency and competitive power of firms is greater, the more stable and committed their workforce: as the success of German and Japanese industry testifies. Their willingness to keep on staff in a recession and cut dividends to shareholders (as opposed to vice versa in the UK) helps to preserve capacity. We have got into the perverse and damaging situation where the roles of the suppliers of risk capital and the members of the company (i.e. its workforce) have become reversed. If profits are hit, dividends are maintained and employees sacked, rather than dividends being cut and workers being kept on. Employees bear a much greater risk than the suppliers of capital.

Even with a less deflationary bias to macro-economic policy, there are bound to be some cyclical movements, with temporary recessions from time to time. These will be more marked in some industries than others. It is important to develop policies which encourage firms to keep open capacity which is temporarily under-utilised, and to hold together their labour force so that they can respond to the following upturn in demand. This is where the Japanese have hitherto been markedly successful. With more spare capacity in hand, the inevitable short-term upward blips in demand are less likely to be inflationary.

COST OF CAPITAL

As well as being dependent on sales prospects, decisions to invest in new capacity are also influenced by the cost and availability of capital and the target rates of return sought by firms and financial institutions. The increasing use of interest rates both to combat inflation and bolster weak currencies has created a global bias towards higher real interest rates. The one point where higher inflation can inhibit investment is that high money, as opposed to real, rates of interest can increase the real interest burden on a project in its early years relative to later years. This may inhibit start-up projects; but on the other hand investment in new products characteristically secures higher prices and better returns in their early rather than their later years.

The availability of capital may be as, or more, important than its cost in inhibiting expansion. As every borrower knows, the market for institutional credit is unlike any other market, in that willingness to pay the going price is no guarantee of being able to buy the product. You cannot just go into a bank, inquire politely how much they are charging for loans and say 'I'll take £X million please'! Bank losses on commercial lending during the recession seem to have led to a stiffening of the banks' lending criteria. The periods for which banks are prepared to lend is also crucial, particularly the traditional reliance of small businesses in the UK on bank overdrafts: although the Bank of England reports that the ratio of term loans to overdrafts rose from 2:3 to 3:2 from 1992 to 1995.[2]

The dependence of so many businesses on bank loans rather

than risk-related capital is an important factor limiting expansion, particularly in high technology or riskier sectors. The supply of industrial capital is clearly not a market where the needs of the customer have been matched by the development of the appropriate products. Banks' 'new products' have mostly been directed at personal customers, where in the case of mortgages, at any rate, the supply of capital was already adequate. Save for the establishment of their venture capital subsidiaries, which are merely replicas of ordinary venture capital companies, the clearing banks have not done very much to widen the range of methods of company financing, particularly by developing performance-related loans or 'structured finance' deals.

In recent years the supply of venture capital has been redirected to the greener pastures of Management Buy-Outs. The supply of risk capital for run-of-the-mill small or medium sized businesses remains unsatisfactory. Most financial institutions are looking for the option to realise their investments after five years and an internal rate of return of at least 20 per cent a year, which is unrealistically high in relation to the general run of results and at a time of low inflation. The criteria for evaluating investment projects, particularly those which will expand capacity, adopted by firms and financial institutions deserves further investigation. A recent inquiry by the Bank of England[3] of 250 (mainly large and medium-sized companies) found that the average post-tax 'threshold' or 'hurdle' rate for the internal rate of return was 20 per cent in money terms. Only 26 per cent of firms had reduced the threshold as inflation abated. Were it not for the arithmetical ingenuity of the project champions putting forward investment proposals, not many projects would be approved!

Once the need to reduce the risk of expanding capacity is recognised as one of the central problems of economic policy today, attention will focus on how this can be assisted by changes in the system of company taxation, the use of grants or the establishment of new financial institutions (such as an Industrial Bank) to provide capital in a sympathetic manner. In so far as the objective is to stimulate the creation of additional capacity rather than investment *per se*, the last two essentially discretionary approaches may be more practical than changes in tax law, because of the difficulties of defining in any water-tight legal sense expenditure on 'additional' capacity.

CAPACITY AND THE BALANCE OF PAYMENTS

The question of expanding capacity is closely linked to that of the balance of payments. The erosion of our manufacturing capacity in the 1980s weakened our competitive position. Consideration of the evolution of the balance of payments will be a key part of any expansionary strategy. In this context it is important to distinguish clearly between the short-term and long-term effects of faster growth of demand, and hence output and employment, on the balance of payments. In the short term a faster growth of domestic demand will tend to lead to a deterioration in the balance of payments. More imported materials will be required and consumers and business will spend more on imported goods and equipment. Exports may also rise more slowly as demand at home strengthens. (This is the picture, based on short-term movements in the past, that is built into most economic forecasting models.)

In the longer term, however, the position is different. Starting from current high levels of unemployment, faster growth of home demand over a period of, say, three to five years will lead to a faster growth of industrial capacity. This means not only that industry will have the advantage of additional capacity, but that a higher proportion of it will be using the latest technology and producing new products. This is bound both to increase our export potential and provide increased competition with imported goods, thus strengthening our balance of payments position. Just as the deflationary effects of restricting demand and a high exchange rate devastated our industrial capacity in the early part of the 1980s, a more expansionary demand regime, combined with a more appropriate exchange rate policy, could gradually help to restore our industrial potential.

This factor is widely ignored because most of the standard economic forecasters' models are essentially short term. But in a recent study,[4] three Cambridge economists have examined the balance of payments implications of moving towards full employment, together with the investment needed for the necessary increase in industrial capacity. The quantitative results are necessarily somewhat tentative but they suggest that the investment in new capacity required to reduce unemployment by one million over the next 10 years would be manageable, and the expansion in our industrial capacity could bring the balance of payments deficit close to zero.

They compare two scenarios: one with a lower, and one with a higher, level of manufacturing investment and capacity. Both are constrained by the need to avoid an insupportable balance of payments. The first 'slow growth' scenario based on past trends postulates a 2.2 per cent growth of GDP leaving unemployment at 2 million at the end of the decade, and the current account deficit remains at just under 2 per cent of GDP throughout the period.

The second 'investment in capacity' scenario postulates a GDP growth of 2.4 per cent a year with unemployment falling to 1.5 million. This scenario examines the increase in manufacturing investment with a zero balance of payments deficit at the end of the period. Assuming a gradual improvement in export and import trends as additional investment takes effect, the current account initially shows a deficit of about 1.0 to 1.5 per cent of GDP, but the improvement in manufacturing trade performance gradually restores the current account to zero balance by 2005. For this to happen, manufacturing investment would need to increase at an average rate of 6 per cent a year, a rate of expansion only achieved in previous periods of expansion. But such a rate of increase in investment is only what is required to bring investment back up to the peak reached in 1989 by the year 2000.

The authors are careful to point out the hypothetical nature of many of the assumptions, but similar limitations apply to any such calculations. They illustrate, however, the direction in which further exploration is needed to draw up a longer-term strategy. It is only when such a strategy commands general support and conviction that industry can be expected to base its investment decisions on the assumption of faster growth in demand and sales consistent with a significant reduction in unemployment.

In drawing up such a strategy, it is essential to distinguish between measures primarily aimed at increasing a country's long-term growth and economic efficiency and measures which will reduce unemployment. We should not confuse the problem of raising the long-term growth rate (as determined by the growth of output per head) with that of raising a country's output, and hence employment, to its full potential at any one time. We should beware of assuming that measures to facilitate long-term growth, such as the ability of firms and individuals to adjust to changing technology, will reduce unemployment. Indeed their real importance comes once we have achieved full employment.

There will always be a variety of rates of long-term growth of output *per head* within the industrialised countries whether unemployment is low, as in the immediate postwar period, or high as it is at present. There is no particular reason why speeding up the growth of productivity all round should restore full employment; or why any one country should improve its employment position by securing a higher place in the productivity growth league unless to do so would remove a balance of payments constraint which would otherwise have held it back. Part of the trouble is the failure to distinguish between measures which may help one country's competitive position and measures which will reduce unemployment in the industrialised countries as a whole. (The 1994 OECD Jobs Study was a case in point.) So-called 'supply-side' policies to speed up the growth of productivity are naturally desirable, but not in themselves a remedy for unemployment.

TECHNICAL CHANGE

Similar considerations apply when considering the relation between technical change and unemployment. For the reasons discussed above, exploiting technical change more fully provides no necessary cure for unemployment; neither can the current unemployment problem be blamed on it. The re-emergence of mass unemployment in the 1980s is so clearly related to the attack on inflation that it is difficult to argue that technical change is in any sense a major cause. (Indeed, as long as the economy is being managed on the principle that unemployment must not be allowed to fall too low for fear of renewed inflation, any reduction in unemployment due to a surge of innovative investment might well lead to more restrictive demand management.) But this is not to deny that technical change can cause severe employment problems in particular industries or areas, or that the measures we take to tackle the unemployment problem should not be affected by the technological changes of the moment. The *overall* effects of technical change in stimulating or reducing demand can be met by adjustments in demand management. It is the *structural* effects on the demand for different skills that call for specific measures to ease or speed up the process of transition. (Though it should also be remembered that the most traumatic of these structural adjustments in recent years, in coal, steel and shipbuilding, have not reflected technical change but displacement of European capacity by ambitious developments elsewhere.)

The most obvious technical changes at the moment, those based on computerisation, have the advantage from this point of view that they (and any consequent labour savings) are spread fairly evenly over a wide range of industries and services, and the skills required have been very quickly forthcoming. Workers at all levels have adapted quickly to the use of computers in their jobs and recent graduates have met the need for the professional staff required for software development, for instance. Clearly our education and training programmes must ensure that these needs will be fully met in future at the highest possible level of skill or effectiveness. But as an immediate structural problem of transition the computer revolution in itself seems in many respects to be much less acute than many of its predecessors.

The most revolutionary changes as far as employment are concerned may well follow, not from changes in technology within the firm, but the ease with which information can now be communicated between firms in different countries or continents. This will make certain parts of the production process (i.e. data handling or engineering design) highly mobile and hence easier to site in developing countries with good educational facilities but cheap labour. There are signs that this is already happening. From a global point of view this is a beneficial factor because it will require employment opportunities and balances of payments in Third World countries and hence speed up their development. This will, however, have an impact on employment patterns in the established industrial countries.

In their assessment of the effects of Computerised Technical Change within the twenty-first century, Chris Freeman and Luc Soete[5] stress the need to adopt measures to stimulate employment in Europe which go with the grain of the change. They argue for 'a new form of Keynesian public investment policy . . . to provide the basic infrastructure for an Information and Communication Technology based economy' and which would 'offer an ideal opportunity to diffuse new technologies and to promote the necessary collaboration between users, construction firms, and equipment and software suppliers'. But as we shall see in the next chapter, European finance ministers in their discussions on the Delors White Paper and their early 1996 discussion of the EU Budget have consistently opposed raising loans or diverting surplus budgetary funds to such projects.

10 Our European Future

Unemployment in the European Union rose sharply in the late 1970s and early 1980s to more than triple its previous levels, and remained around 10 per cent for the rest of the 1980s. From 1991 to 1995 EU unemployment averaged 10 per cent: 21 per cent in Spain, 15 per cent in Ireland, 11 per cent in France and Italy, 9 per cent in the UK, and 7 per cent in Germany.[1] The new phenomenon of mass unemployment has, as in the UK, been associated with a major shift in political priorities and economic philosophy. This was crystallised in the Treaty of Maastricht which has confined European economic policy within a deflationary straitjacket. As the deadlines for Monetary Union draw near, the convergence provisions of the Maastricht Treaty have increasingly led to further deflationary measures being taken, at a time when the immediate need in dealing with Europe's unemployment problem is to focus on ways of expanding demand.

The fact that Germany failed to meet the budget deficit criterion in 1995, and France was some way from satisfying it, led to budget cuts and the intensification of restrictive demand policies despite the urgent need for expansionary measures to counteract rising unemployment. Brian Reading has illustrated the potentially dramatic effects on output if countries' budget deficits were to be cut to meet the Maastricht 3 per cent limit in 1997.[2] He estimates that: 'German growth would be cut by a moderate 1.3 per cent in 1997, but the French GDP would have to fall by 4 per cent and Italy's, Spain's and Sweden's by over 10 per cent. Europe would be plunged into a slump by the severity of the fiscal squeeze.' (The UK is assumed to be within the limit.) Reading makes the point that these effects might be mitigated by lower interest rates; but with European interest rates effectively set by the Bundesbank, the scope for loosening monetary policy is problematical.

His figures have been calculated on a country by country basis without allowing for any loss of exports to neighbouring countries. If several countries tried to cut their deficits at the same time, the loss of output would be greater. The estimates also do not allow for any fall in private investment, which would almost certainly happen if demand fell in this way. Reading concludes that 'the cost of meeting the Maastricht criteria will be intolerable'. The positive side of this analysis is that similar arithmetic could apply in reverse (i.e. any increase in budget deficits designed to stimulate European economies would have a multiple effect on GDP), and if the major countries were to expand together the impact would be considerably greater. Higher demand could lead to increases in industrial investment, and at some point the original fiscal stimulus could be withdrawn leaving unemployment at a permanently lower level and the budgetary position improved.

The perverse effect of the convergence provisions in the Treaty exemplifies the grip that the New Orthodoxy now has on European officials and finance ministers. The economic provisions of the Treaty (derived from the Delors Committee Report on European Monetary Union) were based on a series of monetarist misconceptions, which had the convenient attribute of avoiding the need for any associated political or constitutional change. As we have seen in Chapter 6, the essence of monetarist theory may be summarised as follows:

(a) inflation is solely determined by the money supply which can be controlled by the central bank;
(b) governments should aim to balance their budgets and thus avoid stimulating the growth of the money supply;
(c) unemployment is not (save in the short run) affected by monetary or fiscal policy but by imperfections in the labour market due to collective bargaining or wage regulation.

These three basic precepts were fundamental to the Delors Committee's approach to monetary union. They explain the importance attached to the concept of a European Central Bank whose first duty is to avoid inflation, the emphasis on limiting budget deficits, and the lack of any consideration of the role of fiscal policy in demand management or on unemployment. The weakness in the Maastricht approach reflects the flaws in the monetarist analysis. The rate of inflation is not solely a consequence of monetary policy. It is determined by a variety of factors. In so far as inflation is determined by the strength of demand, both budgetary and monetary policy are important. But on the cost side there are also major institutional factors determining different countries' rates of inflation, of which the most important is the method of pay determination.

The influence of the monetarist approach on Maastricht also partially explains its tendency to under-rate the problems of convergence after a common currency has been adopted: since, if countries' rates of inflation were solely a reflection of the rates of growth of supply of their particular currencies, the adoption of a common currency would automatically remove any problem of differing rates of inflation. Hence in the monetarist canon the most difficult obstacle to speedy monetary integration is removed virtually by definition once the fateful decision has been taken.

The constitutional fallacy of Maastricht is that it postulates a monetary union without any corresponding development of democratic political machinery to determine and implement European economic policy. The only new European institution responsible for economic policy is the proposed Central Bank, which is specifically isolated from political control. Such an approach is only conceivable on the basis of two mutually inconsistent fallacies: that monetary policy is the only aspect of macro-economic policy of sufficient importance to need to be conducted on a European scale; and that this, the only effective policy instrument, should be isolated from democratic control. The need for such control is accentuated by the almost total lack of concern of most central banks for employment objectives – one of the major reasons for opposing the Maastricht concept of independent European, or national, central banks.

Maastricht implicitly dismisses the problem of mass unemployment in the Community and tacitly assumes that employment will continue to be sacrificed in the interests of pursuing low inflation. The attempt to maintain fixed parities within the ERM accentuated existing deflationary tendencies, as French experience with the *franc fort* exemplified. Maastricht merely codified existing pressures and effectively rules out the pursuit of expansionary fiscal policies to combat unemployment.

PROBLEMS OF CONVERGENCE AND ADJUSTMENT

One objective of the ERM was to try to reduce, or keep down, the rate of inflation in other member countries to German levels, by using fixed exchange rates to put pressure on companies to keep down pay and costs in order to remain competitive. This proved effective in France, and rather later in the day in the UK, but only at a disastrously high cost in unemployment. This has led to a revulsion of sentiment in Britain against the ERM, and also by implication against eventual monetary union. It is becoming increasingly realised that the Maastricht concept of using a predetermined date for monetary union to force the necessary degree of convergence in inflation rates and cost levels is only practical at the cost of further deflation and unemployment.

The ERM mechanism, at least in its later years, was incapable of coping with adjustments in rates without major market upheavals and political crises. Such adjustments will, however, still be needed for some time to come, for two main reasons. The first is the continuation of different rates of inflation, which eventually make existing exchange rates untenable. The second, which is partly a consequence of the first but may also reflect other structural factors, is the emergence of unsustainable surpluses or deficits in countries' balance of payments, with the consequent pressure for changes in exchange rates generally falling primarily on deficit countries.

Two main types of factors lead to divergent rates of inflation. First, on the demand side, the pressure of demand may be greater or less in one country than another. Second, on the cost side, pay settlements in one country may be more sensitive to demand than in another, or pay settlements may just show a chronically higher or lower rate reflecting built-in inflationary experience or pay bargaining arrangements in that country. There is also on the cost side the possibility that some countries may be more affected by changes in import prices than others because of their particular pattern of industry or imports. This factor needs, however, to be treated with caution because a sharp rise in oil prices, for example, may be as inflationary in a country which is self-sufficient in oil as one which is wholly dependent on imports.

As far as differences in the pressure of demand are concerned, the growth of trade between Community countries will generally reduce the extent to which such disparities are possible. The reverse of this is, of course, the difficulty of any one country following expansionary demand policies to reduce unemployment unless others do likewise. The most critical factor underlying differences in inflation rates, however, will continue to be differences in the rate of pay increases relative to increases in productivity. What then is the likelihood of the rate of increase in money wages and salaries relative to the rate of increase of productivity in different countries, regions or industries converging of their own accord as the Common Market takes hold?

On the wage front, the existence of national negotiations either on an industry basis, or wider, tends to lead to a 'going rate' for increases in one country in any particular year. Geographical contiguity also leads to similar increases in particular countries or regions; and on the continent, where frontiers may cut across industrial areas, market pressures may tend to equalise pay on either side of the border. A key question therefore is whether the growth of the Common Market will lead trade unions to negotiate on a European rather than a national basis. This could start with multinational companies. The difficulty for both sides in such negotiations is that the various plants of a major European automobile producer, for example, may have different absolute levels of productivity; and any attempt to set standard rates of pay may penalise employment or lead to the closure of works in the places with lower productivity. Negotiations could, of course, still be multinational whilst preserving regional or national differences in rates, but the natural pressure would be to level up.

This raises the further issue as to whether such absolute differences in productivity in different countries will persist as managers and workers become more mobile. The short answer is that with such wide cultural and historical differences across the Community it will take decades, rather than years, for such disparities to narrow significantly. The implication is, however, that if there is a trend towards convergence in productivity levels, there will be scope for convergence in real wage rates.

The most apparent effect of cost levels getting out of line in different member countries would be a rise (or differential rise) in unemployment in a country whose costs had risen relative to those elsewhere. Conversely any country whose costs had risen less than those elsewhere would experience a relative increase in employment and the possible danger of inflationary pressure. There are two ways in which EMU would affect the ability of countries to deal with this situation. The first is that they would be unable to use exchange rate adjustments to bring their costs into line. The second is that with a common interest rate policy they would not have a free hand to use interest rates to stimulate or damp down demand.

A number of 'stabilisation schemes'[3] have been put forward to alleviate the problem of differential increases in unemployment in particular countries after monetary union, of which disparate cost movements are one potential cause. Such schemes would give financial assistance to the hardest hit countries. None of the stabilisation schemes proposed, however, tackle the problem of how to reverse such disparities in cost (unless the grants envisaged for countries with relatively high unemployment were to be used to subsidise or reduce costs). Indeed by mitigating the effects of high costs on employment, such proposals would tend to blunt the pressure to slow down or reverse the rise in relative costs. Such stabilisation measures are not a substitute for exchange rate movements to remedy cost disparities.

Far more attention needs to be given to the effects of the development of the Common Market on (a) the determination of pay rates across the Community and (b) the convergence of levels of efficiency. The rapid establishment of a monetary union is not going to eliminate the fundamental reasons for disparate rates of growth in pay and productivity. If we are to minimise unemployment, monetary union should follow, not precede, convergence and most, if not all members, will not be ready for it for many years to come. If France and Germany stick to the timetable for political reasons, the economic cost is likely to be high. The key issue that the 1996–7 Inter-Governmental Conference (IGC) should be considering is a more gradual timetable. In the meantime there is a case for reconstituting the ERM to provide greater stability, but with scope for orderly adjustment from time to time, as a prelude to eventual monetary union at a later date.

A NEW ERM?

The difficulties with prematurely fixed exchange rates has led to quite unjustifiable enthusiasm for floating rates. Floating is not the easy answer to exchange rate problems. It does not necessarily bring about the desired balance of payments adjustments, as we see with the problems of the dollar and the yen (discussed in Chapter 11). The instability makes long-term industrial planning difficult. The advantages of a common market are difficult to achieve if fluctuations in exchange rates between members make it impossible for companies to make investment decisions with any confidence in the future movement of costs between different members of the Community. It seems clear that the maximum practicable exchange rate stability is desirable in a common market. But the key phrase is 'the maximum practicable'. If complete stability were practical, we should already effectively be in a monetary union.

There is a need to examine constructively the possibilities of a new ERM either as a general staging post on the way to Monetary Union or as an organisation linking those EU members who have not yet joined EMU with the EMU. The initial British rejection of any such proposals in early 1996 appears shortsighted. The history of the ERM suggests that the problem of any such managed exchange rate system is the difficulty of taking intergovernmental decisions on exchange-rate adjustments. Whatever the provisions for mutual adjustment and symmetry for creditors and debtors, in practice the realities of economic power have remained unchanged, in that other members have not been able to bring about an appreciation of the deutschmark or a reduction in German interest rates when these seemed appropriate for the European economy as a whole. The problem has been one of power relationships, and intergovernmental decision making in a discretionary system, as much as the precise provisions of that system. Hence we either need to change the process of decision making or make the system more automatic and less discretionary – a conclusion equally applicable to attempts to operate a 'fixed' exchange rate system on an international scale.

In the short term the best avenue to explore may be to look for some automatic, or semi-automatic, mechanism for changing parities within the ERM without the necessity for intergovernmental agreement. Here the most promising suggestion seems to be to maintain the present system of wide bands, but with a new provision that parities (i.e. the centres of the bands) should automatically be adjusted to the actual rates at the end of a period: say, a quarter. An alternative to such an automatic mechanism for adjusting parities would be the application of majority voting to exchange rate decisions. But to deal with the present problem this would mean in effect the power to out-vote Germany and then the expectation that the German government would in turn over-ride the Bundesbank. This seems even less practical than the more federal solutions discussed later in this chapter.

At the same time, provisions are needed to combat speculative pressures within the new ERM and worldwide. The basic principle should be that central banks (including the new European Central Bank if EMU has started) should be bound to support automatically any currency coming under pressures which might drive it out of its band. This is the opposite of the Bundesbank's initial proposals, but (as we shall argue in Chapter 11) it is as an essential feature of any attempt to establish managed exchange rates in present world markets.

EUROPEAN DEMAND MANAGEMENT

Along with exchange rate policy, the other major components of macro-economic policy to be affected by monetary union are fiscal and monetary policy, both key issues in relation to the question of demand management and the restoration of full employment. Indeed now that we are well down the road to the establishment of a genuine common market, most of the economic factors determining the advantages and disadvantages of closer political integration are bound up with the problems of demand management, and fiscal policy in particular.

This is not to deny that supply-side policies have a major role to play. It is, however, important to distinguish between those measures which are designed to improve the competitive position of one country, or region, relative to another, and those which will boost employment in Europe or the industrial world as a whole. As was suggested in the last chapter, as far as reducing unemployment is concerned, the key measures are those needed to help firms to expand their effective capacity by ensuring access to long-term finance, reducing the risks of expansion and providing adequate training. Most of these supply-side functions can be undertaken on a national rather than a Community-wide basis: though there will need to be some coordination or federal oversight to ensure that subsidiarity does not lead to a self-defeating competition for jobs in the form of local incentives or concessions.

The importance of looking at demand management on a Community-wide, as well as a national basis, stems from the growing interpenetration of each other's markets. Reducing unemployment by expanding demand on a Community-wide basis will both be more effective and run into fewer problems than action by any one country on its own. One country expanding on its own is in danger of running into balance of payments difficulties through increased imports; and the diversion of part of the increase in demand to imports reduces its effect on output and employment at home. In addition, if unilateral expansion in one country increases its rate of inflation relative to other members, this will weaken its competitive position and accentuate any balance of payments problem. Coordinated or joint expansion will minimise any balance of payments problems, and each country will be able to achieve a higher increase in employment from a given stimulus if other countries take similar action. This would be particularly important in present circumstances where fear of increased budget deficits is deterring many governments from fiscal expansion. The greater effectiveness of coordinated expansion would mean that a temporary stimulus would lead to greater expansion and speed up the eventual improvement in countries' budget deficits.

It is, however, no good those who wish to see more expansionary policies followed in the UK calling for greater European coordination unless at the same time there is a reasonable chance of other governments wishing to pursue the same objectives. If the UK were to wish to follow expansionary demand policies to reduce unemployment and the majority of the Community were not, it would be irrational for the UK to support any move to put greater responsibility for demand management on to a Community-wide basis. If it were more effective, it would merely be more effective in a deflationary direction.

REINTERPRETING MAASTRICHT

If the members of the Community are to act together to achieve full employment and faster growth, we have somehow to extricate ourselves from the transitional provisions of the Maastricht Treaty, and reinstate full employment as a major policy objective. Whether or not the IGC will face up to this remains to be seen. A statement, for example, that monetary union could not take place until unemployment in the Community was down to 5 per cent could revolutionise assumptions about policy, and is an approach which should be considered seriously by those who are both 'pro-European' and concerned with full employment. The first step along this road should be to draw up a set of guidelines directed towards full employment and faster growth. It would then have to be agreed that such guidelines would take precedence over the transitional requirements for inflation rates, budget deficits, interest rates and exchange rates in the Treaty of Maastricht. The aim would remain convergence, but would include convergence towards lower levels of unemployment. Discussion of such a change should be a major concern of the IGC. Unless it is, the Maastricht route to EMU is liable to end in disarray.

Article 103 of the Treaty could provide the opportunity for such an approach by establishing the machinery for coordinating macro-economic policy subject to the limitations imposed by the independence of the Central Bank. Article 103 provides that the Council shall draw up broad guidelines for the economic policies of member states and the Community. This broad statement of policy would be approved by a qualified majority of the Council and reported to the European Parliament; and to ensure closer coordination of economic policies, developments in each country would be monitored in the light of these guidelines and the need for convergence.

In the immediate future the most important point is to find a way round the 'excessive government deficits' provisions, and the 3 per cent limit which rule out the use of counter-cyclical fiscal policy in the recession. Article 104c of the Treaty states that 'Member States shall avoid excessive government deficits', and that the Commission shall examine:

(a) whether the ratio of the planned or actual government deficit to gross domestic product exceeds a reference value, unless
   - either the ratio has declined substantially and continuously and reached a level that comes close to the reference value;

- or, alternatively, the excess over the reference value is only exceptional and temporary and the ratio remains close to the reference value;

(b) whether the ratio of government debt to gross domestic product exceeds a reference value, unless the ratio is sufficiently diminishing and approaching the reference value at a satisfactory pace.

The reference values are specified in the relevant protocol as 3 per cent and 60 per cent respectively, and could be amended; but such arithmetical limits are conceptually erroneous. Budgetary policy should be evaluated on much wider criteria, in particular the macro-economic situation prevailing at the time. But as a tactical expedient it could be argued quite convincingly in the present deflationary situation that it would be reasonable for countries to exceed the 3 per cent limit temporarily by giving a deliberate stimulus to demand; instead of which the Community is inflicting untold damage on itself and prolonging the recession by adhering to inappropriate and misconceived limits, whose only rationale was to avoid the danger of inflationary budget policies.

Again, as the policing of Article 104c depends on a report by the Commission which must 'take into account all relevant factors', it would be possible, if the Commission and Ministers were convinced of the need for expansionary policies, to permit higher deficits for a time without infringing the Treaty. In the longer term, whilst some influential members such as Germany might wish to keep these provisions intact as longer-term guidelines, there is a strong case for amending them when the Treaty next comes to be revised. How expansion would affect the operation of the transitional provisions on price and interest rate convergence is uncertain, but the guiding principle in any new initiative should be that satisfaction of such conditions for monetary union must take second place to the needs of expansion and reducing unemployment.

THE DELORS WHITE PAPER ON UNEMPLOYMENT

Such an initiative would, however, require a revolution in official attitudes, as set out, for example, in the European Commission's

1993 report, generally referred to as the Delors White Paper on Unemployment.[4] The White Paper conspicuously fails to recognise that the key problems at the present time are those of demand management and that the immediate questions in tackling unemployment are thus macro-economic ones. Instead, the report concentrates on what it calls 'rigidities in the labour market', which seems to provide a pretext for attacking all forms of legislation or agreements to protect labour, combined with a general call to cut labour costs. A major theme running through the report is that the high level of European unemployment is 'structural', thus implying that it cannot to be reduced by raising the level of demand. This assertion is untenable. At current levels of unemployment there can be little doubt that demand would have to rise a long way before the reduction of unemployment began to be affected by the emergence of 'structural' problems in the normal sense of the word: that is, problems specific to particular regions or industries. It is only 'structural' in the sense that there is now inadequate capacity to employ the labour force fully.

Macro-Economic Policy

The White Paper's approach to fiscal policy is reminiscent of Treasury views in the 1920s and 1930s described in Chapter 2:

> turning on the tap of government spending and creating money can, like a narcotic, produce a short-lived illusion of well-being. But the return to reality would be all the more painful when we had to repair the damage wreaked by inflation and external imbalances. The worst damage would be higher unemployment.

This lurid outburst is almost the sole reference to the possibility of expansionary demand management in 200 pages. The only other references to budgetary policies call for more deflationary action. The bulk of the discussion on unemployment is concerned with labour costs in a manner strongly reminiscent of the 1920s.

The White Paper does cite Article 103 (mentioned above), which provides for coordination of macro-economic policies, as the appropriate framework for tackling the unemployment problem, but then strikingly fails to give any consideration to the question of coordinated demand expansion. The key paragraph on budgetary policy says that:

> Action in the budgetary area depends on an assessment of the likely impact on demand and on business and consumer confidence of changes in the present budgetary stance. In 1991 and 1992, Member States have allowed budget deficits to deteriorate since it was considered that this would lend a measure of support to domestic demand . . . By mid-1993, however, Member States reached a consensus that no room for manoeuvre in the short term was available: any additional deterioration in budget deficits was more likely to depress overall demand through its negative effect on confidence, than to support it.

The reference to confidence has a resonance with similar discussions in the interwar period. What it says in effect is: 'While you and I appreciate that cutting taxes or raising government expenditure would in itself stimulate demand, businessmen and consumers who do not understand these things would lose confidence and hold back their expenditure.' (The more usual version is that financial markets would lose confidence with adverse effects on exchange rates and interest rates.) Such an assertion about business or consumer confidence is questionable, in that at the present time there could be major support in the business community (certainly in this country) for increased public investment, particularly in construction. Neither are consumers likely to have their confidence weakened by tax cuts. The more practical question is how financial markets would be likely to react to any increase in budget deficits. Here the argument is in effect that while Finance Ministers or Treasury officials may realise that cutting taxes or increasing public investment will increase demand, people working in financial institutions are unable to appreciate this and will lose confidence if there is any increase in public deficits. Instead of using such fears as an excuse for inaction, the more appropriate response would be to exercise the necessary political and intellectual leadership to execute expansionary policies with sufficient conviction to minimise any threat to confidence – rather than making self-fulfilling prophecies of disaster.

So much for the short term. The discussion of budgetary policy in the medium term is also somewhat confused, with a call for tighter budget policies to encourage growth and employment! The report says that: 'Budgetary policy will have to contribute to the medium-term goal of more growth and employment essentially in two ways: (i) achieving debt sustainability and (ii) contributing to the necessary increase in national saving. The first goal is necessary to reduce the burden that unbalanced budgetary policies exert on monetary policies and on fiscal flexibility.' The argument appears to be that the deflationary effect of reducing budget deficits would be more than offset by the expansionary effect of a consequent reduction in interest rates. This is clearly unlikely as we saw in Chapter 6. As the experience of any recession will testify, interest rates in Europe (as in the US) are basically determined by central banks and not by the level of government borrowing. Moreover the stimulating effect of any reduction in interest rates seems extremely unlikely to be as strong, or as predictable, as that of changes in government expenditure or taxation. Again it is highly misleading to suggest that the key factor limiting investment in new capacity is lack of saving, rather than lack of confidence in continued expansion. More public saving might be needed as a consequence of industry's desire to invest heavily in new capacity but it is not a means of creating that desire.

Investment in Trans-European Networks

The one positive proposal of the White Paper in terms of demand expansion is the proposal for a European programme of public investment in infrastructure. This would be directed at trans-European networks in transport, energy and telecommunications, and would involve expenditure averaging 20 billion ECU (£16 billion) a year from 1994 to 1999. Of this, 5.3 billion ECU would come from the Community budget, 6.7 billion from the European Investment Bank in the form of loans, 7.0 billion from the issue of new Union Bonds and 1.0 billion from convertible bonds issued by the European Investment Fund. The proceeds from issuing Union Bonds would be lent directly to project promoters (public sector agencies or private companies). By lending directly to non-governmental bodies, this new source of finance would not raise public sector deficits in the countries involved and thus would provide an ingenious way of getting round the inhibitions on further increases in public debt. It would combine the advantage of speeding up the execution of desirable investment projects, which would meet the interest charges out of commercial receipts, with that of stimulating a reduction in unemployment. Unfortunately this constructive proposal has gained little support from finance ministers, or even the more modest proposal by the President of the Commission to use surplus budgetary funds for this purpose.

Labour Costs

Most of the proposals in the White Paper are based on two fallacies discussed in Chapter 8, namely that unemployment is primarily a problem of labour costs, and that the high incidence of unemployment among unskilled workers means that there is an especial shortage of unskilled jobs. The White Paper complains that the 'relatively high cost of unskilled labour is encouraging investment in rationalisation and holding back job creation in services'. It envisages a more 'labour-intensive' European economy with a higher proportion of low-paid service jobs in the private sector, such as domestic service – in effect, a reversion towards prewar society. The one plausible version of a more labour-intensive path for a relatively affluent society, one that would satisfy the demand for better public provision of education and health care, is dismissed on the grounds that 'current levels of public expenditure, particularly in the social field, have become unsustainable and have used up resources which could have been channelled into productive investment'. This is a further example of the political bias against public services that runs through the report rather than of any economic analysis. With the persistently high levels of unemployment in the last decade the allegation that public expenditure has been using resources that might have been devoted to investment is clearly unsupportable. Europe cannot at the same time both be lacking resources for investment and need to create more service jobs to mop up unemployment.

Apart from the economic fallacy underlying the case for cutting the cost of unskilled work, it would have serious social consequences. At some points the document acknowledges this and suggests that these effects should be mitigated by some form of income support. Elsewhere it argues the case for reducing the cost of unskilled labour by reducing 'non-wage costs' (rather than wages) in the form both of employers' social security contributions and income tax payments. (Presumably the latter are regarded as a labour cost in that lowering employees' own tax payments would enable employers to cut wages further.) The report is confused as to whether such measures are to be directed at all labour or only the less skilled. In so far as they are envisaged 'particularly for less skilled labour', the practical difficulties of defining 'less skilled' would mean in practice 'low paid'. In other words, the basic concept is to give employers the maximum financial incentive to cut wages for those who are currently low paid.

One of the proposals linked to the reduction of non-wage costs is to replace any loss of revenue by imposing environmentally friendly taxes on energy and industrial pollution. The latter deserve, however, to be considered in their own right rather than linked to a disputable case for reducing employers' social insurance contributions.

In the EU, as in the UK, however, the most important aspect of wages policy in facilitating the adoption of policies to reduce unemployment concerns the determination of money, rather than real wages: that is the need for bargaining structures that will avoid inflationary wage–price spirals and hence the deflationary demand policies adopted to deal with them during the 1980s. The report does refer to the July 1992 statement by the Social Partners on these lines, but fails to recognise that this is the one most essential requirement for expansion without inflation.

The various policy prescriptions based on the concept of a low wage, labour-intensive path for the European economy (which incidentally conflicts with those parts of the report devoted to high technology industries) should be seen as a whole and rejected. They are the antithesis of what is desirable as a recipe for an acceptable future for Europe either socially or industrially, or for its role in the world economy. For the EU to compete more successfully with low wage industries in Eastern Europe or the Third World would only aggravate the problems of those countries' balance of payments. The need is rather for Europe to compete more successfully with Japan in advanced industrial technology at the expense of the Japanese balance of payments surplus (see Chapter 11).

While the Report's belated recognition of the importance of tackling mass unemployment is to be welcomed, the melange of remedies proposed bears little relation to the present nature of the unemployment problem, above all the need to move away from the present deflationary prescriptions for macroeconomic policies.

A FEDERAL GOVERNMENT FOR EUROPE?

The nature of any European approach to economic policy cannot be separated from the question of its future constitution. Conscious direction of European economic policy requires more than a European Central Bank. Immediately the need for an active role for government in economic policy is admitted, it becomes impossible to separate the problems of achieving full economic integration from those of further political integration: that is, some form of federation. The case for some European machinery (e.g. a Community budget or Central Bank), is that when joint or European-wide action is needed it may be easier for one Federal institution to move in the appropriate direction than to get agreement between a number of national governments. But note the argument is basically a political one about decision making, rather than an economic one: for example, in economic terms, an agreement that every country should cut its national VAT by 5 per cent would have the same effect as reducing a European-wide VAT by 5 per cent.

The gradualist or empirical approach of pursuing integration step by step without considering too closely where it may ultimately lead has now been taken as far, or further, than is productive. As the revolt of the Euro-sceptics demonstrates, further attempts to evade the issue of what sort of Federal constitution the Community is heading for, with or without the UK, can only lead to confusion and frustration. The term 'Federal' is used here to cover a situation in which there is some form of European government (Presidential or Cabinet) either directly elected, or drawn from Parliament, with specified powers not subject to veto by individual states i.e. what is often called a 'Confederal' constitution. The possible variants are numerous: taking existing models, a directly elected executive President, as in the US; a Prime Minister and Cabinet drawn from Parliament, as in the UK; a combination of the two as in France, and so on. There could, for example, be a directly elected Cabinet with a minister from each country but elected by a European electorate.

The major political issue is the question of whether the European Union should have a common foreign and defence policy, frequently the principal foundation for the formation of a Federation. The interrelationship between political and economic integration arises from the effects of creating an elected Federal government with major powers and the consequent European budget. A European defence force under a European government would naturally give rise to a European defence budget financed by Community-wide taxation. A democratic Federal government powerful enough to be responsible for foreign policy and defence would also be a suitable candidate to bear the responsibility for major economic policy issues.

In so far as the Maastricht provisions dealing with foreign policy and defence are as yet untried, it may seem early days to consider further integration in this field. Yet what do we gain from the retention of separate national armed forces? Churchill called for a European Army in 1950. Their main use is now for international policing rather than self-defence, and such action must always be undertaken on an international basis, albeit with differing degrees of success. The US alliance could remain but NATO would be replaced by a bilateral American–European defence agreement.

The political machinery of Federation may be particularly important to potential new members, such as Poland, Hungary and the Czech Republic, who are not yet ready for full economic integration. Membership of a democratic European Federation could be the best guarantee for ex-Communist countries of the preservation of democracy. Of course, further membership of the Community will make it more heterogeneous and hence Federation more difficult. On the other hand, if membership does increase, the difficulty of intergovernmental action will become more acute. The prospect of additional members then cuts both ways in the argument for and against federation.

A Federal Budget

Community countries at present spend about 2.5 per cent of GDP on defence, but considerable savings in manpower and procurement costs might be achieved with a common defence force. Thus even the advanced level of public expenditure resulting from this politically very significant movement towards Federalism would not give a Federal Government much leverage in demand management without spectacular variations in its surplus or deficits. An additional area where there might be a good case for a combined Federal and state regime is in the field of pensions, unemployment pay and other social security benefits. As one of the conditions for increased mobility of labour, social security rights will need to be easily transferable between countries. It will not, however, be practical to have equal levels of benefit in countries within the Community as long as there are significantly different levels of real wages. But there could be a uniform system of *wage-related* unemployment, sickness and retirement contributions and benefits, provided there were different minimum flat rates of benefit in different countries (at any rate for some years), based on the average level of wages in that country. The actual administration would remain on a national basis but the rules would be Community-wide. Such a scheme could be a powerful instrument both for equalisation and stabilisation.

Any initial federal budget is, however, likely to involve a relatively low level of gross federal revenue and expenditure which would limit its impact for purposes of demand management.[5] Any significant changes in the surplus or deficit in macro-economic terms could appear very large in relation to the size of the federal budget. Hence national budgets could not be regarded solely as instruments for dealing with *differences* in macro-economic conditions between countries. A high degree of budgetary coordination between states and linked action would still be needed in conditions, such as those prevailing today, where the whole of the Community is suffering from a major deficiency in demand and heavy unemployment. In other words, while the existence of the type of Federation we are envisaging here, with only defence and social security as major Federal spending functions, would go some way towards giving the Federal government adequate powers of fiscal demand management, there would still need to be some coordination of national budgetary policies. There is no simple way of overcoming this difficulty; but it could be eased by, for example, giving the Federal government power to lower (or raise) VAT across the Community whilst making good the loss to individual states (or keeping the additional revenue) by means of more (or less) Federal borrowing.

Tax Convergence

In considering the factors determining the size, and hence the leverage of the Federal budget, attention naturally tends to be focused primarily on the extent of federal expenditure, which then determines the magnitude of revenue required. But the economic implications of the Federal government's revenue depends not only on its total size, but also how it is raised. Indeed just as there are pressures for centralising or standardising functions involving expenditure, there are also pressures towards uniformity on the tax side. For example, although differences in indirect taxes are still possible within a Federation, there are practical limits on such differences – such as bottle-laden cars and vans streaming through the Port of Dover – which arise from the Common Market and will therefore come into play irrespective of any further political integration. The other major area where there will be growing pressure towards uniformity is the field of company taxation and taxation of the highly mobile rich. Hence where there are taxes which are uniform across the Community (or nearly so), but still remain in national hands, they will only be able to be changed substantially by common agreement. This may come not only to limit individual countries' ability to determine their own levels of public expenditure, but also their ability to adopt differing macro-economic policy stances.

This would suggest that the taxes which are under most pressure to converge would also be the ones most suitable for raising money for federal purposes. This may conflict with the desire of the Federation to have at its disposal taxes which are either good automatic stabilisers or which can be altered quickly as instruments of macro policy. Company taxation and taxation of the very rich do not rate strongly on the latter criteria. But a Community VAT combined with National VATs would satisfy both criteria, as could social security contributions. Tax convergence is just another way in which the development of the Common Market is weakening the ability of individual states to influence their own economies; and unless their lost power is replaced by a corresponding increase in the power of a federal government, we shall be reverting to a potentially unstable, high unemployment pre-Keynesian environment.

Exchange Rates

In an essay on the 'Economic Aspects of Federalism', first published in 1940, the great liberal economist Lionel Robbins wrote:

> It would be wrong to say that economic advantage was the *raison d'être* of federation; the *raison d'être* of federation is the preservation of justice and civilization; and justice and civilization involve much more than economic advantage. But it is none the less true that without a solid basis of harmonious economic relations, these values are likely to be jeopardized. It is no exaggeration to say that a federation will stand or fall by the adequacy of its economic constitution.[6]

It is interesting that Robbins envisaged the possibility of restrictions on interstate trade and the continued existence of separate currencies within a Federation – at any rate for an initial period – but with the important premise in each case that policy should be determined by the Federal, not national, authorities. At this stage in history the question of restrictions on trade within any European Federation would not arise among the mainstream members, but could possibly arise (at least initially) in the case of new Eastern bloc members: we should not automatically exclude them as possible members of a new Federation on this count.

Although the circumstances are different from what he had in mind, Robbins' suggestion of Federal determination of exchange rates could be pertinent to the problems Europe faces today. The ERM was quite realistic in providing that changes in exchange rate parities required mutual agreement; this is to some extent merely an acknowledgement of the fact that adjustments between two countries can never be wholly unilateral. The difficulty has been to secure that agreement. There was nothing in the constitution of the ERM that prevented the necessary realignments taking place except the impracticability of intergovernmental agreement. Is then the condition for a discretionary system of adjustable exchange rates some form of majority voting or Federal institution? It may seem difficult at the moment to think in these terms, but there is a serious case for considering whether the establishment of Federal institutions might well be followed by a period of exchange rate management under Federal control before the establishment of full monetary union. In gradualist terms, the extension of democratic control over European institutions should precede monetary union.

The Federal Vision

The major constitutional question which the IGC should now be discussing is the possible eventual form of a democratic Federal constitution, rather than tinkering with the minutiae of past Treaties. The responsibilities of a Federal government would include foreign policy and defence. It would also have responsibilities in the field of macro-economic policy and a commitment to full employment. If such a Federation were to be established in the 1990s, a monetary union should not be created until the Federation had been in existence for some years and the necessary degree of real convergence achieved by the development of the Common Market. In this initial period an exchange rate mechanism would be needed which put adjustments in exchange rates into the hands of the Federal government. Before, however, any worthwhile progress can be made in this direction, the EU needs to break away from the monetarist philosophy underlying Maastricht and start thinking seriously about restoring full employment. Further integration along the lines set out at Maastricht is merely a prescription for accentuating Europe's unemployment problem.

Continued economic integration without a federal government may well satisfy those who believe that government has no part to play in the stabilisation or development of the economy and would be consistent with the New Orthodoxy. But it represents an effective abandonment of the whole postwar consensus on which the Economic Community was originally based and which underlay the successful economic development of Western Europe in the postwar years. An economic union without a democratic government responsible for economic policy would be a headless monster. We must face the fact that Europe must either adopt some form of Federal government or call a halt to progress to economic union short of monetary union.

Federation will only come, however, if the people of Europe are fired by a vision of what it may achieve. The creation (and break-up) of federations is charged with emotion. The impetus to create a European federation will only come from a heartfelt urge for peace, freedom and prosperity, rather than from any dry calculus of penalties and advantages. But central to such objectives must be the re-establishment of full employment, and any new constitution for Europe must have a bias towards, not against, its achievement. All we have today is a blueprint for a Europe that may seem good for business, but ignores what should be one of the fundamental objectives of a democratic industrialised society: namely, full employment.

11 A Global Payments Strategy

Whilst economic cooperation within the European Union has become progressively closer (albeit without any effective attack on unemployment), cooperation between governments to tackle world-wide economic problems has sunk to a low point. The shift in the emphasis of macro-economic policy during the late 1970s and early 1980s towards combating inflation rather than maintaining full employment represented a watershed in international economic policy. The fixed exchange rate mechanism established at Bretton Woods had broken down; the world economy reverted to the prewar state of chronic mass unemployment; and the prevalence of monetarist and free market thinking among the political leadership of the industrial nations effectively ruled out any major structural reforms in the management of the world economy.

This is a far cry from the spirit of the 1944 Bretton Woods agreement which, as we saw in Chapter 3, set up a framework for effective collaboration between the major powers to operate a new international financial system compatible with full employment. The architects of that agreement recognised that the maintenance of full employment in the industrialised countries would not only benefit the industrialised countries themselves, but the less developed countries would also gain from the increasing demand for their commodities and manufactured goods. Emphasising the need for full employment and steady growth was not to be regarded as a selfish objective of the industrialised countries, but as a key part of any strategy for world-wide growth. A similar common interest lay in minimising fluctuations in industrial activity and thus avoiding violent swings in commodity prices which could harm both the industrialised countries and primary producers.

THE BRETTON WOODS SYSTEM

The fixed exchange rate regime established at Bretton Woods was designed to avoid a situation whereby countries in balance of payments deficit, or whose exchange rates came under pressure, automatically had to deflate to the point where they would no longer enjoy full employment. To this end the system provided that exchange rates could be changed where there was agreed to be a structural imbalance in a country's balance of payments (rather than excessive demand). It also in principle accepted that creditor as well as debtor countries had an obligation to ensure the necessary adjustments: the scarce currency clause (although never in the event invoked) would have allowed debtor countries to discriminate against a persistent creditor. Subject to these provisos, however, it was basic to the system that demand management was the normal means to be employed to remedy short-term imbalances. The underlying assumption was that with exchange rates fixed at appropriate levels such imbalances reflected excessive demand in the debtor countries or (in principle at any rate) deficient demand in creditor countries. This assumption, which was in many ways an inheritance of the old Gold Standard regime, was, however, in practice more pertinent in an era of generally high demand.

As operated by the IMF this system still had a deflationary bias because it was bound to be asymmetrical, with virtually all the pressure being put on those in balance of payments deficit to deflate. This was partly due to the fundamental fact that deficits can put direct financial pressure on countries who incur them (and thus put them in the hands of the IMF), whereas those in surplus can simply accumulate exchange reserves and are liable to no such pressure. Also, with full employment generally prevailing and the US being the main creditor, there was no general case for pressing creditors to increase demand. By the standards of the 1980s and 1990s, however, the deflationary aspects of the system which concerned many of us at the time now appear less significant. Compared with the 1980s and 1990s it was a 'Golden Age'.

The break-up of the Bretton Woods fixed exchange rate system in the early 1970s reflected two main factors, both of which were also fundamental causes of the collapse of the ERM, as we saw in Chapter 10. The first is the difficulty of getting intergovernmental agreement on changes in exchange rates when the existing structure is no longer appropriate. The second is the increasing importance of capital movements in determining or putting pressure on exchange rates. There is also a fashion cycle in which fixed and floating rates tend to alternate as the disadvantages of either system lead to a reaction against it.

The Bretton Woods fixed exchange rate phase was one in which fiscal policy tended to take precedence over monetary policy as the major instrument of macro-economic policy. But the growth of mobile capital and the switch to floating rates during the 1970s increased the importance of interest rate policy as a means of influencing exchange rates; and then by the 1980s the rise of monetarism was making changes in interest rates the only fashionable instrument of macro-economic control. We now face the practical dilemma that an interest rate policy that may be appropriate for exchange rate purposes may be inappropriate for the needs of the domestic economy (as in the case of the UK while it was in the ERM) or vice versa (as in the case of Germany). A further related change is that interest rate policy, like exchange rate policy, has increasingly become a matter of international concern: so that of the two instruments, fiscal policy is the one over which national governments have most effective control.

Under the New Orthodoxy the policy assumptions and the mechanics of the world monetary system have acquired a deflationary bias. This is not a simple matter of floating or fixed exchange rates. The fixed rate system in the ERM had as strong, or stronger, deflationary pressures than the floating regime which replaced it. But the floating rate regime in the world as a whole also has a deflationary bias because the growth of mobile financial capital puts pressure on governments to follow 'orthodox' (i.e. deflationary) policies. Summit meetings and gatherings of finance ministers and the pronouncements of the OECD and the IMF have tended to reinforce these tendencies.

THE MOVEMENT OF CAPITAL

In order to assess the shortcomings, or merits of the present 'system' (if it can be dignified as such), it is first necessary to postulate the objectives of any international exchange and payments system. In the broadest terms it should facilitate worldwide growth of output and living standards; to which should be added a distributional objective in that the fruits of growth should in some sense be 'fairly' distributed between countries; or in more practical terms, the abolition of underemployment, poverty, disease and political autocracy in the poorer countries should rank highly in comparison with further increases in living standards in the richest countries. It should also avoid stimulating inflation, particularly by violent fluctuations in the prices of primary products.

The diffusion of technology and the pace of development are closely dependent on the international movement of capital and aid. With the growth of multinational companies, direct investment has become increasingly important, both through the construction of plant and through the purchase of existing firms or property. In addition in the grey area between direct and purely financial investment, the purchase of shares with or without the immediate achievement of majority control may have longer-term industrial consequences.

In devising a contemporary concept of how the world economy should operate, it is important to consider both the actual and desirable movement of long-term capital and aid between countries or areas. At one time it seemed natural to work on a tacit model whereby the leading industrial country or countries, starting with the UK in the nineteenth century, and in the early postwar period the US, had a substantial balance of payments surplus and invested heavily in less developed countries (as well as in other industrialised countries). The emergence of Japan as a major creditor, with the US in chronic deficit and Western Europe generally more or less in balance, has shattered that model, as has the varying experience of the rest of the world. In addition, the growth of financial capital movements has meant that the pattern of capital flows in total may differ markedly from that of productive investment on its own.

The historic model of more advanced industrial countries with balance of payments surpluses investing in, or granting aid to, less developed countries provided a means of enabling the latter to catch up. This depended, of course, on their loans being at reasonably low rates of interest; the reliance on the international banking system to recycle the OPEC surpluses to developing countries provoked a catastrophic debt crisis when interest rates rose. Nevertheless in seeking a desirable and sustainable pattern of payments surpluses and deficits and the associated flows of long-term investment, it seems reasonable to assume that the richer countries should be in surplus (or at least balance), even though the fact that an advanced country like the US may have highly developed financial markets and also be an attractive area for direct investment means that industrial pre-eminence is no longer necessarily synonymous with being a net exporter of capital. But both the long-term future of the US itself, and the interests of the rest of the world, suggest that this should be the appropriate policy objective.

If, however, the US were in fact to revert to being a rich country in surplus, its role as the main provider of international currency reserves would no longer be tenable. The beneficial effects to the world economy of the US swinging from surplus to deficit, thus ending the dollar shortage and providing a plentiful supply of dollars, the main reserve currency, have gone largely unrecognised. The simple-minded foreign critics of the US deficit should think themselves lucky that it remains so substantial, especially as long as there are no signs of the Japanese surplus declining to a similar extent. Indeed, unless the US could improve its balance of payments solely at the expense of the Japanese, what would happen to the rest of us? While the reduction of the Japanese surplus might be regarded as desirable irrespective of who are the gainers, the reduction of the US deficit cannot be regarded as desirable without consideration of whose balance of payments would deteriorate as a consequence.

The history of the postwar period demonstrates that it is very much easier to operate a system in which the country providing the main reserve currency (i.e. the US) is in deficit rather than surplus, with two provisos: that people in other countries are willing to finance the deficit by holding various forms of dollar assets; and that it does not respond to the deficit by deflating and dragging the rest of the world into a slump. Then other countries' desire to increase their reserves with the growth of trade (and the increasing need to be able to counteract short-term capital movements) can be met by their holding increasing amounts of the reserve currency, thus helping to finance that country's deficit. But if the yen were to become the main reserve currency and Japan were to remain in surplus, there might well be a shortage of reserve currency.

There would then be a need to increase world liquidity, in the sense of the supply of reserve currency, by increases in Special Drawing Rights with the IMF or other means.

THE SURPLUS PROBLEM

Although it is healthy to consider the problems of debtor and surplus countries in general terms, at any period of history these problems are specific to particular countries or groups of countries. In the immediate aftermath of war, the US had the greatest surplus on current account and the scarce currency clause was aimed at the dollar. Today the major imbalances are those of Japan and the US. Over the three years 1992–4 the Japanese current surplus averaged $126 billion a year, but only about one-fifth of this was offset by direct investment and aid which averaged $16 billion and $3 billion a year respectively. In the same period the US current deficit averaged $104 billion; and US official aid averaged $16 billion but the net inflow of direct investment from all sources was only $19 billion a year. The remainder of the gap was closed by foreign investment in US securities and dollar holdings. The growing volume of foreign-held dollar investments has created a potentially dangerous situation if there were any loss of confidence in the dollar or the US economy. A flight from the dollar combined with massive sales of US equities and bonds could seriously jeopardise the stability of world financial markets.

The fact that so much of the problem revolves around the US and Japan should make it easier in a way to resolve, because any bilateral action is likely to work in the desired direction from a world point of view. It also makes it easier to see the basic industrial and technological factors involved and not over-rate the effectiveness of any change in exchange rates. But it does mean that Japan as the major creditor nation must play a much larger part than it has hitherto in any rethinking of international payments arrangements. It is remarkable how little attention has been paid to the Japanese perspective, reflecting perhaps the Japanese reluctance to assume the full role of a major international power. But as the Japanese foreign minister, Yukihiko Ikeda, has remarked, Japan's image as 'economic giant and political infant' is no longer tolerable.[1] An obvious part of any solution would be for Japan to increase substantially its aid to developing countries, particularly if it is concerned about the effects of any reduction of its trade deficit on employment in Japan.

Nevertheless, although the surplus problem is at present largely specific to Japan, any new approach should consider the introduction of general sanctions or pressures on countries whose surpluses exceed the outflow of productive capital to the rest of the world. These new measures should either exert pressure to reduce the current surplus or facilitate its translation into productive investment and aid to the remainder of the world, particularly the poorest parts of it. One solution would be to lay down that a specified proportion of any country's current surplus should be deposited either with the World Bank or a new financing institution with a minimal return: for example, indexed against price increases but with a zero real rate of interest. These deposits would then be used to finance long-term 'soft' loans on favourable terms to developing countries.

The surplus problem is linked to the objective of increasing and stabilising the flow of capital and aid to the Third World, and avoiding the re-emergence of the type of debt problems that were experienced in the 1980s with the consequent series of write-offs and rescheduling. Leaving the OPEC surpluses to be recycled to developing countries by the banking system turned out to be a major disaster, aggravated by the subsequent rise in interest rates (which was itself a consequence of the inflationary effects of the oil price boom). While the OPEC experience may seem an unique event, there will no doubt be other unforeseen scenarios where a *laissez-faire* approach may be equally disastrous. The basic need is to increase very substantially the proportion of capital movements to the Third World going through publicly owned international institutions on terms that do not favour richer creditors and will not impoverish poorer debtors, as was envisaged when the World Bank was founded.[2] One of the Bank's original functions was to develop a rational pattern of long-term investment, both between industrialised countries and from industrialised to developing countries, and that the network of countries' balance of payments surpluses and deficits should be consistent with these movements. The Bank was then seen as a rather more wide-ranging guardian of such movements than it has actually become.

A WORLD PAYMENTS STRATEGY

A long-term strategy for world payments is needed to formulate a coherent approach to the movement of productive investment, the problems of world liquidity and a consistent exchange rate policy. If exchange rates are a major determinant of trade balances, any targeted pattern of rates should depend on the pattern of surpluses and deficits that it is desired to achieve – at least as between the major countries or groupings. Exchange rates will not in themselves, of course, necessarily bring about such a pattern. There may, for example, be no yen/dollar rate which will bring about the desired adjustment in the Japanese/US imbalance.[3] But there is little sense in trying to determine a reasonable target for such a rate without at the same time having in mind a desired outcome in balance of payments terms. Moreover, if we are to achieve full employment and eschew the use of deflationary policies to remedy balance of payments deficits, exchange rate policy must be used as the main macro-economic instrument for adjusting trade balances and directed towards balance of payments objectives.

The difficulty in getting agreement between the major players on exchange rates lies thus partly in the complex interaction of exchange rate changes, but also in the problem (largely ignored) of providing a rational set of objectives in terms of a desired and sustainable world-wide pattern of surpluses and deficits. It is sometimes argued that any attempt to postulate consistent balance of payments objectives is unnecessary and futile on the grounds that a market mechanism is available to perform the reconciliation task.[4] But that is merely to say that in the event different countries' surpluses and deficits must cancel out. It is, however, only by clarifying some form of *target* pattern of surpluses and deficits that there is any rational basis for setting actual exchange rates or adopting other measures to influence the pattern of world payments. Foreign exchange markets left to themselves do not necessarily lead to anything like a desired pattern, because they may be dominated by speculative short-term movements of funds. Neither can the problems of imbalance be resolved solely by domestic demand management, save at the expense of massive unemployment in the deficit countries.

As regards the US in particular, it is one thing to say that if an increase in competitiveness *led* to an improvement in the US trade balance, this would necessitate an increase in domestic saving (i.e. a decrease in the fiscal deficit): this need involve no change in employment. It is quite another thing to imply that a decrease in the US fiscal deficit would of itself automatically improve the trade deficit. Without an increase in competitiveness as a result of a change in the exchange rate, or improved industrial efficiency, deflationary fiscal measures would only achieve such an improvement at the expense of a multiple decline in employment.

The task for an international secretariat of analysing the existing and potential pattern of world payments in this way to devise strategic objectives may seem formidable, but it is analogous to the task facing the planning function in a large multinational company. The fundamental problem is not analytical, but political. The multinational has an over-arching managerial structure and can take decisions. The nation states have as yet to take decisions by negotiation and agreement. One of the fundamental problems of any new settlement is thus to devise a system capable of reaching the necessary decisions, and conversely not trying to implement a system which requires decisions which the political structure is incapable of making (a recent example being the failure to agree on a general adjustment of exchange rates within the ERM). The immediate essential therefore is to concentrate the power of decision making into a relatively small number of hands. This was much easier in 1944 than it is today: at any rate as far as formal structures are concerned, for instance in the United Nations. Informal structures such as G7 can be kept relatively small, but they are undemocratic in the sense that the interests of other countries remain unrepresented. This has led to the suggestion that the UN should have an economic equivalent of the Security

Council, which in many ways has been remarkably successful in the political field.[5]

INSTITUTIONAL REFORM

With the ending of the Bretton Woods fixed exchange rate system, the Fund has become largely isolated from the affairs of the industrialised countries and increasingly concerned with giving assistance to developing countries, including more recently the countries formerly behind the iron curtain.[6] The Fund is thus tending to operate increasingly in what was formerly the Bank's territory. International financial policy, in so far as it exists, emanates from the G7, Group. The OECD has no real operational role but survives as a research secretariat and the club with the widest membership of industrialised countries. The less developed countries look to the UN and its agencies for consideration of the policy issues in which they are mainly concerned. A fundamental external review of this institutional framework is long overdue.

The Bretton Woods institutions were originally set up under the auspices of the UN, although they have always tended to operate separately from it. Any rationalisation of existing organisations should bring them under the UN umbrella. But this must be done in such a way as to create an overall supervising body sufficiently small, but representative, to be effective. This problem will be eased in so far as regional groupings of countries develop. The EU is at the moment a unique case, but over the years other looser groups may well develop. Even at the moment the US, Japan and the EU could provide a powerful nexus for any new initiative if they were prepared to work together.

The degree to which any international system should operate (a) automatically under pre-ordained rules or (b) in an *ad hoc* or discretionary manner depends on the extent to which international (or more accurately supranational) decision taking is practical. The less effective such decision taking, the greater the need to provide some degree of automaticity. There is thus a need to consider the possible creation of new international decision-making machinery hand-in-hand with any new framework of rules and objectives.

A NEW EXCHANGE RATE REGIME

To make the achievement of full employment a key objective in any new structure for world payments (as it originally was in Bretton Woods) we must find ways of obviating the adoption of deflationary demand policies to remedy balance of payments deficits or exchange rate crises. This means that the system must: (a) avoid exchange rates being determined by short-term capital movements rather than basic trade objectives; (b) ensure that rates can be adjusted as changing economic circumstances require (e.g. trade performance and relative inflation rates); whilst (c) having the means to deal with speculative exchange rate crises.

As far as the exchange rate regime itself is concerned, this suggests that any new agreement should be based on a scheme for managed rates, but one which is more flexible than Bretton Woods or the ERM.

> Some critics of exchange rate agreements argue that there is no reason to suppose that policy-makers can take a better long-run view of exchange rates than the market. The difficulty with this view is that the foreign exchange markets are dominated by short-run speculation, including beliefs about what monetary authorities will do next. This short-run focus is due partly to the fact that, in a world of volatile exchange rates, the premium is in assessing short-run market developments, not longer-run trends. Given that larger and volatile funds are driven by expectations, fundamentals work slowly and feebly.[7]

An important part of the case against free floating and the consequent instability is that it is increasingly inappropriate in a world of international industrial investment by multinationals and growing trade interdependence. Exchange rate instability prejudices the rationality of any investment decisions either in plant, or in sales and distribution networks. Moreover the more unstable rates are, the less effective they are as an economic instrument in influencing longer-term industrial decisions.[8] With a high degree of instability, only large changes in rates tend to have any effect on firms' strategies.

On the other hand a 'fixed' rate system is vulnerable to disruptive macro-economic effects of exchange rate crises and the deflationary bias they impose on monetary and fiscal policies. These stem from the inability of countries to make changes in their rates until they are forced upon them by a crisis. There are two possible approaches to remedying this defect. One is to try to make international decision-making on rates more effective, the other to make changes in rates more automatic. The difficulties of reaching such decisions by intergovernmental consultation has not yet been thoroughly analysed. It involves the directly conflicting trade interests of a shift in parity between two countries, the susceptibility of governments to pressure from financial institutions, and not least, the need for finance ministers to deny that any change (particularly a devaluation) will take place until it has done so; as a consequence, for a finance minister to devalue has been virtually equivalent to committing political suicide, a very important practical factor. The problem is to devise an effective and continuing *international* mechanism for taking decisions on exchange rates. This would be easier if any adjustments were relatively small and infrequent, rather than frequent and traumatic as in a fixed rate system. The intrinsic difficulties of international decision making on exchange rates has long been recognised. Harry White's original proposals prior to Bretton Woods envisaged that an international monetary fund would have to have the authority to determine exchange rates.[9] Examination of the corresponding problem in the case of the European Union in Chapter 10 suggested that a European Federal government may be needed to operate the ERM satisfactorily.

TARGET ZONES

In trying to evolve an exchange rate regime which would avoid the more obvious and serious drawbacks of either the original Bretton Woods system or free floating, the Williamson target zone proposals are still a valuable starting point.[10] Williamson envisages the establishment of target zones $\pm x$ per cent of a parity value fixed in real terms. The parities would be based on the concept that they would be such as to establish balance of payments equilibrium for each country. There would be a degree of automaticity in that nominal rates would be adjusted to allow for different rates of inflation, but adjustments in real rates to allow for changing circumstances would still require conscious decision. If the target zones were sufficiently wide, however (say, ±5 to 10 per cent), the new parity could still be within the target zone. Thus changes could be made in parities without large overnight changes in the actual rates, so avoiding the sort of one-way option for speculators that has been a feature of the Bretton Woods and ERM regimes.

Such a system would still be completely discretionary. A variant, however, would be to combine it with form of 'crawling peg' mechanism whereby parities would be automatically adjusted at the end of a period to, for example, the average actual rate in the period or the end part of it. The borders of the target zone would be automatically adjusted with the change in parity. Such a system would give more weight to market forces and might be less vulnerable to the build-up of speculative pressure. But by the same token it would be more influenced by short-term capital movements and less by fundamental trade objectives.

The world has changed since Bretton Woods, and the target zone idea could provide the basis for an appropriate regime for the new situation, avoiding the extremes of fixed or free floating rates. However, in determining rates, 'equilibrium' exchange rates need to be conceived in terms of formulating a world-wide international payments strategy rather than a series of country by country calculations. Williamson goes part of the way to meeting this by envisaging that instead of aiming at situations where everyone is in balance, account should be taken of the expected flow of long-term investment. This still leaves unanswered, however, the difficult – but fundamental – question of whether the existing flow of long-term investment is desirable or sustainable. (Indeed, such flows are partly a reflection of existing exchange rates. Japanese multinationals might invest more abroad if the yen appreciated further and home production was less competitive.) Any world-wide system must be based on a view of target surpluses and deficits, and corresponding capital movements, between the main participating groups. The most important thing about any exchange rate regime is to have the 'right' exchange rates in that they are appropriate to the circumstances of the day. If they are not, they are either vulnerable to speculation, or damaging if they survive. Britain's entry to the ERM at too high a rate was a prime example.

CURRENCY SPECULATION

An essential condition for the successful operation of any new exchange rate system must be to put the international financial markets in their proper place: that is, as instruments for facilitating international trade and payments and the flow of productive investment, not (as at present) potentially dominant forces in their own right and major sources of instability. This was recognised in the Bretton Woods provisions permitting the control of capital movements. The subsequent abolition of virtually all such controls in the major industrial countries in the intended interests of efficiency has created enormous problems.

International capital markets are not exercising the function of channelling investment efficiently between countries. Movements of capital involving real resources are swamped by purely financial transactions that are speculative in the sense that major investment funds are now held in whatever currency and country has the best short-term prospects, and are subject to transfer by instant decision. The Bank for International Settlements' triennial survey of foreign exchange turnover in April 1995 showed a 50 per cent increase since their 1992 Survey. Turnover had reached $1,230 billion per day, and foreign trade only accounted for 3.5 days' turnover a year: the rest was accounted for by capital movements, mainly short term. The problem is to prevent these short-term transactions, rather than trade payments or real investment, dominating the determination of exchange rates.

Following its historic tendency to sacrifice the interests of industry to those of the City, the UK has been in the forefront of this movement. In North America, where there is traditionally more suspicion of the financial fraternity, the reaction may already have set in. The General Accounting Office[11] has published a report advocating tighter regulation of the derivative markets. But any reversion to the previous system of controls, which permitted some transactions and forbade others, now seems difficult to envisage. The two most promising lines of attack seem to be the possible taxation of foreign exchange transactions and the regulation of financial institutions and markets in such a way as to reduce the magnitude of speculative transactions e.g. by increasing margin requirements. To be effective such measures might require foreign exchange transactions to be concentrated in the hands of recognised financial institutions subject to national and/or international regulatory standards. But there is no reason why such regulation should interfere with the efficient operation of foreign exchange markets. This is a highly difficult and complex question, and the first need is to establish a general climate of opinion in which unregulated speculation is no longer taken for granted.

FINANCIAL MARKETS

The problem of curbing foreign exchange speculation by financial institutions and their clients raises fundamental issues about the relationship between governments and financial 'markets', public discussion of which is long overdue. (The very phrase 'financial markets' prejudges the issue because the actions of markets are in a sense not controllable, whereas those of institutions are.) Governments of both left and right are increasingly influenced by the probable reactions of financial markets whether or not they share the ethos on which those reactions are based. Thus a Chancellor who may, quite rightly, believe that he should raise taxes in a boom and reduce them in a recession may be inhibited from acting in this way if he feels that financial markets may disapprove of such actions. In other words, economic policy is increasingly becoming susceptible to the atavistic prejudices of those working in financial institutions, writing their newsletters, appearing on television and advising their clients.

The two fundamental facts are first that financial institutions are eminently controllable by legislation and the executive because they are wholly dependent on the rule of law for the smooth operation of complex transactions; but the second fact is that such action will not be very effective unless it is taken on an international basis, and that requires intergovernmental agreement. Stricter regulation in one financial centre than elsewhere tends to drive away business, as the Japanese found when they tried to tighten up on trading in derivatives.

(Though it should be remembered that while driving away business may exact a balance of payments penalty in the form of a loss of invisible earnings, this may be compensated for by a lesser vulnerability to speculation. The international use of sterling and the magnitude of transactions in the city of London has always been a mixed blessing for the British economy.)

A peculiar difficulty about this problem is that politicians in or near office are reluctant to discuss it for fear of setting in motion the adverse forces they need to control. The problem has two facets. One is that of the viability of financial institutions and the need for further 'prudential' control. The second, and more far reaching, is to devise direct measures to reduce speculative transactions – as for instance Tobin's proposal to levy a small tax on all foreign exchange transactions, which would make little impact on trade and long-term investment but could deter very short-term transactions.[12]

Those present at Bretton Woods – finance ministers, central bankers and civil servants – all subscribed to a regime which assumed that financial institutions would have to submit to control of foreign exchange transactions. Why should we now submit to a tacit dictatorship of the anonymous employees of financial institutions and their clients: a dictatorship, to give them their due, to which they have never made any overt claim? It is neither in the interests of the democratic process nor in the long-term interests of the financial institution themselves. For if it continues there will eventually be a populist backlash of tremendous force which could go much further than is necessary to put things right. This may seem unlikely in the UK, but in North America, with farmers' and businesses' traditional suspicion of East Coast bankers, anything could happen. It is time that some of the more far-sighted members of the financial community woke up to this, and themselves encouraged informed discussion of the problem.

Whatever can be done to limit speculative capital movements, they may still remain a problem. We therefore also need to strengthen the international banking arrangements to counter them. At the moment the critical factor is central bank cooperation, and (as we have seen recently in the ERM) its effectiveness depends crucially on the commitment of the key players to maintaining a given pattern of rates. Central bank action needs to be reinforced by the operations of a new International Stabilisation Fund, with massive resources under its control and with a clearly defined duty to operate to support agreed exchange rate targets at all times, rather than waiting for a crisis to develop and then discussing under what conditions it will support the country under pressure. The essential conditions for a more stable regime are, first, agreement on the bands within which rates are to be managed, and then *automatic* action to counter any speculative action threatening to breach these bands. At the same time, central banks must have an obligation to conduct their interest rate policies in such a way as to support rather than undermine the agreed pattern of exchange rates.

COMMODITY PRICES

Commodity prices are a key link between the economies of the industrialised countries and the developing world, and their instability is deleterious to both sides. As we saw in Chapter 5, the unprecedented boom in commodity prices in the early 1970s was an important catalyst in accelerating world-wide inflation. Non-oil commodity prices, as measured by the *Economist* index, rose by more than 65 per cent in 1973, the largest year-on-year rise ever recorded, steeper even than in the Korean rearmament boom. By the time they reached their peak in 1974, world commodity prices (excluding oil) had more than doubled. Oil prices quadrupled. The resulting inflationary impact on industrialised countries was a key factor in shifting their macro-economic policies away from the maintenance of full employment in the interests of curbing inflation. The consequent slow-down in the growth of output contributed to the decline in real prices of many primary commodities in the 1980s. The balance of payments surpluses of the OPEC countries became a major factor in the world economy, and higher interest rates accentuated developing countries' debt problems. The ensuing debt crises had serious effects for many developing countries. The mass unemployment now plaguing the industrialised countries had its origins in the deflationary measures taken to combat the inflationary effects of the increases in oil and commodity prices. Given that such a price explosion two decades ago has left such a wake of destruction, it is strange that little or no attention has been paid to the question of stabilising commodity prices in the intervening years.

Greater stability of commodity prices would be a major benefit to both primary producers and the industrialised world. But the economic climate of the 1980s has led to the abandonment of postwar buffer stock schemes and a free market approach of letting the fluctuations take their course. It is sometimes suggested that new financial derivatives might dampen down such fluctuations, but experience of derivative markets indicates that they are more likely to be a source of further instability, particularly if speculative activity spills over from financial to commodity markets. Instability in commodity markets is thus a further problem waiting to be tackled.

A TEN-POINT PLAN

In the half century since Bretton Woods, international economic cooperation has declined, partly because of the hold of the New Orthodoxy which sees no role for economic management by national governments, let alone on a wider international scale, and partly because of the increasing practical difficulties of cooperation as the postwar political hegemony of the Allied Powers declined. The Bretton Woods system of fixed rates has given way to a general reversion to floating rates; global movements of financial capital rather than payments for trade now dominate foreign exchange markets; and the growing dependence of developing countries on private investment, together with the rise and fall of the OPEC countries' balance of payments surpluses, has created a series of problems not catered for in the postwar economic blueprint.

Under the Bretton Woods system a prime function of the IMF was to provide credit for countries with temporary balance of payments problems. No corresponding provision was made for countering speculative capital movements because it was assumed that capital movements would continue to be closely controlled. As a consequence, when a country's currency comes under pressure today, it is liable to be subject to several weeks' interrogation by the IMF before receiving any assistance, and any immediate support depends on its relations with the major central banks. The essential conditions for greater stability are: (a) that the parities and bands within which rates are managed should be *agreed* through the IMF; and (b) that any speculative action threatening to breach these bands should *automatically* lead to effective international action to offset it. International agreement on exchange rate targets and automatic action to support them should be the key principles in devising a more stable system.

The key international economic issues which now need to be addressed may be summarised as follows.

1 A fundamental review is required of the existing international economic agencies, some at least of which have outlived their original functions and usefulness. A new structure is required both for intergovernmental decision making and for the relevant executive agencies. The immense professional resources scattered across existing organisations need to be rationalised into an effective economic secretariat to service a world economic 'cabinet' and forum under the aegis of the UN.

2 Careful analysis is needed of the evolving pattern of current surpluses and deficits and flows of 'productive' capital (private or official) and aid. An integrated world economic strategy is required in which (a) the net flow of productive capital will be directed towards the most pressing needs of the developing and ex-Communist world, and (b) exchange rates will reflect the need to establish a pattern of trade surpluses and deficits consistent with these movements.

3 The axis of any effective strategy must be a resolution of the Japanese and US surplus and deficit positions. Part of any such solution should be an increase in Japanese aid to, and investment in, developing countries. It is essential therefore that Japan should play a key role in the formulation of any reforms.

4 A new managed exchange rate regime needs to be devised which should be based on a system of parities and margins agreed between the main players and formally approved by the IMF. Changes in parities should be relatively small

and frequent, rather than large and infrequent as in a fixed rate system.

5 Speculative capital movements between countries and between currencies are now a normal part of every investment portfolio, but their negative effects outweigh their economic usefulness. Any new exchange rate regime needs to be accompanied by measures to curb speculation. The two most obvious instruments for this purpose are taxation and the regulation of financial institutions. This would probably require exchange rate transactions to be limited to regulated financial institutions, but there is no reason why this should interfere with the efficient operation of foreign exchange markets.

6 A new International Stabilisation Fund should be set up under the aegis of the IMF with adequate borrowing powers to enable it to intervene as required to offset speculative movements threatening the agreed pattern of exchange rates. It should have a clearly defined duty to operate automatically in support of agreed rates, rather than waiting for a crisis to develop and then discussing the conditions on which it will give support. Agreement on rates and automatic action to support them are the twin pillars of a new more stable exchange rate regime.

7 There is a longer-term need to consider the problems of world liquidity if the US dollar deficit no longer fills countries' growing needs for a reserve currency. Under existing institutional arrangements these needs might be met by a substantial increase in Special Drawing Rights.

8 The recycling of the OPEC surpluses through the banking system in the late 1970s and early 1980s and the consequent debt crisis illustrate the fallacy of assuming that private financial institutions and capital markets on their own will provide an adequate and stable flow of investment funds to developing countries. An overall strategy for the provision of development capital and aid to the Third World and the former Communist countries is needed, together with a fundamental review of the role and structure of international institutions to make effective the original Bretton Woods concept of the World Bank's role in this field.

9 There are already strong pressures on countries in deficit

to reduce their deficits. There are no corresponding pressures on surplus countries either to reduce their surpluses or to ensure that they reflect a corresponding movement of long-term investment funds rather than the acquisition of financial assets. Consideration should be given to the possibility of raising further development capital by requiring countries to deposit a specified proportion of their surpluses with the IBRD or a new financial institution for lending to developing countries.

10 The industrialised countries have taken little interest recently in commodity policy, but fluctuations in world commodity prices (including oil) remain a potential destabilising factor for both suppliers and consumers.

The most immediate need is to recognise once again the importance of full employment and steady growth in the industrialised countries for the world economy as a whole, and for those countries to agree to follow policies directed to these ends. This does not in itself require any change in the formal system of world payments but is a key prerequisite for building any new structure on sound foundations. In the longer term, the ability to manage, rather than be at the mercy of, the global economy must call for some sacrifice of nominal national sovereignty and the creation of more powerful and effective international institutions.

12 The Way Ahead

The review of the development of economic policy since the Second World War in previous chapters has shown that the principal factor in the abandonment of full employment in recent years has been the resort to deflationary monetary and budgetary policies to control inflation. Full employment cannot, however, simply be restored by reverting to more expansionary demand management: that is essential, but not sufficient. We have at the same time to build up the capacity to employ the potential workforce once again, ensure that the necessary skills are available, and find other means of combating inflation. We have also, with other governments, to establish economic regimes, both in the European Union and in a wider international sphere, that will facilitate expansion rather than exercise a continual deflationary bias.

The first need is to abandon the New Orthodoxy which has blighted economic policy for the last 15 years, and which is in many respects little more than a reversion to the orthodoxy of the 1920s and 1930s. New policies must be based on a revolution in economic aims and objectives, springing from a firm belief that mass unemployment is no longer acceptable as a feature of modern industrial society and a new-found determination that democratic governments should work together to control our economic destiny. The alternative to such a revolution in policy is to continue to work on the assumption (at present dominating official opinion) that once unemployment in the UK is down to around 2 million, demand will need to be restrained to avoid a resurgence of inflation. Whilst paying public lip service to the need to reduce unemployment, in private those responsible for economic policy are watching carefully to see that it does not fall too low for fear of jeopardising the inflation target. This is the standard Treasury and Bank of England approach, although they may differ from time to time as to where that critical point lies – the so-called 'sustainable' or 'natural' rate of unemployment.

COMMON MISCONCEPTIONS

Public discussion of the unemployment problem has been heavily distorted by a number of misconceptions about its causes and cures. One of these is to regard it as a natural consequence of technical progress, particularly in the field of computers and electronics, leading to the replacement of workers by machines. This has been a constant theme since the industrial revolution; even during the full employment era automation was seen as a major threat to jobs; but it is no more true today than it ever was. Although technical progress in electronics and medicine has been rapid in recent years, looking back over the last century there have been equally striking developments: the internal combustion engine, electricity, radio, television, air travel, nuclear power, and so on. Indeed the increase in productivity has slowed down, rather than accelerated, in the period of higher unemployment. In the OECD countries as a whole, productivity increased by 3.7 per cent from 1960 to 1973, 1.8 per cent from 1973 to 1989 and 0.9 per cent from 1989 to 1993.[1] Provided demand is maintained by adopting suitable macro-economic policies, technical progress is not a cause of general unemployment, although it may create problems for particular groups of workers, as it did for the handloom weavers at the start of the industrial revolution.

The next major misconception is the re-emergence of the belief that the level of unemployment is nothing to do with demand or macro-economic policy, but solely a problem of the labour market: if labour were cheaper, more people would be employed. But the market for labour is not like that for goods. Wages are not only a cost to the employers; they are also purchasing power in the hands of the employees. Apart from the social consequences, cutting wages is not a remedy for unemployment because it means cutting demand as well as costs.

Then there are the 'solutions' to the problem of unemployment which accept that an increase in demand is necessary but insist that this will not be effective unless real wages are reduced, at any rate for the marginal workers to be taken on. This misconception rests on the fundamental fallacy (discussed in Chapter 8) of assuming that the average level of labour productivity tends to decrease when output and employment rise. In modern industry the opposite is true. Economies of scale mean that average productivity in a plant generally increases when output increases, mainly because the fixed labour costs of managerial and supervisory staff and support functions are spread over a larger volume; and if higher output necessitates investment in new capacity, this will tend to be more advanced and with higher productivity than existing plant. Reducing real wages is not therefore a necessary condition for increasing output and employment. The various remedies for tackling unemployment which involve cutting labour costs, either by reducing wages or subsidising employment, are thus wide of the mark. The sweatshop route to lower unemployment is both unnecessary and immoral.

There is, however, a genuine problem in that lower unemployment may spark off a wage–price spiral. But it is wrong to suggest that the way to cope with this is to intensify the fight for jobs, either by making life harder for the unemployed or helping one group of the unemployed to get jobs (i.e. the young, or the long-term unemployed, or, indeed, the over-50s) at the expense of the rest. Helping such groups is highly desirable against a background of an expanding demand for labour, but it is not in itself a cure for unemployment, and there is little reason to think that once the demand for labour is restored to higher levels such measures would have much, if any, effect in moderating pay demands.

PAY BARGAINING

To achieve expansion without inflation in the UK, reform of the pay bargaining system is essential. The present solution of relying on a competitive labour market to control inflation will only work if the bargaining position of labour is sufficiently weakened by widespread unemployment and the abandonment of protective legislation for workers, both of which create intolerably low pay and poor working conditions for those at the bottom of the employment ladder. Moreover, once wages have become more sensitive to market conditions, there is no guarantee that they will not increase rapidly if demand gets visibly stronger.

The alternative is to seek once again means of injecting into pay negotiations the consideration of the overall repercussions of individual settlements on inflation for the economy as a whole. This means that there must be some national agreement on the general level of pay increases, which commands the allegiance of the great majority of employers and employees. This is only possible in a society where the government is prepared to work in close consultation with representatives of both sides of industry.

The problems of devising such a strategy for pay were discussed in some detail in Chapter 7. The ultimate objective should be to set up the permanent machinery to solve the problem on a continuing basis. The precise institutional arrangements are essentially a political matter in the sense that they must take a form acceptable to all three main players: the Government, the TUC and the CBI. The whole history of previous pay policies makes it clear that the key factor is not the machinery, but the willingness of the unions to adhere to the guidelines. The first step should be to establish a new forum, an Economic Policy Council, where the three parties can discuss pay as part of an overall economic policy for expansion. From that forum should emerge annual guidance on pay negotiations to which employers and unions will adhere. This must cover both the general level of wage increases in that year's pay round, and the general principles applicable to particular cases, such as the justification for any exceptional increases.

Individual negotiators must know, however, that if they adhere to such an agreement, others will 'play the game'. There must therefore be some machinery for monitoring settlements, considering exceptional cases and bringing pressure to bear on any group threatening to break the policy. It is suggested that an independent Pay Advisory Commission should be set up for this purpose. It should have the power to gather information on pay negotiations, the authority to make representations to both parties in any pay negotiations, and to give advice during any recourse to conciliation procedures. It should cover both the private and public sectors and provide a source of independent advice to the Pay Review bodies and in public sector negotiations. It should also be responsible for setting any minimum wage levels.

There can be no question of any return to the statutory enforcement of such an agreement; and the Commission would not have any power to impose settlements or act as final adjudicator. But serious consideration should be given to investing the Commission with the power to refer a dispute to arbitration which would be binding on both parties. The Commission would then act as a 'friend of the court' and their views would be taken into account in the arbitration proceedings. This power, which would have to be used only sparingly, would provide a means of avoiding (or minimising) damaging and unpopular industrial disputes, particularly in the public services. Making the ultimate process one of 'arbitration' rather than 'adjudication' in difficult cases should help to achieve settlements which not only avoid breaching the agreed guidelines but also take realistic account of such factors as the balance of bargaining power and climate of public opinion.

Any new arrangements should be regarded as a permanent reform and not the temporary response to a particular set of events. The best time to introduce them is therefore when inflation is low and real wages are rising, so that the new machinery can start operating without being under strain. Then when the inevitable adverse 'shock' does occur and, for example, wage restraint is needed in the face of a sharp rise in commodity prices, the necessary trust and goodwill on all sides will have been built up to cope with the inevitable pressures. We should not leave tackling the incipient pay problem on one side merely because wage increases are not excessive for the time being.

There will always be problems of conflict and potential breakdowns in any pay policy, as there are indeed in any society that permits free collective bargaining: embarrassing labour disputes are not avoided merely by governments trying to abdicate any responsibility in these matters. Any Government is bound to have a public sector pay policy and if a Labour Government introduces a minimum wage this will inevitably be a factor in private sector negotiations. If we wish to restore full employment and avoid serious inflation, we cannot avoid the issue of pay policy just because there are bound to be difficulties and occasional failures. These occur with any instrument of economic policy, but we cannot therefore cast them all aside.

INDUSTRIAL CAPACITY

One of the consequences of the prolonged period of depressed demand and high unemployment has been the erosion of industrial capacity through closures and inadequate new investment. This applies to 'capacity' in the widest sense, not just of physical plant, but in managerial organisation, sales staff and so on. 'Down-sizing' has become the keyword, rather than expansion. As a result we no longer have the capacity to employ our potential labour force fully and any substantial rise in demand is likely to bring an increasing number of firms up against capacity limitations with potentially inflationary consequences. The need to stimulate the growth of capacity is thus an essential part of any policy to restore full employment. One of the consequences of the relative decline of such capital-intensive industries as steel, however, is that capacity limitations other than of plant may in many cases be of greater relative importance and may be removed more quickly and cheaply.

Stimulating the expansion of capacity will not be an easy task. Decisions to invest in new capacity involve the risk that it will not be fully utilised; and the formative experience of managers now in key positions has been that the risk of losses through over-expansion is much more severe than that of forgoing potential additional profits through failure to expand: the penalty for expanding unsuccessfully may be business failure and bankruptcy. To overcome these inhibitions it will be necessary to consider what financial measures can be taken to tilt the balance of risk more favourably towards expansion. This must include tackling the high cost and inadequate supply of risk capital for small and medium-sized businesses. But above all capacity decisions rest on sales expectations, and industry needs to be convinced that the economy is firmly set on an expansionary course that will not be speedily reversed by the re-emergence of deflationary policies to limit inflation. One prerequisite for this is to assuage fears that expansion will lead to inflation by tackling the pay bargaining problem before there are any signs of inflationary wage demands.

BALANCE OF PAYMENTS

A traditional limit on the ability of the UK to follow expansionary policies is the possible effect on the balance of payments. There is, however, some danger of confusion as to the precise significance of this threat. The previous review of post-war history shows that an increase in the pressure of domestic demand tends to lead to a deterioration in the balance of payments, by weakening the incentive to export and by increasing imports of materials, machinery and consumer goods. But it should be remembered that in the years of full employment, this only occurred when unemployment fell to exceptionally low levels by current standards. Nevertheless it is probably correct to assume that in the short term increasing demand at home will, if anything, have an adverse effect on the balance of payments. But in the longer term the more rapid growth in demand and industrial capacity associated with a reduction in unemployment will strengthen our balance of payments. More capacity will mean a greater diversity of firms competing in home and export markets, more modern capacity employing the latest technology and a greater variety of new products. Just as deflation and deindustrialisation have had an adverse effect on our competitive power, so a more rapid expansion of industrial capacity should improve it. It may therefore be necessary to accept some short-term deterioration in the balance of payments in order to achieve a long-term strengthening.

A FULL EMPLOYMENT STRATEGY

Any return to full employment will have to be phased over a period of years to enable industrial capacity to be rebuilt *pari passu* with increased demand and to allow any potential shortage in the supply of skilled labour to be met by appropriate education or training, although it is doubtful whether the latter is a serious bottleneck. Expanding 'capacity' may involve a variety of actions, from constructing new plant to setting up new manufacturing or sales divisions. In some cases this is a relatively speedy process; in others it may take four or five years. The government must therefore be seen to be working to a convincing long-term strategy.

A strategy for full employment should set out the general objectives of the government over a five year period and the policies by which it intends to achieve them. The three key factors in reducing unemployment will be: a sustained expansion of demand; an effective agreement on pay increases; and investment in additional capacity. But any statement of long-term strategy would also embrace other aspects of economic policy, in particular measures to improve efficiency, training and education, and help the long-term unemployed back into work. Within the framework of that strategy, the government should publish an annual economic review, akin to the present Financial Statement or 'Red Book', but ranging more widely. Although one should be very wary of trying to extend the techniques of business management to the management of the economy as a whole, there is in this case a legitimate analogy with a longer-term strategy for a business and its annual operating plans. While the annual operating plan or economic review should automatically be updated every 12 months, the longer-term strategy should be revised less frequently and the emphasis should be on objectives and policies rather than on figures *per se.*[2] It should, however, include broad targets for unemployment as well as inflation, if only because that is the one sure way of avoiding any ambiguity in Whitehall or with the Bank of England as to government policy and objectives.

If we are to embark on an era of more positive management of the economy, it is important to remove the confusion between objectives and forecasts. Macro-economic forecasting was originally designed (like business forecasting) as a means of determining what adjustments in policy were required to reach the desired objectives. In recent years, however, the growing band of forecasting models has been concerned almost exclusively with forecasting what will actually happen on (often unstated) guesses or assumptions about future government action. This meets a legitimate need of decision makers in business (though it is important that the assumptions about Government policy should be made explicit); but it tends to confuse public discussion of government policy, by creating a fatalistic outlook that what the forecasters suggest will happen is a predetermined outcome not susceptible to Government action.

FASTER GROWTH IN DEMAND AND OUTPUT

Just as the medium-term projections in the Red Book have in the past provided a reference point for discussing public expenditure and tax policy so, in a wider-ranging Annual Economic Review, such projections could provide a basis for discussing pay policy, the efficacy of measures to encourage the expansion of capacity, the development of the balance of payments and other elements in the Full Employment Strategy. The fundamental respect in which such a strategy would differ from past policies is that it would deliberately aim at a rate of growth of GDP sufficient to reduce unemployment to below one million over, say, the next five years, rather than a continuation of existing trends with unemployment tacitly assumed to remain between 2 and 3 million.

In recent years the Treasury's Red Books have made clear their belief that, if inflation is to be kept in check, GDP should not be allowed to rise above trend and unemployment to fall below 'the sustainable rate'. For example, the 1995 Financial Statement shows the economy as growing slightly above trend, at 3 per cent in 1996–7 and 1997–8 as spare capacity is taken up, but at the trend rate of 2.5 per cent thereafter. (This implies that they considered that there was about 1 per cent spare capacity.) It does not indicate what they consider this implies for unemployment, except to say that 'there is evidence that the sustainable rate of unemployment has declined'. Indeed it is highly significant that the Statements specifically set inflation targets and forecast future inflation rates but make no attempt to set any objectives for unemployment or forecast future unemployment levels. The fact that their approach is entirely dominated by inflation-targeting and does not aim at any significant reduction in unemployment is a clear indication of the values and objectives behind current policy.

Any new strategy must postulate as its aim the achievement of a faster rate of growth of GDP with a corresponding lower rate of unemployment, and make clear the Government's determination to manage demand accordingly. (Such a speeding-up in the growth of demand and output to reduce unemployment should not be confused with the supply-side measures to improve productivity and hence the growth in GDP possible without any reduction in unemployment.) This means more expansionary budgetary and monetary policies than hitherto assumed. How far this should come from lower interest rates and how far from a more expansionary fiscal stance depends partly on external factors, in particular the level of German interest rates. But there should so far as possible be a bias towards low interest rates for a number of reasons. First, it will encourage industrial investment. Second, in a period of floating exchange rates it will keep down the level of sterling and maintain or improve our international competitive position: again, encouraging more industrial investment. Third, it will ease any budgetary problems by cutting the cost of public borrowing.

BUDGETARY POLICY

Nevertheless the room for manoeuvre on monetary policy may be limited, and at some point a more expansionary budgetary policy is likely to be needed. The precise nature of any fiscal stimulus must depend on the circumstances prevailing at the time. The options are either to cut taxation or to increase government current or capital expenditure. The choice will depend partly on the political stance of the Government in power and whether they consider that continuing expenditure programmes on such services as health or education are adequate or need to be increased: for current expenditure or employment in these services cannot be temporarily increased and then cut back. Public investment, on the other hand, could be raised for a time and then reduced later when the required boost in demand had taken effect. More public investment in hospitals, schools, housing and so on is badly needed, and there could also be a strong case for increasing the load on the construction industry to prevent any further erosion of its capacity; but there are practical limits to the extent to which the timing of public investment projects can be altered. Changes in taxation, on the other hand, are more flexible: the main problem in this case is the political one of raising taxes again after they have been lowered.

In analysing the impact of any budgetary stimulus it is important to distinguish between (a) measures which increase employment in the public sector (including contracted-out services) and (b) those which increase employment in the private industrial sector. Increases in public expenditure in order to employ more staff in hospitals or schools, for instance, come into the first category. Extra demand on the private sector may, however, come either from increasing public expenditure on say, construction or computers, or from additional personal consumption or investment resulting from tax cuts. Increasing public expenditure is not synonomous with increasing employment in the public sector. In devising a long-term strategy for restoring full employment, the extent to which it is dependent on an increase in jobs in the public sector must be determined by a judgement on the adequacy or inadequacy of staffing in the main public services. A high proportion of the additional jobs would be in the private sector; but how far these came from additional public expenditure or from lower taxation would be largely a matter of political judgement.

Given that part of any increase in demand will fall on the private industrial sector (whether immediately or through the subsequent 'multiplier' effects) the consequent increase in output and employment should in turn lead to badly needed investment in new capacity. Stimulating additional private investment in this way is an important facet of any strategy, and the major reason why the need for a budgetary stimulus to demand should only be temporary. Once the economy is firmly established as operating at a higher level of demand, experience suggests that industrialists will invest on the assumption that it will continue to do so; just as at present they are implicitly working on the assumption that the economy will continue to operate with something like recent levels of unemployment.

A temporary stimulus would involve a short-term increase in the PSBR. The net increase would reflect the difference between (a) the cost of the additional expenditure or tax cuts and (b) the saving in unemployment benefits and the extra tax receipts as more people were in work. The longer-term impact would depend on the extent of the multiplier effect as people receiving wages instead of unemployment pay spend more, and on the increase in investment as industrial activity recovered. The direct cost of creating 750,000 new jobs by increased public expenditure has been put at approximately £22,500 per annum per head, which would be partly offset by reductions in expenditure on benefits and higher tax revenue of between £11,000 and £12,000 per annum per head.[3] Similar savings would accrue from the creation of a further 250,000 new jobs from the 'multiplier' effect[4] (i.e. the additional spending of the first 750,000). The net increase in the PSBR in the short run to create one million new jobs is thus put at £5 to 6 billion (depending on the precise assumptions taken): less than 1 per cent of GDP. The 1995 forecasts of the PSBR showed it as falling to 2 per cent in 1997–8 and lower thereafter.[5] A more expansionary budget at around this time would imply some modest increase in the PSBR, which might or might not threaten the achievement of the Maastricht convergence condition that the public sector deficit should be less than 3 per cent of GDP. This would be a further reason for avoiding any speedy entry to the EMU, whose timetable is in any event threatened by the difficulties of France and other potential members. As a result of such a stimulus, however, output and employment would grow more rapidly than on existing Treasury assumptions, and the PSBR would subsequently improve more quickly. Thus, when the initial stimulus had taken full effect, the PSBR would be lower than as present projected – a reflection of the fact that the major factor increasing public sector deficits both here and elsewhere in the EU is the high level of unemployment.

EUROPEAN UNION

The problem of achieving full employment is an international one. The growth of trade, particularly between closely integrated economies, as in the EU, means that changes in the level of demand in one country have immediate effects on its trading partners. Thus expanding demand in one country will tend both to increase output in that country and imports from elsewhere. This may cause balance of payments problems if one country tries to expand on its own, although there have been cases where countries like Sweden have succeeded in maintaining appreciably lower levels of unemployment than elsewhere. There is, however, a strong case for coordinating expansion policies between the major industrial countries, and particularly within the EU. Not only will this be more effective in reducing unemployment, but as a result it will also ease any budgetary problems.

Whatever political or cultural reservations Britain may have about its future in Europe, there is no escape from the fact that our economy is becoming increasingly integrated into that of the European Union as a whole. There are thus potentially powerful economic and political forces limiting our ability to pursue a radically different economic philosophy. At present economic policy in Europe is dominated by the New Orthodoxy and the monetarist philosophy underlying the Treaty of Maastricht (which was discussed in Chapter 10). As is now becoming increasingly apparent, the convergence and budgetary provisions in the Treaty are leading to further deflation and aggravating the unemployment problem.

If European governments were to have the necessary change of heart, there is probably just about sufficient flexibility in the provisions of the Treaty to enable more expansionary policies to be pursued, provided monetary union was delayed. In any event the Treaty could always be amended. It would be tragic if the whole future of European political and economic union should founder on the rocks of ill conceived and arithmetically arbitrary convergence provisions about budget deficits and national debt.

Any such change in heart would logically go hand-in-hand with a fundamental review of the whole Maastricht approach. The concept of an economic community with monetary policy in the hands of an independent European Central Bank without an elected European government responsible for macroeconomic policy would make the pursuit of full employment on a European scale difficult. The Central Bank would inevitably have a deflationary bias, and there would be no machinery for coordinating the use of monetary and fiscal policy at a European level.

Unless monetary union is deferred for some years until the European economies have achieved a much greater degree of convergence, it would tend to aggravate the unemployment problem. Such a union (i.e. fixing exchange rates irrevocably between those who enter) would mean that any country whose costs got out of line would automatically suffer increased unemployment, whereas there would be no incentive to further expansion for those who are most competitive – shades of the old Gold Standard with a vengeance! Monetary union would mean the end of sterling crises; but until a much greater degree of convergence is achieved, the UK has more chance of achieving full employment with a flexible exchange rate.

For those who see the need for further European economic integration but also believe in the pursuit of full employment, Maastricht was a potentially disastrous wrong turning on the road to European economic union. It is not a matter of being 'for' or 'against Europe', but for or against unemployment. Further integration without a change in economic philosophy will only intensify the deflationary pressures which may lead once again to growth of nationalism, racism and anti-democratic forces. In the end only the establishment of a European Federal government with responsibility for economic policy on a European level and with its members pledged to the achievement of full employment can ensure that Economic and Monetary Union is consistent with the restoration and maintenance of full employment.

THE GLOBAL ECONOMY

While the development of the UK economy and her ability to deal with the problem of unemployment are closely bound up with the future of European integration, it is equally important to create a new international financial regime which will assist in the restoration of full employment. The most cursory glance at the economic history of the interwar years shows that there is nothing new in national economies being susceptible to buffeting by international financial storms. What is new is the increasing tendency in recent years for governments to abdicate from any attempt to control these forces. Even though the movement to European union has been distorted by the monetarist prescription emanating from the Delors Committee, at least the governments involved have been concerned for many years to work together on economic problems: the mistake has been to conceive such cooperation almost entirely in terms of establishing the regime for a competitive common market without any attempt to cooperate on the key issues of macro-economic policy. But, on a wider international plane, the corresponding effect of the dominance of free market ideology has in practice been even more limiting. International cooperation has been mainly confined to reducing trade barriers in the GATT negotiations. Collaboration on exchange rate policy and the flow of development capital, or on updating the role of international institutions, has declined rather than improved.

The determination of the architects of Bretton Woods to exercise such control contrasts tragically with the current lack of will either to coordinate economic policies or to reform the present out-dated collection of international agencies and payments arrangements (see Chapter 11). A new structure is required both for intergovernmental decision making and for the relevant executive agencies. These need to be seen to be operating on the basis of an agreed world economic strategy whose axis must be a resolution of the Japanese and US balance of payments surplus and deficit positions, which makes it essential that Japan should play a leading role in any new international settlement.

The resort to floating exchange rates in recent years has merely substituted a slightly different set of problems for those experienced under the previous 'fixed' rate regime. Floating reduces the risk of acute speculative crises when a country on a fixed rate is expected to devalue, but has created instead a continuing state of instability. This inhibits rational decision making by industry on investment in plant or export policy; and the exchange rates prevailing are more influenced by short-term capital movements than economic fundamentals, such as trade or productive investment, as the behaviour of the dollar/yen rate illustrates.

A new exchange rate regime needs to be devised based on a system of parities and margins agreed between the main players and formally approved by the IMF. Changes in parities should be relatively small and frequent, rather than large and infrequent as in a fixed rate system. Such arrangements need to be accompanied by measures to curb speculation. A new International Stabilisation Fund should be set up under the aegis of the IMF with adequate borrowing powers to enable it to intervene as required to offset speculative movements threatening the agreed pattern of exchange rates. Intervention should be *automatic* and not held back until discussions have been held with the country whose currency is under pressure. The key principles in devising a new and more stable system must be international agreement on exchange rates and automatic action to counter speculation against them.

In the international economic field, as in Europe, there is a vacuum in leadership. Admittedly the growing number of countries involved makes negotiations difficult, but at the present time the US, EU and Japan are still sufficiently dominant for any lead they may take to be effective. They could and should pave the way for a new round of international discussions by detailed negotiations between themselves, as the US and UK did in preparation for the Bretton Woods conference. But again such proposals are only likely to be worthwhile if they reflect a new and more positive attitude to the problem of international instability and unemployment. In the longer term our ability to control economic developments, rather than be helplessly buffeted by international events, depends on recreating and strengthening the postwar international institutions, which are weaker now than they were 50 years ago. The major political and economic challenge of the twenty-first century is to establish new and democratic international institutions designed to cope with present day problems. These may, as in Europe, be most close-knit at a continental or regional level, but there can ultimately be no escape from tackling the problem of international economic governance at a world level.

FINANCIAL MARKETS

Although achieving full employment will be easier if the major European economies all move in the same direction, that does not mean that Britain is powerless to act on her own, if necessary; and it should not be used as an excuse for inaction. If Britain were the only country to adopt more expansionary policies, however, this would make the potential balance of payments problem greater and it would be essential to remain outside any fixed exchange rate regime. This would also lessen the danger of speculative exchange crises.

There is always a danger of international speculation against the pound if financial markets disapprove of any more expansionary policies; but it is dangerously defeatist to believe that financial markets are now all-powerful and will rule out any expansionary action or return to full employment. This is a particularly insidious fear for any left-of-centre government, because it leads inexorably to the pursuit of conservative financial policies. But ill-placed orthodoxy may equally generate market reactions. As the Major government discovered in the ERM débâcle, trying to govern to please the markets is no guarantee of either economic or political success. The only sensible approach is to adopt policies best suited to the development of the economy and explain them with courage and conviction.

In so far as the veto on expansion is believed to come from a potential flight from sterling, it should be remembered that in the last resort the key to such crises lies with other governments and central banks rather than the markets themselves. In every sterling crisis since 1945 it has been the willingness or otherwise of the American and then the German authorities to support sterling that has decided the issue. The key to the sustainability of any European exchange rate under the ERM was the willingness or otherwise of the Bundesbank to signal its support.

It does neither democratic governments, nor in the long run financial institutions themselves, a service to propagate the view that the authorities are helpless in the face of all-powerful markets: that we should submit to what President Roosevelt called 'government by organised money'. As George Soros himself has said: 'If people like me can crash a currency system, there is certainly something wrong with the system.'[6] Financial institutions are ultimately dependent on the statutory and regulatory framework set by governments; but the key point is that such institutions operate globally, and hence the power of individual governments acting on their own has become attenuated. If, however, they are prepared to act together, governments still have the whip-hand.

CONCLUSION

The future depends on our ability to reassert the will to control our own economic destiny. The restoration of full employment is perfectly possible once it is genuinely re-established as an essential objective of economic policy. It would be possible for the UK to act on its own, but more effective if the EU and other industrialised countries were to act together. For this to happen the voters in the industrial democracies and their leaders must be prepared to move towards a more cooperative and less inequitable society, and withdraw their allegiance from the belief that markets rule supreme. But no such movement will be of any avail unless at the same time we are prepared to overthrow the 'tyranny of prevailing opinion' and break the grip of the New Orthodoxy on economic policy. Budgetary and monetary policy must both once again be used as instruments of demand management directed to assuring an adequate demand for labour.

It is incompatible with the basic values of our democratic society to accept the continued existence of mass unemployment as a necessary condition for the smooth running of the industrial system. Just as the majority must respect the rights of minorities to political liberty and participation in political society, so too the majority must accept the right of all citizens to participate in industrial society by being able to get a job. The idea that a million to two million of our fellow citizens are dispensable is unacceptable. We are still living in the aftermath of a war in which a generation fought, and many died, for the preservation of freedom and democracy; they were determined that the postwar world should banish the spectre of unemployment. How much longer are we to countenance this betrayal of their hopes and sacrifice?

Appendix 1: Measuring Unemployment

HISTORICAL SERIES

The figures for UK unemployment in Tables 2.1, 2.2, 3.1 and 4.1 are taken from the series 'Unemployment Statistics from 1881 to the Present Day' published by the Department of Employment in January 1996[1] and are based on administrative sources (as opposed to household surveys).

Before 1912, the statistics refer to the percentage of members of certain trade unions which paid out unemployment benefits to those members who were unemployed; by 1912 they covered 1.4 million workers.

From 1912 to 1916 the statistics refer to the percentage of people covered by the National Insurance Act of 1911 who were unemployed. This covered some 2.25 million manual workers.

From 1916 to 1920 the coverage was extended by a further 1.25 million workers by the 1916 Unemployment Insurance Act.

The National Insurance Act of 1920 brought an additional 8 million workers within the scope of the scheme, which then covered most manual workers (11 to 12 million in all), but excluded agricultural workers, domestic servants, civil servants, miners, teachers, police, railway and local authority workers and those earning more than £250 a year. The series from 1920 to the outbreak of the Second World War is broadly consistent.

CLAIMANT COUNT

From 1948 to 1982 administrative unemployment statistics were based on numbers registered as unemployed at Employment Exchanges. The percentage rate expressed the number of unemployed as a proportion of the registered unemployed plus the numbers of employees in employment. After September 1982 (when this series reached its highest level of 3.3 million, or 14 per cent) it was replaced by a new measure, called the 'Claimant Count': that is, the number of people receiving unemployment (or unemployment-related) benefit. This change itself reduced the percentage unemployment rate by a half to 1 per cent. The Department of Employment's recalculation of the 1981 average on the new basis would have reduced it from 11.4 to 10.5 per cent.

The new approach was an administrative necessity because the unemployed were no longer required to register at Job Centres in order to draw benefit; but the change in method has meant that the statistical value of the series since then has been undermined by a series of changes in the rules for administering benefit which have, in virtually every case, had the effect of reducing the claimant count. The Royal Statistical Society's 1995 *Report on the Measurement of Unemployment in the UK*[2] lists 30 such changes, of which, according to the Department of Employment, eight have been significant in statistical terms. It is difficult to estimate how many people have been excluded from the unemployment count by these revisions, and this has led to a search for alternative measures which might give a more reliable measure, both of month to month changes and of the absolute level of unemployment.

LABOUR FORCE SURVEY

The other main source of data about unemployment is the quarterly Labour Force Survey which provides the data on which unemployment can be measured on the standard ILO definition of unemployment used for international comparisons. This differs from the claimant count definition in excluding people on benefit who are not actively seeking work, but it includes people not on benefit who are unemployed and are actively seeking work. In the summer of 1994, for example, the Claimant Count put unemployment at 2.53 million and the Labour Force Survey at 2.68 million: 1.62 million were unemployed on both definitions, but a further 1.06 million were unemployed only on the ILO definition and a further 0.91 million only unemployed on the Claimant Count definition.[3] In terms of differences in absolute levels or month to month movements there is not a great difference between the two measures; but the one million additional people revealed in the Labour Force Surveys as unemployed but not receiving benefit drew attention to the serious problem of hidden unemployment.[4]

Appendix 2: Tax-Based Incomes Policies

The concept of Tax-Based Incomes Policy is that wage and salary increases which offend certain criteria automatically incur a tax penalty, and there is no need for a separate controlling body or sanctions. There are two approaches to any proposal to impose a tax on such increases. One is to impose a penalty on the employer; the other is to tax the employees. The choice should depend on whether the problem is seen to be the need to stiffen up employers' resistance to excessive wage demands or curb the unions' pressure for such increases. American discussions in the early 1970s[1] tended to concentrate on proposals to tax profits if wage increases exceed the limit. This may have reflected the relatively low degree of unionisation there and hence the feeling that the problem could be tackled by putting pressure on employers.

To be administratively practical the policy would have to be based on the increase in the wage and salary bill per head of the firm relative to a base period. There would be no allowance for the effects of changes in the proportions of technical or unskilled staff on average earnings per head, or the effects of overtime. On this basis it might be practical to administer a tax on employers to penalise excessive increases in wages and salaries. (If, however, tax penalties were assessed as part of the usual corporate tax system, they would of course, be paid some time after the event.)

Consideration of the detailed administrative problems illustrates vividly the extremely inflexible nature of the tax approach. The rules governing wage increases would have to be specified by law in sufficient detail to cover the innumerable boundary and transition problems: the position of new firms, the effect of take-overs, and so on. Moreover, it seems unlikely that a formula would be acceptable in practice that did not allow for changes in the composition of the labour force and hours worked. In that case tax officials would become deeply involved in detailed analysis of each firm's wage bill in order to administer the provisions. There is also the problem of whether or not small firms can be excluded from a system which is in fact part of the tax system.

Any annual changes in the policy would require revised tax legislation. In British conditions this would mean that the details would be under parliamentary discussion for some months.

Layard and Nickell[2] have proposed a tax on any increase in average hourly earnings in excess of a specified norm, collected from firms along with PAYE receipts. This proposal would seem to suffer both from all the disadvantages of imposing a uniform percentage ceiling across all firms irrespective of circumstances, and also to ignore any justifiable reasons for such an excess in terms of shifts in the composition of a firm's labour force or a change in the composition or level of activity.

More fundamentally, a system based on penalising the *employer* would not seem to meet the British situation where wage increases which contravene the prevailing incomes policy rules have virtually always come about after strikes or threats of strikes, and have been strongly resisted by the employer. Hence to have the necessary effect, logic would suggest imposing tax penalties on the workers pressing the demands. But proposals to tax *employees* on any excessive increases raise even greater problems. First, unless the tax takes back 100 per cent of the increase, there remains an incentive to get the greatest possible increase in money wages: indeed the existence of a high marginal tax rate could stimulate, rather than modify, wage demands. Second, what is to be the criterion? Fogarty[3] suggested that it should be the increase in the average wage and salary bill per head of the firm. If this is excessive, a penalty tax would be levied on all employees irrespective of their actual individual increases. The manifest injustice of this leads inevitably to the proposal that the tax on employees should be levied on their individual excesses over the norm. Moreover, this would also cope with the problem that any scheme based on the firm's total wage bill as shown in the accounts would be working well in arrears.

It is, however, difficult to take seriously a proposal where increases in an individual's earnings (not his or her pay scale) are limited by law. It is one thing to try to influence the settlement of the collective bargaining process, but quite another to seek to regulate what the individual can earn in the situation so established.

There remains the question of a tax-based system to restrain price increases. There is general agreement that any automatic system is difficult to conceive because of the large number of different products made by even quite small firms. Any system of taxation linked to whether individual price increases are justified would necessitate an impossibly large bureaucracy to police it. Schemes based on average price rises for each firm raise similar problems of determining what is justified. In the end such an approach tends to end up as a proposal for an excess profits tax. Save in wartime conditions, taxes on *increases* in profits rather than profits *per se* seem inimical both to expansion and improvements in efficiency.

The tax approach to incomes policy is the least flexible of all: first, because it postulates a uniform rate of increase in pay for every firm; second, because the detailed rules have to be laid down and turned into tax law in advance. There can be little or no provision for exceptional cases. Furthermore, while such a system may avoid a clash between the government and the unions over individual settlements, if any consequential increases are effectively taxed away, there could be a revolt against the tax system. Effective tax systems are dependent on a wide measure of tacit consent to their operation, and any attempt to introduce penal elements into the system to enforce an unpopular incomes policy would risk undermining the whole system of direct taxation.

Notes

1 A Pledge Betrayed

1. See Table 4.1 and Appendix 1 on Measuring Unemployment. Figures for Greater London from Labour Force Survey for Summer 1994.
2. Schmitt, J. and Wadsworth, J., *Why are 2 million Men Inactive? The Decline in Male Labour Force Participation in Britain*, CEPR Working Paper No. 338 (1994).
3. Churchill to Otto Niemeyer (22 February 1925) quoted in Moggeridge, D.E., *Maynard Keynes, An Economist's Biography.*
4. Kalecki, M., *Political Aspects of Full Employment* (1943), reprinted in *Selected Essays on the Dynamics of the Capitalist Economy, 1933–70.*
5. Galbraith, J.K., *The Culture of Contentment.*

2 Unemployment and Economic Policy before 1939

1. Beveridge, W.H., *Full Employment in a Free Society*, paras 90 to 93.
2. Beveridge, *Full Employment in a Free Society*, Tables 12 and 13.
3. Panić, M., *European Monetary Union: Lessons from the Classical Gold Standard.*
4. Eichengreen, B., *Golden Fetters.*
5. Lewis, W.A., *Economic Survey 1919–1939.*
6. Moggeridge, D.E., *Maynard Keynes, An Economist's Biography*, p. 429.
7. Keynes, J.M., *The Economic Consequences of Mr. Churchill.*
8. Hodson, H.Y., *Slump and Recovery, 1929–1937.*
9. Estimates of international unemployment between the wars differ widely: for example unemployment in Germany from 1930 to 1932 is variously estimated at 13.5 per cent and 33.6 per cent: see Kitson, M. and Michie, J., 'Depression and Recovery, Lessons from the Interwar Period', in Michie, J. and Grieve Smith, J., *Unemployment in Europe.*

   The figures quoted in the text for unemployment and GDP in the USA are taken from Maddison, A., *Dynamic Forces in Capitalist Development.* The estimate of the level of world unemployment in 1932 was made by the ILO.

   The fall in GDP in the UK is taken from Feinstein, C.H., *National Income, Expenditure and Output of the UK 1855–1965.*
10. Youngson, A.J., *The British Economy 1920–1957.*
11. Reproduced in *Unemployment: A Labour Policy* (Labour Party, 1921).
12. Bullock, A., *The Life and Times of Ernest Bevin, Vol. I.*

3 The Birth of Full Employment

1. Preface to Keynes, J.M., *The General Theory of Employment, Interest and Money.*
2. Kahn, R.F., 'The Relation of Home Investment to Unemployment', *Economic Journal*, June 1931.

3. Keynes, J.M., 'Relative Movements of Real Wages and Output', *Economic Journal*, March 1939.
4. Keynes, *The General Theory of Employment, Interest and Money*, Chapter 19.
5. Beveridge, W.H., *Full Employment in a Free Society*, Introduction.
6. Cairncross, A. and Watts, N., *The Economic Section 1939–1961.*
7. *The Times*, 23 January 1943, quoted by Beveridge.
8. *Socialism and the Condition of the People.*
9. Keynes papers, Vol. XXV.
10. Cmd 6437, *Proposals for an International Clearing Union.*
11. Ibid.
12. Cmd 6519, *Joint Statement by Experts on the Establishment of an International Monetary Fund.*
13. *Bretton Woods, Proceedings and Documents of United Nations Monetary and Financial Conference 1944.*
14. *Articles of Agreement of the International Bank for Reconstruction and Development.*

4 The Years of Full Employment: 1946–70

1. Cairncross, A., *The British Economy since 1945.*
2. *The Economist*, 4 August 1951, quoted in Dow, J.C.R., *The British Economy 1945–60.*
3. Dow, *The British Economy 1945–60.*
4. *Robert Hall Diaries* (ed. Cairncross, A.), 20 August 1957.
5. *Robert Hall Diaries*, 20 November 1958; Cairncross, A. and Watts, N., *The Economic Section 1939–1961.*
6. Hansard, 17 May 1956.
7. Macmillan, H., *At the End of the Day.*
8. Blackaby, F.T. (ed.), *British Economic Policy, 1960–74*, Chapter 9.
9. Macmillan, *At the End of the Day.*
10. Cairncross, *The British Economy since 1945*: the initial meeting is well documented in the memoirs of those concerned.
11. Wilson, H., *The Labour Government 1964–1970.*
12. Gaitskell, H., *Economic Planning and Liberalisation*, EPC (50) 9 (PRO CSB 134 1225).
13. Grieve Smith, J., 'Facing Economic Reality, Devaluation and After', in *Matters of Principle, Labour's Last Chance.*

5 Transition and Revolution: 1970–95

1. Keynes, J.M., *How to Pay for the War.*
2. First quarter to first quarter.
3. Stewart, M., *The Jekyll and Hyde Years: Politics and Economic Policy since 1964.*
4. *Collective Bargaining and the Social Contract* (TUC, 1974).
5. *National Institute Economic Review*, May 1975.
6. Cairncross, A., *The British Economy since 1945.*
7. Healey, D., *The Time of My Life.*
8. Callaghan, J., *Time and Chance.*

9. Healey, *The Time of My Life.*
10. Healey, *The Time of My Life.*
11. Lecture to the British Association (quoted by John Cole, *As It Seemed To Me*).
12. Howe, G., *Conflict of Loyalty.*
13. *National Institute Economic Review,* February 1981.
14. Within the Cabinet, Jim Prior, Ian Gilmour and Peter Walker: see Howe, *Conflict of Loyalty.*
15. The letter was drafted by two Cambridge economists, Robert Neild and Frank Hahn.
16. Keegan, W., *Mr. Lawson's Gamble.*
17. IMF effective exchange rates: annual averages.
18. Evidence to the Treasury Select Committee, 19 December 1983.
19. Keegan, *Mr. Lawson's Gamble.*
20. Lawson, N., *The View from No. 11.*
21. Thatcher, M., *The Downing Street Years.*
22. Lawson, *The View from No. 11.*
23. Stewart, M., *Keynes in the 1990s.*
24. Connolly, B., *The Rotten Heart of Europe.*

6 Demand Management

1. Friedman, M., *The Role of Monetary Policy.*
2. Phillips, A.W., 'The Relation between Unemployment and the Rate of Change of Money Wage Rates in the United Kingdom 1861–1957', *Economica,* November 1958.
3. For an analysis of the unemployment problem largely based on the NAIRU approach, see Layard, R., Nickell, S. and Jackman, J., *Unemployment.*
4. *The Times,* 19 October 1995.
5. For a review of macro-economic policy in the Thatcher era, see Britton, A.J.C., *Macroeconomic Policy in Britain, 1974–87.*
6. The Governor of the Bank of England giving evidence to the House of Commons Treasury Committee on 7 December 1995.
7. For a statement of this view using IMF figures, see *Bank of England Quarterly Review,* February 1996 (Box on p. 20).
8. Put forward by James Meade and popularised by Samuel Brittan.

7 Pay and Inflation

1. Blackaby, F.T., 'An Array of Proposals', in *The Future of Pay Bargaining.*
2. See for example: Robinson, P., 'Stagflation: Lessons from Other Places', *Campaign for Work Research Report,* Vol. 1, No. 7 (November 1989) and Layard, R., 'How to End Pay Leapfrogging', *Employment Institute Economic Report,* Vol. 5 (July 1990).
3. Soskice, D., 'Wage Determination: The Changing Role of Institutions in Advanced Industrialised Countries', *Oxford Review of Economic Policy,* Vol. 6, No. 4.
4. Calmfors, L. and Driffil, J., 'Centralisation of Wage Bargaining', *Economic Policy,* April 1988.

5. Brown, W.A., 'Incomes Policy in Britain: Lessons from Experience', in Dore, R. *et al.* (eds), *The Return to Incomes Policy.*
6. Soskice, 'Wage Determination'.
7. Edmonds, J. and Tuffin, A., *A New Agenda, Bargaining for Prosperity in the 1990s,* Joint paper by the GMB and UCW (1990).
8. Such a 'cut' is largely illusory. In a period of rapid inflation wage-earners' pay will have been declining significantly over the period since their last increase. Taking the level of real wages temporarily reached 12 months ago as the starting-point for this year's negotiations may represent an abortive attempt to build on an unsustainable level of real wages which was temporarily above trend. Starting from today, any increase in money wages is always an immediate real increase, but how long it lasts depends on the rate of inflation. Thus a 10 per cent increase in money wages will indeed represent a 10 per cent real increase for a brief time, and a 6 per cent money increase only a 6 per cent immediate real increase. But if everybody has 10 per cent pay increase rather than 6 per cent, it will only be a matter of months before the 10 per cent increases are worth as little as the 6 per cent would have been. There may be a temporary loss in real wages in holding down the going rate, but the difference is far less than it appears at first sight because it is relatively short-lived.
9. Marquand, D., *The Unprincipled Society.* See also Hirst, P., *After Thatcher.*
10. Hutton, W., *The State We're In.*

8 Jobs and People

1. Keynes, J.M., 'Relative Movements of Real Wages and Output', *Economic Journal,* March 1939.
2. There is a classic statement of this in Hicks, J.R., *Value and Capital.*
3. Jonathan Michie reviews the literature on this in *Wages in the Business Cycle.*
4. Harrod, R., 'Increasing Returns', in *Economic Essays.*
5. The accounting treatment of the cost of existing, as opposed to new, capital equipment may, however, distort the lower real cost of new equipment.
6. Galbraith, J.K., *The Culture of Contentment.*
7. Layard, R., Nickell, S. and Jackman, R., *Unemployment, Macroeconomic Performance and the Labour Market.*
8. Wells, J., 'The Costs of Unemployment', mimeo (1993). Calculated from the DSS Reports on *Incomes In and Out of Work.*
9. Garman, A., Redmond, G. and Lonsdale, S., *Incomes In and Out of Work,* DSS Research Report No. 7.
10. DSS, *Households below Average Income, A Statistical Analysis 1979–1992/3* (1995).
11. TUC, *Black and Betrayed* (October 1995).
12. Atkinson, J. and Meager, N., 'Evaluation of Work Start Pilots', *Institute of Employment Studies,* Report 279.
13. Rosewell, B., 'Employment, Households and Earnings', in Meadows, P. (ed.), *Work out – or Work in?*

14. Hewitt, P., 'The Place of Part-Time Work', in Meadows, *Work out – or Work in?*
15. Rowntree Foundation, *Inquiry into Income and Wealth.*
16. Hewitt, 'The Place of Part-Time Work'.
17. Royal Statistical Society, *Report of Working Party on the Measurement of Unemployment in the UK* (April 1995).
18. House of Commons Employment Committee, *Unemployment and Employment Statistics* (February 1996).
19. Unemployment Unit, *Working Brief* (February 1996).
20. Wells, J., 'Unemployment, Job Creation and Job Destruction in the UK since 1979', in Arestis, P. and Marshall, M. (eds), *The Political Economy of Full Employment.*
21. Nickell, S. and Bell, L.A., 'The Collapse of Demand for the Unskilled and Unemployment Across the OECD', *Oxford Review of Economic Policy* (Spring, 1995).
22. Wood, A., *North–South Trade, Employment and Inequality.*
23. Robinson, P., 'Skills, Qualifications and Unemployment', *Economic Affairs*, Vol. 16, No. 2 (Spring, 1996).
24. Rowntree Foundation, *Inquiry into Income and Wealth.*
25. DSS, *Households below Average Income, A Statistical Analysis 1979–1992/3.*

9 The Capacity Problem

1. Hutton, W., *The State We're In.*
2. *Competitiveness, Forging Ahead* (Cmnd 2867).
3. Wardlow, A., 'Investment Appraisal Criteria and the Impact of Low Inflation', *Bank of England Bulletin*, August 1994.
4. Cosh, A., Coutts, K. and Hughes, A., 'Manufacturing, the Balance of Payments and Capacity', in Michie, J. and Grieve Smith, J. (eds), *Creating Industrial Capacity.*
5. Freeman, C. and Soete, L., *Work for all or Mass Unemployment?*

10 Our European Future

1. OECD standardised unemployment rates.
2. Lombard Street Research Ltd, *Monthly International Review* 47.
3. Majocchi, A. and Rey, M., *A Special Financial Support Scheme in EMU: Need and Nature*; Goodhart, C.A.E. and Smith, S., *Stabilisation* (Commission of the European Communities, 1994).
4. *Growth, Competitiveness, Employment: The Challenges and Ways Forward into the 21st Century* (Commission of the European Communities, December 1993).
5. MacDougall, D., *The Role of Public Finance in European Integration* (*MacDougall Report*) (Commission of the European Communities, 1977). See also MacDougall, D., 'Economic and Monetary Union and the European Community Budget', *National Institute Economic Review*, May 1992.
6. Robbins, L., 'Economic Aspects of Federalism', in Channing Pearce, N. (ed.), *Federal Union, A Symposium.*

11 A Global Payments Strategy

1. *Financial Times,* 1 May 1996.
2. Two of the original purposes of the International Bank, set out in Article 1 of the 1944 Bretton Woods Agreement, were:

> To promote private foreign investment by means of guarantees or participation in loans and other investments made by private investors; and when private capital is not available on reasonable terms, to supplement private investment by providing, on suitable conditions, finance for productive purposes out of its own capital, funds raised by it and its other resources.
>
> To promote the long-range balanced growth of international trade and the maintenance of equilibrium in balances of payments by encouraging international investment for the development of the productive resources of members, thereby assisting in raising productivity, the standard of living and conditions of labour in their territories.

3. The IMF suggests, however, that there is some evidence that the yen's sustained appreciation beginning in mid-1985 did have a significant effect on its trade balance (*World Economic Outlook,* February 1994). Between 1986 and 1991, Japan's export volume growth was only 2.75 per cent a year compared with the industrial country average of 5 per cent and US export growth of 10 per cent. Japan's import volume growth during this period averaged 8.5 per cent a year compared with the industrial country average of 6.25 per cent and the US average of 4 per cent.
4. For example, in a detailed discussion of the problem of setting a co-ordinated set of targets for surpluses and deficits, Polak argues that it is impractical and reconciliation is best left to the market. Polak, J.J., 'Comment on Andrew Crockett, "The Role of International Institutions in Surveillance and Policy Coordination"', in Bryant, R.C. *et al.* (eds), *Macro-Economic Policies in an Interdependent World* (Brookings, CEPR, IMF, 1989).

   See also Currie, D.A., Holtham, G. and Hughes Hallett, A., 'The Theory and Practice of International Policy Coordination: Does Coordination Pay?', in Bryant *et al.*, *Macro-Economic Policies in an Interdependent World.*
5. Stewart, F., 'Biasses in global markets: can the forces of inequity and marginalisation be modified?', in Haq, M. ul, Jolly, R. and Haq, K. (eds), *The UN and the Bretton Woods Institutions: New Challenges for the Twenty-First Century* (1995).
6. For discussions of the present role of the Fund see: Crockett, A., 'The Role of International Institutions in Surveillance and Policy Coordination', in Bryant *et al.*, *Macro-Economic Policies in an Interdependent World;* Finch, C.D., *IMF Surveillance and the G24, International Monetary and Financial Issues for the 1990s,* Vol. II (UNCTAD, 1993); *Pulling Together: The IMF in a Multipolar World* (Overseas Development Council, Washington, DC, 1989).

7. Currie, Holtham, and Hughes Hallett, 'The Theory and Practice of International Policy Coordination'.
8. See Krugman, P.R., *Exchange Instability*. Krugman's theoretical exposition reinforces my own experience in the steel industry that decisions to invest (or not to invest) in plant, distributive facilities or sales organisations in other countries depend heavily on confidence in the robustness of any exchange rate assumptions, in particular that current rates will remain unchanged for the foreseeable future.
9. Van Dormael, A., *Bretton Woods: Birth of a Monetary System.*
10. Williamson, J. and Miller, M.H., 'Targets and Indicators: A Blueprint for the Coordination of Economic Policy', Institute for International Economics, Washington DC: *Policy Analyses in International Economics,* No. 22 (September 1987).
11. US General Accounting Office, *Financial Derivatives: Actions Needed to Protect the Financial System.*
12. Tobin, J., *A Proposal for International Reform.*

12 The Way Ahead

1. Singh, A., 'Liberalisation and Globalisation: An Unhealthy Euphoria', in Michie, J. and Grieve Smith, J., *Full Employment Without Inflation.*
2. See the author's *Business Strategy.*
3. Michie, J., Kitson, M. and Sutherland, H., 'The Fiscal and Distributional Effects of Job Generation', in Michie and Grieve Smith, *Employment and Social Justice: Policies for Full Employment.*
4. See Chapter 3, page 37.
5. Budget Statement (1995).
6. 'Soros Wants Regulation Against Excessive Speculation', Reuter News Service, 9 June 1996.

Appendix 1: Measuring Unemployment

1. *Labour Market Trends* (January 1996).
2. Report of Working Party on *The Measurement of Unemployment in the UK* (Royal Statistical Society, April 1995).
3. Royal Statistical Society Report.
4. Wells, J., 'Unemployment, Job Creation and Job Destruction in the UK since 1979', in Arestis, P. and Marshall, M. (eds), *The Political Economy of Full Employment.*

Appendix 2: Tax-Based Incomes Policies

1. Wallich, H.C. and Weintraub, S., 'A Tax-Based Incomes Policy', *Journal of Economic Issues,* June 1971; Dildine, L.L. and Sunley, E.M., 'Problems of Tax-Based Incomes Policies', *Brookings Papers on Economic Activity,* No. 2 (1978).
2. Layard, R. and Nickell, S., *An Incomes Policy to Help the Unemployed* (Employment Institute, 1986).
3. Fogarty, M.P., 'Fiscal Measures and Wage Settlements', *British Journal of Industrial Relations,* March 1973.

Select Bibliography

Arestis, P. and Marshall, M., *The Political Economy of Full Employment* (Edward Elgar, 1995).

Arndt, H.W., *The Economic Lessons of the Nineteen-Thirties* (Royal Institute of International Affairs, Oxford University Press, 1994).

Atkinson, J. and Meager, N., 'Evaluation of Work Start Pilots', *Institute of Employment Studies,* Report 279.

Beckerman, W. (ed.), *The Labour Government's Economic Record: 1964–70* (Duckworth, 1972).

Berry, R., Kitson, M. and Michie, J., *Towards Full Employment: The First Million Jobs* (Full Employment Forum, 1995).

Beveridge, W.H., *Unemployment: A Problem of Industry* (Longmans, 1909 and 1930).

—— *Full Employment in a Free Society* (George Allen & Unwin, 1944).

Blackaby, F.T., *British Economic Policy, 1960–74* (Cambridge University Press, 1978).

—— (ed.), *The Future of Pay Bargaining* (Heinemann, 1980).

Bosco, A. (ed.), *The Federal Idea, Volumes 1 and 2* (Lothian Foundation Press, 1991 and 1992).

Breton, A. and Scott, A., *The Economic Constitution of Federal States* (University of Toronto Press, 1978).

Bretton Woods, Proceedings and Documents of United Nations Monetary and Financial Conference, 1944 (US State Department).

Britton, A.J.C., *Macroeconomic Policy in Britain, 1974–87* (Cambridge University Press, 1991).

Bryant, R.C. *et al.* (eds), *Macroeconomic Policies in an Interdependent World* (Brookings, CEPR, IMF, 1989).

Bullock, A., *The Life and Times of Ernest Bevin, Vols. 1 and 2* (Heinemann, 1960 and 1967).

Burgess, T. (ed.), *Matters of Principle, Labour's Last Chance* (Penguin, 1968).

Cairncross, A., *Years of Recovery, British Economic Policy 1945–51* (Methuen, 1985).

—— (ed.), *The Robert Hall Diaries 1947–1953 and 1954–1961* (Unwin Hyman, 1989 and 1991).

—— *The British Economy since 1945* (Blackwell, 1992).

Cairncross, A. and Watts, N., *The Economic Section 1939–1961: A Study in Economic Advising* (Routledge, 1989).

Callaghan, J., *Time and Chance* (Collins, 1987).

Calmfors, L. and Driffil, J., 'Centralisation of Wage Bargaining', *Economic Policy,* April 1988.

Channing Pearce, N. (ed.), *Federal Union, A Symposium* (Croom Helm, 1940).

Coates, K. and Holland, S., *Full Employment for Europe* (Spokesman, 1995).

Cole, J., *As It Seemed To Me* (Weidenfeld & Nicolson, 1995).

Commission of the European Communities, *Growth, Competitiveness, Employment: The Challenges and Ways Forward into the 21st Century* (The Delors Report on Unemployment), 1993.
Connolly, B., *The Rotten Heart of Europe* (Faber & Faber, 1995).
Dildine, L.L. and Sunley, E.M., 'Problems of Tax-Based Incomes Policies', *Brookings Papers on Economic Activity*, No. 2 (1978).
Dow, J.C.R., *The British Economy 1945–60* (Cambridge University Press, 1964).
Dore, R., Boyer, R. and Mars, Z., *The Return to Incomes Policy* (Pinter, 1994).
DSS, *Households below Average Income, A Statistical Analysis 1979–1992/3* (1995).
Edmonds, J. and Tuffin, A., *A New Agenda, Bargaining for Prosperity in the 1990s*, Joint paper by the GMB and UCW (1990).
Eichengreen, B., *Golden Fetters, The Gold Standard and the Great Depression 1919–1939* (Oxford University Press, 1992).
Feinstein, C.H., *National Income, Expenditure and Output of the UK 1855–1965* (Cambridge, Department of Applied Economics, 1972).
Finch, C.D., *IMF Surveillance and the G24, International Monetary and Financial Issues for the 1990s*, Vol. II (UNCTAD, 1993).
Fogarty, M.P., 'Fiscal Measures and Wage Settlements', *British Journal of Industrial Relations*, March 1973.
Forsyth, M., *Unions of States: The Theory and Practice of Confederation* (Leicester University Press, 1981).
Freeman, C. and Soete, L., *Work for all or Mass Unemployment? Computerised Technical Change into the Twenty-First Century* (Pinter, 1994).
Friedman, M., 'The Role of Monetary Policy', *American Economic Review*, No. 58 (1968).
Gaitskell, H., *Economic Planning and Liberalisation*, EPC (50) 9 (PRO CSB 134 1225).
Galbraith, J.K., *The Culture of Contentment* (Sinclair-Stevenson, 1992).
Garman, A., Redmond, G. and Lonsdale, S., *Incomes In and Out of Work*, DSS Research Report No. 7.
Goodhart, C.A.E. and Smith, S., *Stabilisation* (Commission of the European Communities, 1994).
Gregg, P. and Wadsworth, J., *More Work for Fewer Households?*, NIESR Discussion Paper No. 72 (1995).
Haq, M. ul, Jolly, R. and Haq, K. (eds), *The UN and the Bretton Woods Institutions: New Challenges for the Twenty First Century* (Macmillan, 1995).
Harrod, R., 'Increasing Returns', in *Economic Essays*, 2nd edn (Macmillan, 1972); first published in *Essays in Honour of E.N. Chamberlain* (1967).
Healey, D., *The Time of My Life* (Michael Joseph, 1989).
Hicks, J.R., *Value and Capital* (Oxford University Press, 1939).
Hirst, P., *After Thatcher* (Collins, 1989).
Hodson, H.Y., *Slump and Recovery 1929–1937* (Oxford University Press, 1938).
House of Commons, Employment Committee Third Report, *Unemployment and Employment Statistics* (February 1996).
Howe, G., *Conflict of Loyalty* (Macmillan, 1994).
Hutton, W., *The State We're In* (Cape, 1995).
Johnson, C., *The Economy under Mrs. Thatcher, 1979–1990* (Penguin, 1991).
Jones, K., *An Economist among Mandarins, A Biography of Robert Hall, 1901–1988* (Cambridge University Press, 1994).

Kahn, R.F., 'The Relation of Home Investment to Unemployment', *Economic Journal*, June 1931.

Kaldor, N., *The Scourge of Monetarism* (Oxford University Press, 1942).

Kalecki, M., *Selected Essays on the Dynamics of the Capitalist Economy, 1933–70* (Cambridge University Press, 1971).

Keegan, W., *Mrs. Thatcher's Economic Experiment* (Allen Lane, 1984).

—— *Mr. Lawson's Gamble* (Hodder & Stoughton, 1989).

Keynes, J.M., *The General Theory of Employment, Interest and Money* (Macmillan, 1936).

—— 'Relative Movements of Real Wages and Output', *Economic Journal*, March 1939.

—— *Shaping the Post-War World*, The Collected Papers, Vols XXV and XXVI (1940–4).

—— *Essays in Persuasion* (Macmillan/Cambridge University Press, 1972; 1st edition 1931).

—— *The Economic Consequences of Mr. Churchill* (1925) reprinted in *Essays in Persuasion* (Macmillan/Cambridge University Press, 1972).

—— *How to Pay for the War* (1940) reprinted in *Essays in Persuasion* (Macmillan/Cambridge University Press, 1972).

Keynes, J.M. and Henderson, H.D., *Can Lloyd George Do It?* (1929) reprinted in *Essays in Persuasion* (Macmillan/Cambridge University Press, 1972).

King, P., *Federalism and Federation* (Croom Helm, 1982).

Kitson, M. and Michie, J., 'Depression and Recovery, Lessons from the Interwar Period', in Michie, J. and Grieve Smith J. (eds), *Unemployment in Europe* (Academic Press, 1994).

Kreisky Commission, *A Programme for Full Employment in the 1990's* (Pergamon, 1989).

Krugman, P.R., *Exchange Instability* (MIT Press, 1989).

Labour Party, *Unemployment: A Labour Policy* (1921).

—— *Labour and the Nation* (1929).

—— *How to Conquer Unemployment: Labour's Reply to Lloyd George* (1929).

—— *Socialism and the Condition of the People* (1933).

Lawson, N., *The View From No. 11* (Bantam, 1992).

Layard, R., 'How to End Pay Leapfrogging', *Employment Institute Economic Report*, Vol. 5 (July 1990).

Layard, R. and Nickell, S., *An Incomes Policy to Help the Unemployed* (Employment Institute, 1986).

Layard, R., Nickell, S. and Jackman, J., *Unemployment: Macroeconomic Performance and the Labour Market* (Oxford University Press, 1991).

Lewis, W.A., *Economic Survey 1919–1939* (George Allen & Unwin, 1949).

Liberal Party, *Britain's Industrial Future*, Report of the Liberal Industrial Inquiry (Ernest Benn, 1928).

MacDougall, D., *The Role of Public Finance in European Integration* (Commission of the European Communities, 1977).

—— 'Economic and Monetary Union and the European Community Budget', *National Institute Economic Review*, May 1992.

Macmillan, H., *At the End of the Day, 1961–3* (Macmillan, 1973).

Maddison, A., *Dynamic Forces in Capitalist Development* (Oxford University Press, 1991).

Majocchi, A. and Rey, M., *A Special Financial Support Scheme in EMU: Need and Nature* (Commission of the European Communities, 1994).
Marquand, D., *The Unprincipled Society* (Fontana, 1988).
Meade, J., *Full Employment Regained?* (Cambridge University Press, 1995).
Meadows, P. (ed.), *Work out – or Work in?* (Joseph Rowntree Foundation, 1996).
Michie, J., *Wages in the Business Cycle* (Pinter, 1987).
Michie, J. and Grieve Smith, J. (eds), *Unemployment in Europe* (Academic Press, 1994).
—— (eds), *Managing the Global Economy* (Oxford University Press, 1995).
—— (eds), *Creating Industrial Capacity: Towards Full Employment* (Oxford University Press, 1996).
—— (eds), *Employment and Economic Performance: Jobs, Inflation and Growth* (Oxford University Press, 1997).
Moggeridge, D.E., *Maynard Keynes, An Economist's Biography* (Routledge, 1992).
Nickell, S. and Bell, L.A., 'The Collapse of Demand for the Unskilled and Unemployment Across the OECD', *Oxford Review of Economic Policy* (Spring, 1995).
Panić, M., *European Monetary Union: Lessons From the Classical Gold Standard* (Macmillan, 1992).
Phillips, A.W., 'The Relation between Unemployment and the Rate of Change of Money Wage Rates in the United Kingdom 1861–1957', *Economica*, (November 1958).
Robinson, P., 'Stagflation: Lessons from Other Places', *Campaign for Work Research Report*, Vol. 1, No. 7 (November 1989).
—— *Full Employment in Britain in the 1990's* (Avebury, 1991).
—— *The British Labour Market in Historical Perspective: Changes in the Structure of Employment and Unemployment*, CEPR Discussion Paper 20 (1994).
—— 'Skills, Qualifications and Unemployment', *Economic Affairs*, Vol. 16, No. 2 (Spring 1996).
Rowntree Foundation, *Inquiry into Income and Wealth* (Joseph Rowntree Foundation, 1995).
Royal Statistical Society, *Report of the Working Party on the Measurement of Unemployment in the UK* (April 1965).
Schmitt, J. and Wadsworth, J., *Why are 2 million Men Inactive? The Decline in Male Labour Force Participation in Britain*, CEPR Working Paper No. 338 (1994).
Skidelsky, R., *Politicians and the Slump: The Labour Government 1929–1931* (Macmillan, 1967).
—— *John Maynard Keynes, The Economist as Saviour, 1920–1937* (Macmillan, 1992).
Soskice, D., 'Wage Determination: The Changing Role of Institutions in Advanced Industrialised Countries', *Oxford Review of Economic Policy*, Vol. 6, No. 4.
Stewart, M., *Keynes and After* (Penguin, 1967, 1972 and 1986).
—— *The Jekyll and Hyde Years, Politics and Economic Policy since 1964* (Dent, 1977).
—— *Keynes in the 1990s: A Return to Economic Sanity* (Penguin, 1993).
Thatcher, M., *The Downing Street Years* (HarperCollins, 1993).

Tobin, J., A Proposal for International Economic Reform, *Eastern Economic Journal*, July–October 1978.

Trades Union Congress, *Collective Bargaining and the Social Contract* (1974).

—— *Black and Betrayed* (1995).

H.M.Treasury, Financial Statements and Budget Report, 1996–7 (Red Book) (1995).

Tumin, P., *Lessons from the Great Depression* (MIT Press, 1989).

United Nations, *National and International Measures For Full Employment* (1949).

US General Accounting Office, *Financial Derivatives: Actions Needed to Protect the Financial System* (1994).

Van Dormael, A., *Bretton Woods, Birth of a Monetary System* (Macmillan, 1978).

Wallich, H.C. and Weintraub, S., 'A Tax-Based Incomes Policy', *Journal of Economic Issues* (June 1971).

Wardlow, A. 'Investment Appraisal Criteria and the Impact of Low Inflation', *Bank of England Bulletin* (August 1994).

Wells, J., 'The Costs of Unemployment', mimeo, 1993. Calculated from the DSS Reports on *Incomes In and Out of Work*.

White Papers, *Memoranda on Certain Proposals Relating to Unemployment*, Cmd 3331, 1929.

—— *Report of May Committee on National Expenditure*, Cmd 3920, 1931.

—— *Proposals for an International Clearing Union*, Cmd 6437, 1943.

—— *Employment Policy*, Cmd 6527, 1944.

—— *Joint Statement by Experts on the Establishment of an International Monetary Fund*, Cmd 6519, 1944.

—— *The National Plan*, Cmnd 2764, 1965.

—— *Competitiveness: Forging Ahead*, Cmnd 2867, 1995.

Williamson, J. and Miller, M.H., *Targets and Indicators: A Blueprint for the Coordination of Economic Policy* (Institute for International Economics, Washington DC, Policy Analyses in International Economics No. 22, September 1987).

Wilson, H., *The Labour Government 1964–70: A Personal Record* (Weidenfeld & Joseph, 1971).

Wood, A., *North-South Trade, Employment and Inequality* (Oxford University Press, 1994).

Worswick, G.D.N. and Ady, P.H. (eds), *The British Economy 1945–50* (Clarendon, 1952).

Youngson, A.J., *The British Economy 1920–1937* (George Allen & Unwin, 1960).

Index